Study Guide

Management
A Competency-Based Approach
TENTH EDITION

Don Hellriegel

Mays Business School
Texas A & M University

Susan E. Jackson

School of Management and Labor Relations
Rutgers University

John W. Slocum, Jr.

Edwin L. Cox School of Business
Southern Methodist University

Prepared by

Andre Honoree
Spring Hill College

THOMSON

™

SOUTH-WESTERN

Australia · Canada · Mexico · Singapore · Spain · United Kingdom · United States

THOMSON

SOUTH-WESTERN

Study Guide t/a Management: A Competency-Based Approach, 10/e

Don Hellriegel, Susan E. Jackson, and John W. Slocum, Jr.
Prepared by Andre Honoree

VP/Editorial Director:
Jack W. Calhoun

VP/Editor-in-Chief:
Michael P. Roche

Acquisitions Editor:
Joseph A. Sabatino

Developmental Editor:
Leslie Kauffman, Litten Editing and Productions, Inc.

Marketing Manager:
Jacque Carrillo

Production Editor:
Margaret M. Bril

Technology Project Editor:
Kristen Meere

Media Editor:
Karen Schaffer

Manufacturing Coordinator:
Rhonda Utley

Printer:
Thomson/West
Eagan, Minnesota

Sr. Design Project Manager:
Michelle Kunkler

For more information
contact South-Western,
5191 Natorp Boulevard,
Mason, Ohio 45040.
Or you can visit our Internet site at:
http://www.swlearning.com

Preface

INTRODUCTION

This study guide was designed from a student's perspective, with the tools necessary to help students succeed in a management course. It is intended to accompany Hellriegel, Jackson, and Slocum's *Management: A Competency-Based Approach*, 10th edition. The purpose of this study guide is for you to test your knowledge and improve your performance on exams.

This guide is meant to complement the textbook and your professor's lectures. It is not intended as a substitute for attending class or reading the textbook—you must do both to succeed.

Note that extensive endnotes are provided for each chapter at the end of your textbook. These endnotes provide detailed references for material covered in the textbook and study guide, and are excellent sources for additional readings.

EXAM PREPARATION PLAN

The following are recommendations for preparing for exams in your management course.

1. Read the chapter in your textbook before attending class. It is amazing how much more you will remember from your professor's lecture if the material has been read in advance.

2. Take the outline for each chapter to class with you and add the instructor's notes. This will consolidate your outline and make a great study guide for you. Also, you will have more time to concentrate on what is being said, because you will not need to write everything down.

3. Do not "store up" chapters in this study guide until the day before the exam. This guide will only help you if it is used in conjunction with the other course materials. Practice each study guide chapter after you have read the text chapter and studied the material presented in class. If you do this on a regular basis, studying for the examination will be much more friendly and a whole lot less frustrating.

4. Read each chapter, study it, and then complete the chapter in the study guide like a sample test. Do not read the question and then look at the answer—this method is very ineffective. Complete all questions in the chapter and then grade yourself like the professor would. This will tell you honestly whether or not you know the material.

DISCLAIMERS

The following are disclaimers and words of caution to students using this study guide.

1. There are many essay questions that could have been asked for each chapter. When writing the essay questions for the study guide, we tried not to duplicate the essay questions that the authors of the text posed in the chapter summary.

2. It is important to remember that most professors will use a combination of lecture notes and text material from which to test students. Therefore, make sure you know the material and pay careful attention to the key focus of your professor's lectures.

3. Make sure you really understand the content of the material. Memorizing the questions and answers in this study guide will not help you, since most professors can create thousands of original questions for tests.

4. We intentionally provided some duplication of definitions and key phrases in the solution sections because repetition helps one to remember things.

5. The names used in this book are fictitious and any name you may recognize is purely a coincidence.

Contents

❖2❖

____ 6. Planning involves creating a structure by setting up departments and job descriptions.

____ 7. Leading is a crucial element of the planning and organizing functions.

____ 8. Karen Zaler is a bakery manager who spends most of her time with the bakery employees. She is considered a first-line manager.

____ 9. Doug Relston is a plant manager for the Relston Carpet Manufacturer who spends his time reviewing the work plans of various groups, developing evaluation criteria for performance, and deciding which projects should be given resources. He is considered a top manager.

____ 10. Top managers spend 25 percent of their day planning and leading.

❖3❖

____ 11. Herb Kelleher, former CEO of Southwest Airlines, visits with employees on the job and parties with them after hours. He listens to his employees and observes their body language; thus he is utilizing the communication competency.

____ 12. Of the six managerial competencies, teamwork competency is the most fundamental.

____ 13. Time management and problem solving are dimensions of the planning and administration competency.

____ 14. A well-designed team is capable of high performance, but it needs a supportive environment to achieve its full potential.

____ 15. Strategic action competency is a competency that only top managers need to gain.

____ 16. Managers today are expected to develop a knowledge and an understanding of at least a few other cultures.

MULTIPLE CHOICE

Directions: Select the best answer in the space provided.

❖1❖

____ 1. All of the following are key managerial competencies except:
   a. teamwork.
   b. self-management.
   c. global awareness.
   d. ethics.

_____ 2. Any structured group of people working together to achieve certain goals that the same individuals could not reach alone is a(n) _____.
   a. goal
   b. organization
   c. network group
   d. management team

_____ 3. Which of the following job titles typically represents the role of a manager?
   a. coach
   b. stockbroker
   c. chief knowledge officer
   d. a. and c.

_____ 4. The head of the payroll department for the Target store in Reston, Virginia, is a _____ manager.
   a. network
   b. general
   c. matrix
   d. functional

❖2❖

_____ 5. The four functions of management are:
   a. scheduling, leading, planning, and organizing.
   b. planning, controlling, employing, and leading.
   c. organizing, planning, controlling, and managing.
   d. organizing, planning, leading, and controlling.

_____ 6. _____ is the process of deciding where decisions will be made, who will perform what jobs and tasks, and who will report to whom in the company.
   a. Organizing
   b. Planning
   c. Networking
   d. Controlling

_____ 7. Which of the following is <u>not</u> a step in the control process?
   a. create more structure
   b. take action to correct deviations
   c. set standards of performance
   d. adjust the standards if necessary

_____ 8. John Morson works in the construction industry and supervises the crews for the metal framing and wall-building activities and he sometimes operates machinery and participates in the building process. John is considered to be a _____ manager.
   a. first-line
   b. top
   c. general
   d. middle

_____ 9. Which of the following is a <u>false</u> statement regarding first-line managers?
a. First-line managers in most companies spend little time with higher management or with people from other organizations.
b. First-line managers may be called sales managers, section heads, or production supervisors.
c. First-line managers spend a great deal of time planning and organizing.
d. First-line managers need strong technical expertise.

_____ 10. _____ managers set objectives that are consistent with top management's goals and translate them into specific goals and plans for first-line managers to implement.
a. General
b. Middle
c. Executive
d. Functional

_____ 11. Margie Miller spends most of her time planning and leading while at work. She is considered a _____ manager.
a. first-line
b. top
c. middle
d. strategic

❖3❖

_____ 12. Jack Welch, General Electric's CEO, believes that to beat competitors and maximize the company's profitability GE must improve quality control. As a manager, Jack builds strong interpersonal relationships with a diverse range of people and solicits feedback from employees. Nevertheless, Jack recently informed his managers that they wouldn't have a future with the company if they failed to produce results. Jack is exhibiting the _____ competency.
a. strategic action
b. planning and administration
c. communication
d. global awareness

_____ 13. Which of the following competencies is typified by managerial negotiation skills?
a. planning and administration
b. teamwork
c. organization
d. communication

_____ 14. This managerial competency includes: information gathering, time management, financial management, and problem solving.
a. strategic action
b. planning and administration
c. organization
d. managerial effectiveness

_____ 15. Team design involves _____.
   a. formulating goals to be achieved
   b. defining tasks to be done
   c. identifying the staffing needed to accomplish tasks
   d. All of the above.

_____ 16. Understanding the overall mission and values of the company and ensuring that employee's actions match with them involves the _____ competency.
   a. global awareness
   b. strategic alliance
   c. strategic action
   d. teamwork

_____ 17. An open attitude about cultural differences and a sensitivity to them are important for mastering the _____ competency.
   a. global awareness
   b. leadership
   c. multicultural
   d. communication

_____ 18. Which of the following statements is true regarding self-management competency?
   a. Companies today are much more concerned with prospective employees' technical skills and aptitude than their integrity.
   b. Research shows that people who take advantage of the development and training opportunities that employers offer learn much from them and advance more quickly.
   c. A derailed manager is one who has little managerial responsibility in a high risk functional area.
   d. Successful managers normally devote all their attention to their careers and neglect their personal lives.

ESSAY QUESTIONS

❖1❖

1. Explain the difference between functional and general managers.

❖2❖

2. Identify and discuss the four basic managerial functions.

❖1❖   ❖2❖

3.   Define *management* and *managers*. Discuss the duties and responsibilities of first-line managers, middle managers, and top managers.

❖1❖   ❖3❖

4.   Define *managerial competencies* and explain the six key managerial competencies.

CHAPTER 1
MANAGING IN A DYNAMIC ENVIRONMENT

MATCHING SOLUTIONS

1.   J   - Communication Competency
2.   N - Top Manager
3.   A - Teamwork Competency
4.   O - Opennes and Sensitivity
5.   H - Middle Manager
6.   B - Organization
7.   R - Functional Manager
8.   E - Organizing
9.   T - First-Line Manager
10.   G - Controlling
11.   L - Supportive Environment
12.   F - Management
13.   M - Global Awareness Competency
14.   C - Leading
15.   K - General Manager
16.   I   - Formal Communication
17.   P - Strategic Action Competency
18.   Q - Planning
19.   D - Derailed Manager
20.   S - Managerial Competencies

TRUE/FALSE SOLUTIONS

<u>Question</u>	<u>Answer</u>	<u>Page</u>	<u>Explanation</u>
1.	False	4–5	<u>Managerial competencies</u> are sets of knowledge, skills, behaviors, and attitudes that a person needs to be effective in a wide range of managerial jobs and various types of organizations. The six key managerial competencies are: communication, planning and administration, teamwork, strategic action, global awareness, and self-management.
2.	False	5–6	Profit-oriented businesses are one type of organizational setting in which managers are found, but they also are found in organizations such as: hospitals, schools, museums, sports teams, stores, amusement parks, restaurants, orchestras, community clubs and groups, government agencies, and others. A <u>manager</u> is a person who plans, organizes, directs, and controls the allocation of human, material, financial, and information resources in pursuit of the organization's goals.
3.	True		
4.	True		
5.	False	8	<u>Functional managers</u> supervise employees having expertise in one area, such as accounting, human resources, sales, finance, marketing, or production. For example, the head of a payroll department is a functional manager. Usually, functional managers have a great deal of experience and technical expertise in the areas of operation they supervise. <u>General managers</u> are responsible for the operations of a more complex unit, such as a company or a division. Usually they oversee the work of functional managers.
6.	False	9	<u>Planning</u> involves determining organizational goals and means to reach them. <u>Organizing</u> involves creating a structure by setting up departments and job descriptions.
7.	True		
8.	True		

9.   False   13–14   Middle managers set objectives that are consistent with top management goals and translate them into specific goals and plans for first-line managers to implement. Middle managers typically have titles such as department head, plant manager, and director of finance. Middle managers often are involved in reviewing the work plans of various groups, helping them set priorities, and negotiating and coordinating their activities. They are involved in establishing target dates for products or services to be completed; developing evaluation criteria for performance; deciding which projects should be given money, personnel, and materials; and translating top management's general goals into specific operational plans, schedules, and procedures. Top managers are responsible for the overall direction of the company. Typical titles of top managers are chief executive officer, president, division president, and executive vice-president.

10.   False   14   Top managers spend most of their day (over 75 percent) planning and leading. They spend most of their leading time with key people and organizations outside their own organization.

11.   True

12.   False   15   The six managerial competencies are: communication competency, planning and administration competency, teamwork competency, strategic action competency, global awareness competency, and self-management competency. They are all important. However, communication is the most fundamental because unless you can express yourself and understand others in written, oral, and nonverbal communication, you can't use the other competencies effectively to accomplish tasks through other people.

13.   True

14.   True

15.   False   21   <u>Strategic action competency</u> involves understanding the overall mission and values of the company and ensuring that employees' actions match with them. Strategic action competency includes understanding the industry, understanding the organization, and taking strategic action. All managers, but especially top managers, need strategic action competency.

16.   True

MULTIPLE CHOICE SOLUTIONS

<u>Question</u>	<u>Answer</u>	<u>Page</u>	<u>Explanation</u>
1.	d	5	<u>Managerial competencies</u> are sets of knowledge, skills, behaviors, and attitudes that a person needs to be effective in a wide range of managerial jobs and various types of organizations. The six key managerial competencies are: communication, planning and administration, teamwork, strategic action, global awareness, and self-management.
2.	b	6	An <u>organization</u> is a coordinated group of people who function to achieve a particular goal.
3.	d	7	A <u>manager</u> is a person who plans, organizes, directs, and controls the allocation of human, material, financial, and information resources in pursuit of the organization's goals. Some managers have unique and creative titles, such as chief knowledge officer and chief information officer. People with the job titles of chief executive officer (CEO), president, managing director, supervisor, and coach also have the responsibility for helping a group of people achieve a common goal, so they too are managers. Most employees contribute to organizations through their own individual work, not by directing other employees. Journalists, computer programmers, insurance agents, machine operators, newscasters, graphic designers, sales associates, stockbrokers, accountants, and lawyers are essential to achieving their organizations' goals, but many people with these job titles aren't managers.

4.	d	8	Functional managers supervise employees having expertise in one area, such as accounting, human resources, sales, finance, marketing, or production. General managers are responsible for the operations of a more complex unit, such as a company or a division. Usually they oversee the work of functional managers.
5.	d	9	The four basic functions of management are: planning, organizing, leading, and controlling.
6.	a	9	Organizing is the process of deciding where decisions will be made, who will perform what jobs and tasks, and who will report to whom in the company.
7.	a	10	Controlling is the process by which a person, group, or organization consciously monitors performance and takes corrective action. In the control process, managers: set standards of performance, measure current performance against those standards, take action to correct any deviations, and adjust the standards if necessary.
8.	a	12–13	First-line managers are directly responsible for the production of goods and services. They spend most of their time with the people they supervise and with other first-line managers. This level of management is the link between the operations of each department and the rest of the organization.
9.	c	12–13	First-line managers are directly responsible for the production of goods and services. First-line managers spend relatively little time planning and organizing. Most of their time is spent leading and controlling.
10.	b	13	Middle managers are responsible for setting objectives that are consistent with top management's goals and translating them into specific goals and plans for first-line managers to implement.
11.	b	13–14	Top managers set the overall direction of an organization. They spend most of their day (over 75 percent) planning and leading.
12.	c	15–16	The communication competency involves the effective transfer and exchange of information and understanding between yourself and others. It includes informal communication, formal communication, and negotiation.

13.   d   15–16   Communication competency is the ability to transfer and exchange effectively information that leads to understanding between yourself and others. It includes informal/formal communication and negotiation skills.

14.   b   17   Planning and administration competency involves deciding what tasks need to be done, determining how they can be done, allocating resources to enable them to be done, and then monitoring progress to ensure that they are done. Included is this competency are: information gathering, analysis, and problem solving; planning and organizing projects; time management; and budgeting and financial management.

15.   d   19   Designing the team is the first step for any team project and usually is the responsibility of a manager or team leader. Team design involves formulating goals to be achieved, defining tasks to be done, and identifying the staffing needed to accomplish those tasks.

16.   c   20   Strategic action competency involves understanding the overall mission and values of the company and ensuring that employees' actions match with them. Strategic action competency includes: understanding the industry, understanding the organization, and taking strategic actions.

17.   a   22–24   Global awareness competency includes performing managerial work for an organization that utilizes human, financial, informational, and material resources from multiple countries and serves markets that span multiple cultures. An open attitude about cultural differences and a sensitivity to them are especially important for anyone who must operate across cultural boundaries.

18.   b   25   Self-management competency means taking responsibility for your life at work and beyond. Organizations expect their employees to show integrity and act ethically. A derailed manager is one who has moved into a position of managerial responsibility but has little chance of future advancement or gaining new responsibilities. Future managers won't succeed unless they can balance work and life demands.

ESSAY SOLUTIONS

[Page 8]

1. <u>Functional managers</u> supervise employees having expertise in one area, such as accounting, human resources, sales, finance, marketing, or production. For example, the head of a payroll department is a functional manager. Usually, functional managers have a great deal of experience and technical expertise in the areas of operation they supervise.

   <u>General managers</u> are responsible for the operations of a more complex unit, such as a company or a division. Usually they oversee the work of functional managers. General managers must have a broad range of well-developed competencies to do their jobs well.

[Pages 9–10]

2. <u>Planning</u> involves determining organizational goals and means to reach them. Managers plan for three reasons: (1) to establish an overall direction for the organization's future, such as increased profit, expanded market share, and social responsibility; (2) to identify and commit the organization's resources to achieving its goals; and (3) to decide which tasks must be done to reach those goals.

   <u>Organizing</u> is the process of deciding where decisions will be made, who will perform what jobs and tasks, and who will report to whom in the company. By organizing effectively, managers can better coordinate human, material, and informational resources.

   <u>Leading</u> involves communicating with and motivating others to perform the tasks necessary to achieve the organization's goals. Leading isn't done only after planning and organizing end; it is a crucial element of those functions.

   <u>Controlling</u> is the process by which a person, group, or organization consciously monitors performance and takes corrective action. A management control system sends signals to managers that things aren't working out as planned and that corrective action is needed.

[Pages 7, 12–14]

3. <u>Management</u> refers to the tasks or activities involved in managing an organization: planning, organizing, leading, and controlling. A <u>manager</u> is a person who plans, organizes, directs, and controls the allocation of human, material, financial, and information resources in pursuit of the organization's goals.

   <u>First-line managers</u> are directly responsible for the production of goods or services. They may be called sales managers, section heads, or production supervisors. This level of management is the link between the operations of each department and the rest of the organization. Most of their time is spent with the people they supervise and with other first-line managers. First-line managers spend relatively little time planning and organizing. Most of their time is spent leading and controlling. They usually need strong technical expertise to teach subordinates and supervise their day-to-day tasks.

Middle managers are responsible for setting objectives that are consistent with top management's goals and translating them into specific goals and plans for first-line managers to implement. They typically have titles such as department head, plant manager, and director of finance. They are responsible for directing and coordinating the activities of first-line managers and nonmanagerial personnel. They review the work plans of various groups, help them set priorities, and negotiate and coordinate their activities.

Top managers are responsible for the overall direction of the company. They develop goals, policies, and strategies for the entire organization. Typical titles are: CEO, president, and executive vice president. They spend most of their day (over 75 percent) planning and leading.

[Pages 4, 14–25]

4. Managerial competencies are sets of knowledge, skills, behaviors, and attitudes that a person needs to be effective in a wide range of managerial jobs and various types of organizations.

   The six key managerial competencies are:

   a. *Communication competency* refers to the effective transfer and exchange of information that leads to understanding between yourself and others. It includes: informal communication, formal communication, and negotiation. Of the six managerial competencies, it is the most fundamental.

   b. *Planning and administration competency* involves deciding what tasks need to be done, determining how they can be done, allocating resources to enable them to be done, and then monitoring progress to ensure that they are done. Included in this category are: information gathering, analysis, and problem solving; planning and organizing projects; time management; and budgeting and financial management.

   c. *Teamwork competency* requires accomplishing tasks through small groups of people who are collectively responsible and whose job requires coordination. Managers in companies that utilize teams can become more effective by: designing teams properly, creating a supportive team environment, and managing team dynamics appropriately.

   d. *Strategic action competency* involves understanding the overall mission and values of the company and ensuring that employees' actions match with them. It includes: understanding the industry, understanding the organization, and taking strategic actions.

   e. *Global awareness competency* means performing managerial work for an organization that utilizes human, financial, and material resources from multiple countries and serves markets that span multiple cultures. It includes: cultural knowledge and understanding, and cultural openness and sensitivity.

   f. *Self-management competency* refers to taking responsibility for your life at work and beyond. It includes: integrity and ethical conduct, personal drive and resilience, balancing work/life issues, and self-awareness and development.

CHAPTER 2
THE EVOLUTION OF MANAGEMENT

LEARNING OBJECTIVES

After studying this chapter, you should be able to:

❖**1**❖ Describe the three branches of the traditional viewpoint of management: bureaucratic, scientific, and administrative.

❖**2**❖ Explain the behavioral viewpoint's contribution to management.

❖**3**❖ Describe how managers can use systems and quantitative techniques to improve employee performance.

❖**4**❖ State the two major components of the contingency viewpoint.

❖**5**❖ Explain the impact of the need for quality on management practices.

OUTLINE

❖**1**❖ Describe the three branches of the traditional viewpoint of management: bureaucratic, scientific, and administrative.

   I.   **The Evolution of Management Thought**

      1. **Overview**—management today reflects the evolution of concepts, viewpoints, and experience gained over many decades.

         a. Henry R. Towne (1844–1924), an engineer, proposed "shop management" and "shop accounting" to the American Society of Mechanical Engineers.

         b. During the 1886 business boom, employers generally regarded labor as a commodity to be purchased as cheaply as possible and maintained at minimal expense.

         c. The American Federation of Labor (AFL), organized in 1886 by Samuel Gompers and Adolph Strasser, grouped skilled workers by craft lines (carpenters, plumbers, bricklayers, and other trades).

         d. There are many reasons why the evolution of management is important to managers today such as:

            1. Many of the principles established in the early days of management are still used today.

2. The past is a good teacher, identifying practices that have been successful and practices that have failed.

3. History gives a feel for the types of problems that managers long have struggled to solve.

4. Many of the same problems, such as low morale, high absenteeism, and poor workmanship, still exist in many organizations and continue to plague managers.

5. The fact that professional management hasn't been around all that long.

6. The emergence of large-scale business enterprises around the world has raised issues and created challenges that previously applied only to governments.

2. **Traditional (Classical) Viewpoint**—the oldest and most widely accepted view of management. It is split into three main branches: bureaucratic management, scientific management, and administrative management.

   a. All three emerged during roughly the same time period, the late 1890s through the early 1900s, when engineers were trying to make organizations run like well-oiled machines.

3. **Bureaucratic Management**—a system that relies on rules, a set hierarchy, a clear division of labor, and detailed rules and procedures. It provides a blueprint of how an entire organization should operate.

   a. Max Weber (1864–1920), a German social historian, is recognized as creating the seven characteristics of bureaucratic management.

      1. *Rules*—formal guidelines for the behavior of employees while they are on the job.

      2. *Impersonality*—all employees are evaluated according to rules and objective data, such as sales or units produced.

      3. *Division of Labor*—refers to the splitting of work into specialized positions. It enables the organization to use personnel and job-training resources efficiently.

      4. *Hierarchical Structure*—ranks jobs according to the amount of authority (the right to decide) in each job. Typically, authority increases at each higher level to the top of the hierarchy.

      5. *Authority Structure*—determines who has the right to make decisions of varying importance at different levels within the organization.

         a. Traditional Authority—is based on custom, ancestry, gender, birth order, and the like.

         b. Charismatic Authority—is evident when subordinates suspend their own judgment and comply voluntarily with a leader because of special personal qualities or abilities they perceive in that individual.

         c. Rational-Legal Authority—is based on established laws and rules that are applied uniformly.

6. *Lifelong Career Commitment*—where both the employee and the organization view themselves as being committed to each other over the working life of the employee.

7. *Rationality*—is the use of the most efficient means available to accomplish a goal.

b. The benefits of bureaucracy are efficiency and consistency. A bureaucracy functions best when many routine tasks need to be done.

c. The costs of bureaucratic management include: (1) rigid rules and red tape, (2) protection of authority, (3) slow decision making, (4) incompatibility with changing technology, and (5) incompatibility with professional values.

d. The bureaucratic approach is most effective when (1) large amounts of standard information have to be processed and an efficient processing method has been found (e.g., banks, the IRS); (2) the needs of the customer are known and aren't likely to change; (3) the technology is routine and stable, so employees can be taught easily and quickly how to operate machines; and (4) the organization has to coordinate the activities of numerous employees in order to deliver a standardized service or product to the customer.

4. **Scientific Management**—is a philosophy and set of management practices that are based on fact and observation, not on hearsay or guesswork.

a. Pioneering work in scientific management done by Frederick W. Taylor (1856–1915) focused on individuals and their machines or tools.

b. Time-and-Motion Study—involves identifying and measuring a worker's physical movements when performing a task and then analyzing how these impact a worker's productivity.

c. Functional Foremanship—a division of labor that assigns a set number of foremen to each work area, with each one being responsible for the workers in his line of expertise.

d. Taylor believed that money was the answer. He supported the individual piecework system as the basis for pay.

e. Gilbreths—Frank (1868–1924) and Lillian (1878–1972) Gilbreth were a husband-and-wife engineering team who made significant contributions to scientific management.

1. Used motion pictures to study and improve the motion process—resulting in a more than 200 percent increase in workers' productivity.

2. Lillian championed the idea that workers should have standard days, scheduled rest breaks, and normal lunch periods. Her work influenced child-labor laws and rules for protecting workers from unsafe working conditions.

f. <u>Henry Gantt</u> (1861–1919)—focused on "control" systems for production scheduling.

1. *Gantt Chart*—a visual plan and progress report that identifies various stages of work that must be carried out to complete a project, sets deadlines for each stage, and documents accomplishments.

2. Gantt also established quota systems and bonuses for workers who exceeded their quotas.

5. **Assessing Scientific Management**—unfortunately, most proponents of scientific management misread the human side of work. They thought that workers were primarily motivated by money and failed to recognize that workers also have social needs and that working conditions and job satisfaction often are as important.

   a. Managers today cannot assume that workers are only interested in higher wages, and that dividing jobs into their simplest tasks won't always lead to a quality product, high morale, and an effective organization.

6. **Administrative Management**—focuses on the manager and basic managerial functions.

   a. Henri Fayol (1841–1925), a French industrialist, was the first person to group management functions that today are summarized as: planning, organizing, leading, and controlling.

   b. Fayol emphasized formal structure and processes, believing they are necessary for the adequate performance of all important tasks.

   c. Manager's today use many of Fayol's principles of administrative management including:

   1. *Authority Principle*—managers have the right to give orders to get things done.

   2. *Unity of Command Prinicple*—each employee should report to only one manager.

7. **Assessing the Traditional Viewpoint**

   a. All the branches (bureaucratic, scientific, and administrative) emphasize the formal aspects of organization.

   b. Traditionalists are concerned with the formal relations among an organization's departments, tasks, and processes.

   c. The manager's role in a hierarchy is crucial. The relationship between expertise and organizational level is strong. Superiors are to be obeyed by subordinates due to their higher position and presumed expertise.

   d. Traditionalists' overriding focus is on efficient and effective job performance rather than recognizing informal or social relationships among employees at work.

❖**5**❖ Explain the impact of the need for quality on management practices.

V. Quality Viewpoint

1. **Quality**—how well a product does what it is supposed to do—how closely and reliably it satisfies the specifications to which it is built or provided.

    a. Customer demand for high-quality products and services may be the dominant theme for the foreseeable future.

2. **Quality Viewpoint**—emphasizes achieving customer satisfaction through the provision of high-quality goods and services.

3. **Total Quality Management** (TQM)—is the continuous process of ensuring that every aspect of production builds quality into the product.

    a. Quality must be stressed repeatedly so that it becomes second nature to everyone in an organization and its suppliers.

    b. W. Edwards Deming (1900–1993) is considered the godfather of the quality movement.

        1. Believed that poor quality is 85 percent a management problem and 15 percent a worker problem.

4. **Quality Control Process**—generally focuses on measuring inputs, transformation operations, and outputs. The results of these measurements enable managers and employees to make decisions about product or service quality at each stage of the transformation process.

    a. Inputs—Quality control begins with inputs, especially the raw materials and parts used in the transformation process.

    b. Transformation Operations—quality control inspections are made during and between successive transformation stages. Work-in-progress (WIP) inspection can result in the reworking or rejecting of an item before the next operation is performed on it.

        1. *Statistical process control*—is the use of quantitative methods and procedures to determine whether transformation operations are being done correctly, to detect any deviations, and, if there are any, to find and eliminate their causes.

        2. *Sigma*—is a unit of statistical measurement that is used to illustrate the quality of a process.

    c. Outputs—the most traditional form of quality control is the assessment made after completion of a component or an entire product, or provision of a service.

        1. *Measuring by Variable*—assesses the product characteristics for which there are quantifiable standards.

        2. *Measuring by Attribute*—evaluates the product or service characteristics as acceptable or unacceptable.

5. **Importance of Quality**—successfully offering high-quality goods and services to the customer typically results in three important benefits for the organization:

   a. <u>Positive Company Image</u>—a reputation for high-quality products creates a positive image and helps recruit new employees, increases sales of new products, and helps obtain funds from various lending agencies.

   b. <u>Lower Costs and Higher Market Share</u>—improved performance increases productivity and lowers rework time, scrap costs, and warranty costs, leading to increased profits.

   c. <u>Decreased Product Liability</u>—successful TQM efforts typically result in improved products and product performance and lower product liability costs.

6. **Integration of Management Viewpoints and Competencies**—each of the five managerial viewpoints stresses at least one of the managerial competencies.

   a. <u>Traditional Viewpoint</u>—utilizes the planning and administration competency. Managers plan, organize, and lay out the tasks of employees.

   b. <u>Behavioral Viewpoint</u>—focuses on two competencies: communication and teamwork. This viewpoint stresses that employees' behaviors are greatly affected by their interactions with peers.

   c. <u>Systems Viewpoint</u>—stresses that managers should focus on how various inputs, transformation processes, and outputs are related to the organization's goals. The organization is viewed as a "whole," rather than the sum of its various departments or divisions. This wholeness requires managers to develop their communication, strategic thinking and action, and global awareness competencies.

   d. <u>Contingency Viewpoint</u>—draws from each of the other viewpoints and involves the communication, planning and administration, and teamwork competencies.

   e. <u>Quality Viewpoint</u>—stresses meeting customers' expectations in terms of the value (performance and quality) of goods and services. This viewpoint integrates communication, strategic action, self-management, global awareness, and teamwork competencies.

MATCHING

<u>Directions</u>: Select the term that best identifies the statement listed below. Place the letter of the correct term in the space provided.

A. Gantt Chart
B. Total Quality Management
C. System
D. Max Weber
E. Outputs
F. Authority Prinicple
G. Contingency Viewpoint
H. Frank Gilbreth
I. Systems Viewpoint
J. Bureaucratic Management

K. Rules
L. Frederick W. Taylor
M. Hawthorne Effect
N. Behavioral Viewpoint
O. Functional Foremanship
P. Traditional Authority
Q. Administrative Management
R. Mary Parker Follett
S. Acceptance Theory of Authority
T. Sigma

_____ 1. Formal guidelines for the behavior of employees while they are on the job.

_____ 2. Managers have the right to give orders to get things done.

_____ 3. Stressed involvement of workers in solving problems and that management is dynamic, not static.

_____ 4. A visual plan and progress report that identifies various stages of work that must be carried out in order to complete a project, sets deadlines for a stage, and documents accomplishments.

_____ 5. Represents an approach to solving problems by diagnosing them within a framework of inputs, transformation processes, outputs, and feedback.

_____ 6. Organizational philosophy and strategy that makes quality a responsibility of all employees.

_____ 7. A system that relies on rules, a set hierarchy, a clear division of labor, and detailed rules and procedures.

_____ 8. A division of labor that assigns a set number of foremen to each work area, with each one being responsible for the workers in his line of expertise.

_____ 9. An association of interrelated and interdependent parts.

_____ 10. Focuses on the manager and basic managerial functions.

_____ 11. When workers receive special attention, productivity is likely to improve whether or not working conditions actually change.

_____ 12. Management practices should be consistent with the requirements of the external environment, the technology used to make a product or provide a service, and capabilities of the people who work for the organization.

_____ 13. A unit of statistical measurement used to illustrate the quality of a process.

_____ 14. Studied bricklaying to develop principles that contributed to scientific management.

____ 15. Authority based on custom, ancestry, gender, birth order, and the like.

____ 16. Conducted shoveling experiments to develop scientific management principles.

____ 17. The original inputs (human, physical, material, information, and financial resources) as changed by a transformation process.

____ 18. Focuses on dealing more effectively with the human aspects of organizations.

____ 19. Holds that employees have free wills and thus will choose whether or not to follow management's orders.

____ 20. One of the first theorists to deal with the problems of organizations and prescribed a formal system of rules, hierarchical structure, and division of labor for organizations to operate.

TRUE OR FALSE

Directions: Write True or False in the space provided.

❖1❖

____ 1. Henry Gantt proposed that the American Society of Mechanical Engineers create a forum for "shop management" and "shop accounting."

____ 2. Max Weber, a German social historian, is the individual most closely associated with bureaucratic management.

____ 3. Highly bureaucratic organizations have quick decision making and high productivity.

____ 4. Bureaucratic management is typified as being impersonal and containing a hierarchical structure.

____ 5. Fayol is often called the pioneer of scientific management.

____ 6. One goal of time-and-motion studies is to make a job highly routine and efficient.

❖2❖

____ 7. The behavioral or human relations viewpoint stresses the manager's role in a strict hierarchy and focuses on efficient and consistent job performance.

____ 8. Allowing a production manager to decide the priority of the order in which equipment should be purchased would be an example of Mary Parker Follett's beliefs.

____ 9. Traditional management recognizes informal and social relationships among employees at work.

____ 10. The managerial philosophy at Microsoft, Kodak and Mattel is best described as the behavioral viewpoint.

____ 11. The Hawthorne studies proved that productivity will increase when lighting is increased on the production floor and productivity decreases when employees have insufficient light to work from.

❖3❖

_____ 12. Transformation processes at a university include lectures, reading assignments, term papers, and tests.

_____ 13. An example of feedback at a university would be the graduates' ability to get jobs.

_____ 14. A closed system is one in which an organization is limited in its interactions with its environment.

❖4❖

_____ 15. Proponents of the contingency viewpoint contend that different situations require different practices depending on the circumstances.

_____ 16. Proponents of the contingency viewpoint advocate using the other three management viewpoints independently in all situations.

_____ 17. A firm choosing a managerial viewpoint that complements its technology is more likely to succeed than a firm choosing a design that doesn't fit its technology.

❖5❖

_____ 18. Transformational management is the continuous process of ensuring that every aspect of production builds quality into the product.

_____ 19. Deming believed that poor quality was an 80 percent employee problem and at most only reflected a 20 percent defective material problem.

_____ 20. An organization that follows the contingency viewpoint would have managers that exhibit the communications and teamwork competencies.

MULTIPLE CHOICE

<u>Directions</u>: Select the best answer in the space provided.

❖1❖

_____ 1. Which of the following statements reflect a reason to study the evolution of management?
   a. Past problems, such as low morale, high absenteeism, and poor workmanship, still exist in corporations today.
   b. Many of the principles established in the early 1900s are still used today.
   c. The past is a good teacher.
   d. All of the above.

___ 2. Martin Luther King's leadership authority would be best characterized as
_____.
   a. traditional
   b. rational-legal
   c. behavioralistic
   d. charismatic

___ 3. Which of the following would <u>not</u> be a drawback of bureaucratic management?
   a. rigid adherence to rules and routines
   b. consistency of routine tasks that need to be done
   c. managers who focus on protecting and expanding their own authority
   d. rapidly changing technology

___ 4. Which individual in the history of management is responsible for the following statement: "What kinds of shovels work best with which materials?"
   a. Fayol
   b. Gilbreth
   c. Taylor
   d. Gantt

___ 5. Kentucky Fried Chicken (KFC) increased its quality through the application of
_____.
   a. Gantt charts
   b. Hawthorne studies recommendations
   c. scientific management
   d. a and c.

___ 6. Which of the following is <u>not</u> a management principle developed by Weber?
   a. impersonality
   b. authority structure
   c. unity of command
   d. rules

___ 7. Job security, career progression, and protection of workers from employers' whims are considered important by _____ management theorists.
   a. traditional
   b. behavioral
   c. systems
   d. contingency

❖2❖

___ 8. Proponents of the _____ viewpoint look at how managers do what they do, how managers lead subordinates and communicate with them, and why managers need to change their assumptions about people.
   a. behavioral
   b. contingency
   c. traditional
   d. communications

_____ 9. Which of the following would <u>not</u> be included in Chester Barnard's acceptance theory of authority, which states that employees will follow a manager's orders if they _____.
a. understand what is required
b. believe that the orders are consistent with the goals of the organization
c. are involved in the decision-making process
d. see a positive benefit to themselves in carrying out the orders

_____ 10. Which of the following statements reflects the principles of Mary Parker Follett?
a. The more people specialize, the more efficiently they can perform their work.
b. First-line managers are in the best position to coordinate production tasks.
c. Employees will follow orders if they see positive benefits to themselves in carrying out the orders.
d. Protection of authority is important to successful management.

_____ 11. Which conclusion(s) emerged from the Hawthorne studies?
a. Informal work groups greatly influence productivity.
b. Peer pressure has a significant impact on employee productivity.
c. Group pride motivates employees to improve their performance.
d. All of the above.

❖3❖

_____ 12. A(n) _____ is an association of interrelated and interdependent parts.
a. process
b. system
c. organization
d. group

_____ 13. Which of the following utilizes technologies to convert inputs into outputs?
a. performance reviews
b. transformation processes
c. motivation techniques
d. employee reward systems

_____ 14. Managers in Sprint's marketing department continually develop new products or services to satisfy customers' telecommunications desires. They monitor what competitors are doing and then develop ways to deliver better quality and service at a lower price. This illustrates a(n) _____ system.
a. marketing
b. closed
c. open
d. quality

___ 15. Which of the following would be considered a basic characteristic of quantitative techniques?
     a. Computers are essential.
     b. Alternatives are based on economic criteria.
     c. The primary focus is on decision making.
     d. All of the above.

❖4❖

___ 16. The _____ viewpoint means "it all depends."
     a. contingency
     b. behavioral
     c. traditional
     d. modern

___ 17. All of the following statements regarding technology are true <u>except</u>:
     a. A simple technology involves decision-making rules to help employees do routine jobs.
     b. A complex technology is one that requires employees to make numerous decisions, sometimes with limited information to guide them.
     c. Lillian Gilbreth was one of the pioneers in developing the contingency of management to help managers understand one contingency variable—technology.
     d. A firm choosing a managerial viewpoint that complements its technology is more likely to succeed than a firm choosing a design that doesn't fit its technology.

___ 18. The relative importance of each _____ variable—external environment, technology, and people—depends on the type of managerial problem being considered.
     a. scientific
     b. contingency
     c. administrative
     d. behavioral

❖5❖

___ 19. Which of the following is <u>not</u> a quality insight presented by Deming?
     a. Poor quality is unacceptable.
     b. Statistical evidence of quality should be gathered during the process, not at the end.
     c. Employees should feel free to report any conditions that detract from quality.
     d. Suppliers' goods should be sampled by inspection to determine the quality of each delivery.

_____ 20. Nema Noley, an employee of the Promise Sugar Company, a candy manufacturer, noticed a major problem with the quality of the candy she was making due to one particular shipment of sugar. Nema went to her manager to discuss the problem. Her manager was very grateful and took action immediately. By allowing Nema to voice her concerns, this manager exhibited behavior that supports the _____ viewpoint.
   a. administrative
   b. traditional
   c. quality
   d. scientific

ESSAY QUESTIONS

❖1❖

1. Define the traditional viewpoint of management and discuss its three main branches: bureaucratic management, scientific management, and administrative management.

2. Explain administrative management and briefly explain two of Fayol's management principles.

❖2❖

3. Discuss the behavioral viewpoint of management and its basic assumptions.

❖3❖

4. Define the systems viewpoint and discuss its components.

❖**4**❖

5.   Explain why proponents of the contingency viewpoint contend that "it all depends."

❖**5**❖

6.   Define *TQM* and discuss the benefits of offering high-quality goods and services.

7.   Discuss W. Edwards Deming's contribution to the quality movement.

CHAPTER 2
THE EVOLUTION OF MANAGEMENT

MATCHING SOLUTIONS

1.   K - Rules
2.   F - Authority People
3.   R - Mary Parker Follett
4.   A - Gantt Chart
5.   I   - Systems Viewpoint
6.   B - Total Quality Management
7.   J   - Bureaucratic Management
8.   O - Functional Foremanship
9.   C - System
10. Q - Administrative Management
11. M - Hawthorne Effect
12. G - Contingency viewpoint
13. T - Sigma
14. H - Frank Gilbreth
15. P - Traditional Authority
16. L - Frederick W. Taylor
17. E - Outputs

18. N - Behavioral Viewpoint
19. S - Acceptance Theory of Authority
20. D - Max Weber

TRUE/FALSE SOLUTIONS

Question	Answer	Page	Explanation
1.	False	36–37, 45	Henry R. Towne was the presenter of "shop management" and "shop accounting." Henri Gantt focused on "control" systems for production scheduling. Henry Gantt is known for the Gantt Chart, which is a progress report in visual form that identifies various stages of work that must be carried out to complete a project.
2.	True		
3.	False	39–43	Bureaucratic management relies on rules, a set hierarchy, a clear division of labor, and detailed procedures. In a highly bureaucratic organization adherence to rules and procedures may take precedence over effective, timely decision making. Also, managers in a bureaucratic organization may ignore issues of employee productivity while protecting and expanding their own authority.
4.	True		
5.	False	44	Frederick W. Taylor did the pioneering work in scientific management. Scientific management focuses on individual worker–machine relationships in manufacturing plants. Henri Fayol is identified with administrative management. He was the first person to group management functions known today as planning, organizing, leading, and controlling.
6.	True		
7.	False	42	The behavioral (human relations) viewpoint focuses on dealing more effectively with the human side of organizations. The traditional viewpoint stresses the manager's role in a strict hierarchy and focuses on efficient and consistent job performance.
8.	True		

9.	False	47	Traditionalists are concerned with the formal relations among an organization's departments, tasks, and processes. Job security, career progression, and protection of workers from employers' whims are considered important by traditionalists. However, they do not recognize informal or social relationships among employees at work.
10.	False	41	Scientific management focuses on individuals and their machines or tools. Its philosophy is that management practices should be based on proven fact and observation, not on hearsay or guesswork.
11.	False	49	The Hawthorne Contributions illustrated that when employees are given special attention, productivity is likely to change regardless of whether working conditions change. This phenomenon is known as the Hawthorne effect.
12.	True		
13.	True		
14.	True		
15.	True		
16.	False	55	Proponents of the contingency viewpoint advocate using the other three management viewpoints independently or in combination, as necessary, to deal with various situations.
17.	True		
18.	False	56	Total quality management (TQM) is the continuous process of ensuring that every aspect of production builds quality into the product.
19.	False	56	The godfather of the quality movement was W. Edwards Deming. He stressed the need for all employees to use statistics to improve quality and productivity, build trust, and work closely with customers. Deming believed that poor quality is 85 percent a management problem and 15 percent a worker problem.
20.	True		

MULTIPLE CHOICE SOLUTIONS

Question	Answer	Page	Explanation
1.	d	37	These are all reasons why the history of management is important to today's managers.
2.	d	41	Charismatic authority is evident when subordinates suspend their own judgment and comply voluntarily with a leader because of special personal qualities or abilities they perceive in that individual. Social, political, and religious movements are often headed by charismatic leaders. Leaders such as Jesus, Joan of Arc, Gandhi, and Martin Luther King are considered to have exhibited charismatic authority.
3.	b	42	Efficiency and consistency are benefits of bureaucratic management, whereas rigid rules and red tape, protection of authority, slow decision making, incompatibility with changing technology, and incompatibility with professional values are considered drawbacks.
4.	c	44	Frederick Taylor, a pioneer of scientific management, conducted a shovel experiment at the Bethlehem Steel Company. Henri Fayol developed fourteen principles of management which today are referred to as the functions of management. Frank Gilbreth also worked on motion studies and conducted the bricklaying experiment. Lastly, Henry Gantt focused on "control systems" and is noted for the Gantt chart.
5.	d	45	KFC was utilizing scientific management principles. They also used time-and-motion studies, Gantt charts, and teamwork. The team developed administrative procedures for eliminating wasted motions by employees.
6.	c	39, 46	Max Weber introduced bureaucratic management, which relies on rules, a set hierarchy, a clear division of labor, and detailed procedures. He presented seven characteristics: a formal system of rules, impersonality, division of labor, hierarchical structure, a detailed authority structure, lifelong career commitment, and rationality. Henri Fayol is most closely associated with administrative management. Unity of command states that an employee should report to only one manager. This is one of Fayol's principles.

7.	a	47	Traditionalists focused on efficient and effective job performance. Job security, career progression, and protection of workers were considered important elements of enhancing efficient and effective performance.
8.	a	48	The <u>behavioral viewpoint</u> focuses on dealing effectively with the human aspects of organizations. Its proponents look at how managers do what they do, how managers lead subordinates and communicate with them, and why managers need to change their assumptions about people if they want to lead high-performance teams and organizations.
9.	c	49	Chester Barnard believed that managers should have a good working relationship with their subordinates. One way to do this is to involve subordinates in the decision-making process. Barnard's acceptance theory of authority states that employees have free will and thus will choose whether or not to follow management's orders (a, b, and d are included in this theory).
10.	b	48	Mary Parker Follett believed that management is a flowing, continuous process, not a static one, and that coordination is vital to effective management. She believed the people closest to the action could make the best decisions. She was convinced that first-line managers are in the best position to coordinate production tasks. And by increasing communication among themselves and with workers, these managers can make better decisions regarding such tasks than managers up the hierarchy can.
11.	d	49–50	All are true. When employees are given special attention, productivity is likely to change regardless of whether working conditions change—known as the Hawthorne effect.
12.	b	51	A <u>system</u> is an association of interrelated and interdependent parts.
13.	b	52	<u>Transformation processes</u> comprise the technologies used to convert inputs into outputs.
14.	c	52	An <u>open system</u> interacts with the external environment as with Sprint's marketing department. A <u>closed system</u> limits its interactions with its environment. Some production departments operate as closed systems, producing standardized products in an uninterrupted stream.

15.	d	53	Quantitative techniques have four basic characteristics: (1) The primary focus is on decision making. The solution identifies direct actions that managers can take, such as JIT to reduce inventory costs. (2) Alternatives are based on economic criteria. Alternative actions are presented in terms of measurable criteria, such as costs, revenues, and dealer returns. (3) Mathematical models are used. Situations are simulated and problems are analyzed by means of mathematical models. (4) Computers are essential. Computers are used to solve complex mathematical models that would be too costly and time-consuming to process manually, such as statistical process controls.
16.	a	55	The contingency viewpoint (situational approach) really means that it all depends on the situation. Its essence is that management practices should be consistent with the requirements of the external environment, the technology used to make a product or provide a service, and capabilities of the people who work for the organization.
17.	c	55	Joan Woodward was one of the pioneers in developing the contingency viewpoint of management. Lillian Gilbreth worked with her husband Frank Gilbreth on motion studies.
18.	b	55	The relative importance of each contingency variable—external environment, technology, and people—depends on the type of managerial problem being considered.
19.	d	56	Deming believed that managers should rely on only a few suppliers that have historically provided quality, not on sampling inspections of each delivery.
20.	c	56	This manager was encouraging the quality viewpoint by ensuring that an error was caught early.

ESSAY SOLUTIONS

[Pages 36–47]

1. The traditional or classical viewpoint stresses the manager's role in a strict hierarchy and focuses on efficient and consistent job performance. The three main branches are bureaucratic, scientific, and administrative management. All three branches emerged during roughly the same time period—the late 1890s through the early 1900s—when engineers were seeking to make organizations run like well-oiled machines.

    Bureaucratic management is a system that relies on rules, a set hierarchy, a clear division of labor, and detailed rules and procedures. Max Weber is recognized as creating the seven characteristics of bureaucratic management. They are: (1) rules, (2) impersonality, (3) division of labor, (4) hierarchical structure, (5) authority structure, (6) lifelong career commitment, and (7) rationality. The benefits of bureaucracy are efficiency and consistency. The drawbacks include: (1) rigid rules and red tape, (2) protection of authority, (3) slow decision making, (4) incompatibility with changing technology, and (5) incompatibility with professional values.

    Scientific management focuses on individual worker-machine relationships in manufacturing plants. Pioneering work was done by Frederick W. Taylor. Two concepts were used during this time, time-and-motion studies and functional foremanship. Time-and-motion studies involve identifying and measuring a worker's physical movements when performing a task and then analyzing the results. Functional foremanship is a division of labor that links each foreman's area of specialization to that foreman's scope of authority. Frank and Lillian Gilbreth used motion pictures to study the process and arrange motions to eliminate wasted motions and create greater efficiency. Henry Gantt focused on "control" systems for production scheduling and created the Gantt chart.

    Administrative management focuses on the manager and basic managerial functions. Henri Fayol was the first person to group managers' functions that today are summarized as planning, organizing, leading, and controlling. He also developed fourteen management principles and suggested that managers receive formal training in their application.

[Page 46]

2. <u>Administrative management</u> focuses on the manager and basic managerial functions. It evolved early in this century and is most closely identified with Henri Fayol, a French industrialist. He felt strongly that, to be successful, managers had only to understand the basic managerial functions—planning, organizing, leading, and controlling—and apply management principles to them.

    Two of Fayol's management principles described in the text are:
    a. *Authority principle*—Managers have the right to give orders to get things done.
    b. *Unity of command principle*—Each employee should report to only one manager.

[Pages 48, 51]

3. The <u>behavioral viewpoint</u> focuses on dealing more effectively with the human aspects of organizations. It goes beyond the traditionalists' mechanical view of work by stressing the importance of group dynamics, complex human motivations, and the manager's leadership style. It emphasizes the employee's social and economic needs and the influence of the organization's social setting on the quality and quantity of work produced.

    The basic assumptions of the behavioral viewpoint include:

    a. Employees are motivated by social needs and get a sense of identity through their associations with one another.
    b. Employees are more responsive to the social forces exerted by their peers than to management's financial incentives and rules.
    c. Employees are most likely to respond to managers who can help them satisfy their needs.
    d. Managers need to coordinate work with the participation of their subordinates to improve efficiency.

[Pages 51–52]

4. The <u>systems viewpoint</u> of management represents an approach to solving problems by diagnosing them within a framework of inputs, transformation processes, outputs, and feedback. A <u>system</u> is an association of interrelated and interdependent parts. An organization is a system with many teams, departments, and levels that are linked to achieve the organization's goals. <u>Inputs</u> are the physical, human, material, financial, and information resources that enter the transformation process. <u>Transformation processes</u> compromise the technologies used to convert inputs into outputs. <u>Outputs</u> are the original inputs (human, physical, material, informational, and financial resources) as changed by a transformation process. <u>Feedback</u> is information about a system's status and performance. In an organization, feedback may include marketing surveys, financial reports, production records, performance appraisals, etc. Management's role in the systems viewpoint is to ease the transformation process by planning, organizing, leading, and controlling the system.

[Pages 54–55]

5. The <u>contingency viewpoint</u> (situational approach) suggests that management practices should be consistent with the requirements of the external environment, the technology used to make a product or provide a service, and capabilities of the people who work for the organization. It contends that different situations require different practices and advocates the use of the other viewpoints separately or in combination to deal with various situations. Applying the contingency viewpoint requires the development and use of conceptual skills. Managers must be able to diagnose and understand a situation thoroughly to determine which approach is most likely to be successful before making a decision. The contingency viewpoint holds that the effectiveness of different managerial

works in all situations. It all depends on the type of managerial problem and the facts involved.

[Pages 56, 58–59]

6. <u>Total Quality Management</u> (TQM) is the continuous process of ensuring that every aspect of production builds in product quality. Quality must be stressed repeatedly so that it becomes second nature to everyone in an organization and its suppliers.

Successfully offering high-quality goods and services to the customer typically results in three important benefits for the organization:

a. *Positive Company Image*. Organizations can gain advantages from having a positive image. It helps them recruit new employees, increase sales of new products, and helps them obtain funds from various lending agencies.

b. *Lower Costs and Higher Market Share*. Improved performance increases productivity and lowers rework time, scrap costs, and warranty costs, leading to increased profits.

c. *Decreased Product Liability*. Successful TQM efforts typically result in improved products and product performance and lower product liability costs.

[Page 56]

7. W. Edwards Deming (1900–1993) is considered the godfather of the quality movement. His ideas were initially rejected by U.S. managers. He helped rebuild Japan's industrial empire and taught Japanese managers how to use statistics to assess and improve quality.

CHAPTER 3
ENVIRONMENTAL FORCES

LEARNING OBJECTIVES

After studying this chapter, you should be able to:

❖**1**❖ Describe how economic and cultural factors influence organizations.

❖**2**❖ Identify the five competitive forces that affect organizations in an industry.

❖**3**❖ Describe the principal political and legal strategies used by managers to cope with changes in the environment.

❖**4**❖ Explain how technological changes influence the structure of industries.

OUTLINE

❖**1**❖ Describe how economic and cultural factors influence organizations.

1. **The General Environment**—sometimes called the macroenvironment, includes the external factors that usually affect all or most organizations.

   a. Includes: type of economic system, economic conditions, type of political system, condition of the ecosystem, demographics, and cultural background.

   b. All of the above aspects of the general environment have long-range implications for managing organizations.

2. **The Economy**

   a. <u>Economics</u>—the discipline that focuses on understanding how a group of people or a nation produce, distribute, and consume various goods and services.

   b. Free-market competition, private contracts, profit incentives, technological advancement, and organized labor with collective bargaining rights are essential elements of the U.S. economic system.

   c. The government (part of the political system) acts as a watchdog over business, providing direction in antitrust, monetary policy, human rights, defense, and environmental matters.

d. Several trends are currently affecting the U.S. and Canadian economies:

1. *Value Matters*—major emphasis on value where value has shifted from the tangible to the intangible.

2. *Borderless Competition*—the limitations of geographic borders apply less and less. Firms can increasingly reach customers directly without regard to their physical location or that of their customers.

3. *Customer Convenience*—organizations in the new economy will succeed by creating convenience for their customers.

4. *Human Capital*—in the new economy, organizations must manage knowledge, not just data or information.

    a. <u>Knowledge Management</u>—the creation, protection, development, and sharing of knowledge assets.

    b. In the new economy, human capital will gave greater power because it is people who create and share knowledge.

3. **The Environment**

    a. <u>Environmental Stewardship</u>—a policy that an organization adopts to protect or enhance the natural resources in the conduct of its business activities.

    b. <u>Management Action Plans</u>—managers can take the following specific actions to respond to environmental concerns:

        1. Give a senior-level person well defined environmental responsibilities.

        2. Measure everything and set measurable goals and target dates for improvement.

        3. Consider reformulating products in order to use less toxic chemicals in the manufacturing and cleanup.

        4. Consider business opportunities for recycling and disposing of products.

        5. Recognize that environmental regulations are likely to stay and become and become even more restrictive.

    c. Environmental concerns have changed the way producers and consumers alike think about products, the raw materials used to make them, and the byproducts of manufacturing processes.

4. **Demographics**—the characteristics of work groups, organizations, specific markets, or various populations.

    a. <u>Demographics</u>—and in particular, changes in demographics—play an important role in marketing, advertising, and human resource management.

    b. <u>Increasing Diversity</u>—the U.S. workforce is becoming more diverse. The U.S. labor force is becoming more diverse as women and people of color will gradually represent a larger percentage of the labor force.

    c. The U.S. economy has shifted from industrial production to services and information analysis.

d. This shift means that jobs of all kinds are likely to require some type of specialized skill and thus individuals will require more education and training.

e. Employers are likely to face new pressures from an increasingly diverse workforce and must learn how to manage diversity.

   1. *Contingent Workers*—employees who are independent contractors.

5. **Cultural Forces**

   a. Culture—the unique pattern of shared characteristics such as values, that distinguish the members of one group of people from those of another.

   b. Value—a basic belief about a condition that has considerable importance and meaning to individuals and is relatively stable over time.

   c. Value System—comprises multiple beliefs (values) that are compatible and supportive of one another.

   d. Values can greatly affect how a manager:

      1. Views other people and groups, thus influencing interpersonal relationships.

      2. Perceives situations and problems.

      3. Goes about solving problems.

      4. Determines what is and is not ethical behavior.

      5. Leads and controls employees.

   e. By diagnosing a culture's values, managers and employees can understand and predict others' expectations and avoid some cultural pitfalls.

   f. Geert Hofstede, director of the Institute for Research on Intercultural Cooperation in the Netherlands, developed a framework of work-related values that uncovered some intriguing differences among countries in terms of the following five dimensions.

      1. *Power Distance*—the degree to which less powerful members of society accept that influence is unequally divided.

      2. *Uncertainty Avoidance*—the extent to which members of a culture feel threatened by risky or unknown situations.

      3. *Individualism*—a combination of the degree to which society expects people to take care of themselves and their immediate families and the degree to which individuals believe they are masters of their own destinies.

      4. *Collectivism*—opposite of individualism. Refers to a tight social framework in which group members (e.g., family, clan, organization, and nation) focus on the common welfare and feel strong loyalty toward one another.

5. *Masculinity*—the degree to which assertiveness and the acquisition of money and material things are valued, as well as the degree of indifference to others' quality of life.

6. *Femininity*—opposite of masculinity. Refers to a more nurturing, people-oriented approach to life.

7. *Long-Term/Short-Term Orientation*—this value was originally developed to reflect the teaching of Confucius who developed a pragmatic set of rules for daily life.

   a. Hofstede has extended his earlier work and labeled this dimension long-term/short-term – which reflects the extent to which a culture stresses that its members accept delayed gratification of material, social, and emotional needs.

   b. In long-term oriented cultures, families stress the importance of thrift, ordering relationships by status and observing this order, persistence, and education.

   c. The family is the prototype of all social organizations.

   d. People should treat others as they would like to be treated.

g. Managerial Implications—understanding culture can make you a better manager even if you never leave your own country. For in this ever increasing global market, managers in every country must think globally.

❖**2**❖   Identify the five competitive forces that affect organizations in an industry.

II.   **Competitive Forces in an Industry**

1. **Competitors**—the single most important day-to-day force facing organizations, aside from customers.

2. **New Entrants**—the relative ease with which new firms can compete with established firms.

   a. Common factors to diagnose in assessing barriers to entry:

     1. *Economies of Scale*—achieved when increased volume lowers the unit cost of a good or service produced by a firm.

     2. *Production Differentiation*—uniqueness in quality, price, design, brand image, or customer service that gives one firm's product an edge over another firm's.

     3. *Capital Requirements*—the dollars needed to finance equipment, purchase supplies, purchase or lease land, hire staff, and the like.

     4. *Government Regulation*—a barrier to entry if it bars or severely restricts potential new entrants to an industry.

3. **Substitute Goods and Services**—goods or services that can easily replace other goods or services.

4. **Customers**—by playing one against the other, try to force down prices, obtain more or higher quality products (while holding prices constant), and increase competition among sellers.

   a. Customer bargaining power is likely to be great when:

      1. The customer purchases a large volume relative to the supplier's total sales.

      2. The product or service represents a significant expenditure by the customer.

      3. Large volume customers pose a threat of backward integration. *Backward integration* is the purchase of one or more of its suppliers by a larger corporation as a cost-cutting or quality enhancing strategy.

      4. Customers have readily available alternatives for the same services or products.

5. **Suppliers**—their bargaining power often controls how much they can raise prices above their costs or reduce the quality of goods and services before losing customers.

❖**3**❖ Describe the principal political and legal strategies used by managers to cope with changes in the environment.

III. **Political–Legal Forces**

1. To achieve organizational goals, managers must accurately diagnose political and legal forces and find useful ways to anticipate, respond to, or avoid the disturbances they cause.

2. **Equal Credit Opportunity Act**—entitles the customer to be considered for credit without regard to race, color, age, sex, or marital status.

3. **Truth in Lending Act**—states that credit grantors must reveal the "true" cost of using credit—for instance, the annual interest rate the customer will be paying.

4. The five basic political strategies to assist managers in coping with turbulence in their task environments are the following:

   a. <u>Negotiation</u>—the process by which two or more individuals or groups having both common and conflicting goals present and discuss proposals in an attempt to reach an agreement. It is probably the most important political strategy because each of the other four strategies involves to some degree the use of negotiation.

   b. <u>Lobbying</u>—an attempt to influence government decisions by providing officials with information on the anticipated effects of legislation or regulatory rulings.

    c. <u>Alliance</u>—a unified effort involving two or more organizations, groups, or individuals to achieve common goals with respect to a particular issue.

       1. Alliances often are used for the following purposes:

         a. Oppose or support legislation, nomination of heads of regulatory agencies, and regulations issued by such agencies.

         b. Improve competitiveness of two or more organizations through collaboration.

         c. Promote particular products or services, such as oranges, computers, and electricity.

         d. Construct facilities that would be beyond the resources of any one organization, such as new plants.

         e. Represent the interests of specific groups, such as women, the elderly, minorities, and particular industries.

       2. <u>Joint Venture</u>—typically involves two or more firms becoming partners to form a separate entity. Each partner benefits from the others' competence, which allows them to achieve their goals more quickly and efficiently.

       3. <u>Representation</u>—membership in an outside organization that is intended to serve the interests of the member's organization or group.

       4. <u>Socialization</u>—the process by which people learn the values held by an organization and the broader society.

❖**4**❖   Explain how technological forces influence changes in industries

IV. Technological Forces

    1. **Technology**—the tools, knowledge, techniques, and actions used to transform materials, information, and other inputs into finished goods and services.

    2. **Impact of Technology**—technological forces play an increasingly pivotal role in creating and changing an organization's task environment.

      a. Computer-based information technologies are now essential in most organizations.

      b. Information technology creates options including the following, that simply weren't feasible with older technologies:

        1. Computer-aided design linked to versatile, computer-controlled machines.

        2. Consumers shopping via home pages on the Internet and "electronic shopping malls."

        3. Online, real-time financial management systems.

        4. Retail banking.

c. Advances in design and manufacturing technology have made it possible to reduce substantially the amount of time required to introduce a new product into the market.

d. In the late 1990s, perhaps the single greatest change in distribution was the strong presence of the Internet and the World Wide Web, which provided online ordering, distribution, and sales.

e. Satellites, cellular towers, and fiber-optic telephone cables allow individuals and companies to exchange voice, data, and graphic messages in real time.

f. The Information Superhighway will provide opportunities for firms in the future and will affect every organization in the years ahead.

MATCHING

Directions: Select the term that best identifies the statement listed below. Place the letter of the correct term in the space provided.

A. Value System
B. Capital Requirements
C. Socialization
D. Alliance
E. Economics
F. Negotiation
G. Culture
H. Representation
I. Technology

J. Power Distance
K. Uncertainty Avoidance
L. Truth in Lending Act
M. Contingent Workers
N. Demographics
O. Lobbying
P. Femininity
Q. Joint Venture

_____ 1. The tools, knowledge, techniques, and actions used to transform materials, information, and other inputs into finished goods and services.

_____ 2. Typically involving two or more firms becoming partners to form a separate entity, which allows them to achieve their goals more quickly and efficiently.

_____ 3. Hofstede's value dimension that measures the degree to which less powerful members of society accept that influence is unequally divided.

_____ 4. The process by which people learn the values held by an organization and the broader society.

_____ 5. An attempt to influence government decisions by providing officials with information on the anticipated effects of legislation or regulatory rulings.

_____ 6. States that credit grantors must reveal the "true" cost of using credit.

_____ 7. The discipline that focuses on understanding how people of a group or nation produce, distribute, purchase, and use various goods and services.

_____ 8. Comprises multiple beliefs that are compatible and supportive of one another.

_____ 9. The characteristics of a work group, organization, specific market, or national population.

_____ 10. Membership in an outside organization for the purpose of furthering the interests of the member's organization.

_____ 11. The dollars needed to finance equipment, purchase supplies, purchase or lease land, hire staff, and the like.

_____ 12. The shared characteristics and values that distinguish one group of people from another.

_____ 13. Hofstede's value dimension that measures the tendency to be nurturing and people oriented.

_____ 14. The unity of two or more organizations, groups, or individuals to achieve common goals with respect to a particular issue.

_____ 15. The consequence of the massive downsizing of organizations has been an increase in the number of these.

_____ 16. The process by which two or more individuals or groups, having both common and conflicting goals, present and discuss proposals in an attempt to reach an agreement.

_____ 17. Hofstede's value dimension that measures the degree to which members of a culture feel threatened by risky or unknown situations.

TRUE OR FALSE

<u>Directions</u>: Write True or False in the space provided.

❖1❖

_____ 1. The general environment includes the external factors that usually affect all or most organizations.

_____ 2. Micromanagement is the creation, protection, development, and sharing of knowledge assets.

_____ 3. Although most consumers believe environmental issues are important, the demand for better, more technologically advanced products means that producers and consumers have not changed the way they think about products.

_____ 4. The U.S. economy is shifting from a service industry to industrial technological production that requires less specialized skill.

_____ 5. Austria is considered a low-masculinity culture where women now hold many managerial jobs.

_____ 6. According to Confucius, the family is the prototype of all social organizations.

❖2❖

_____   7.   Capital requirements are the dollars needed to finance equipment, purchase supplies, purchase or lease land, hire staff, and the like.

_____   8.   Economies of scale refers to the relative ease with which new firms can compete with established firms.

_____   9.   Product differentiation is found in such items as a product's uniqueness of quality, price, design, brand image or the customer service it offers its customers.

_____   10.   Aside from customers, suppliers are the single most important day-to-day force facing organizations.

_____   11.   Ronald McDonald and Happy Meals serve to differentiate McDonald's from its competitors.

_____   12.   The U.S. Postal Service has a monopoly on the products and services it provides, and competitors have not been able to produce substitute goods or services.

_____   13.   Rivalry among competitors produces strategies such as price cutting, advertising promotions, enhanced customer service or warranties, and improvements in product or service quality.

_____   14.   If McDonald's grows its own potatoes to obtain a direct source of raw materials for french fries, this would be an example of forward integration.

❖3❖

_____   15.   The Equal Credit Opportunity Act says that credit grantors must reveal the "true" cost of using credit to the customer.

_____   16.   The National Football League is an example of an organization utilizing the concept of alliance.

_____   17.   Representation includes formal and informal attempts by organizations to mold new employees to accept certain desired attitudes and ways of dealing with others and their jobs.

❖4❖

_____   18.   Technological forces play an increasingly pivotal role in creating and changing an organization's task environment.

_____   19.   Advances in design and manufacturing technology have made it possible to reduce substantially the amount of time required to introduce a new product into the market.

_____   20.   The only organizations that will be affected by the Information Superhighway are high-tech companies and the computer industry.

MULTIPLE CHOICE

Directions: Select the best answer in the space provided.

❖1❖

____ 1. Which of the following is <u>not</u> considered part of the general environment of a company?
     a. economic conditions
     b. employees
     c. culture
     d. demographics

____ 2. Which of the following statements is <u>false</u> regarding the U.S. economic system?
     a. Government ownership of enterprise is the exception rather than the norm.
     b. Free market competition and technological advancements are essential elements.
     c. The government acts as a watchdog over business, providing direction in antitrust and environmental matters.
     d. The economy is centrally planned.

____ 3. Firms such as Travelocity, Wells Fargo, and Charles Schwab exemplify which trend of the new economy?
     a. value matters
     b. human capital
     c. borderless competition
     d. customer convenience

____ 4. Which of the following statements is true relating to U.S. demographics?
     a. The number of Hispanic workers is expected to be 13 percent by 2010.
     b. During the next decade, 45 million workers will enter the U.S. labor force; one-half will be minorities.
     c. Most of the participation of working women will come from second-career women.
     d. The percentage of African-American workers will increase by 25 percent by 2005.

____ 5. As a result of massive downsizing in the country today, which of the following workers is in greatest demand?
     a. child-care workers
     b. computer engineers
     c. special education teachers
     d. contingent workers

____ 6. A _____ is a basic belief about a condition that has considerable importance and meaning to individuals and is relatively stable over time.
     a. culture
     b. religion
     c. heritage
     d. None of the above.

TRUE/FALSE SOLUTIONS

Question	Answer	Page	Explanation
1.	True		
2.	False	73	Knowledge management is the creation, protection, development, and sharing of knowledge assets.
3.	False	73–74	Environmental concerns have changed the way producers and consumers alike think about products, the raw materials used to make them, and the byproducts of manufacturing processes. In fact, industries have developed a whole new generation of successful products in response to the Clean Air Act and reuse and recycling regulations.
4.	False	75	The U.S. economy has shifted from industrial production to services and information analysis. This shift means that jobs of all kinds are more likely to require some type of specialized skill. One result is that people with little education or training will continue to have a hard time finding meaningful and well-paying work and experience long spells of "labor market inactivity."
5.	False	80	Austria, Mexico, Japan, and Italy are considered high-masculinity cultures, and women still do not hold many managerial jobs in these countries. Masculinity is the degree to which assertiveness and the acquisition of money and material things are valued, as well as the degree of indifference to others' quality of life.
6.	True		
7.	True		
8.	False	82	Economies of scale refers to decreases in per unit costs as the volume of goods and services produced by a firm increases.
9.	True		
10.	False	81	Competitors are the single most important day-to-day forces facing organizations.
11.	True		

12.	False	82	In a general sense, all competitors produce substitute goods or services, or goods or services that can easily replace another's goods or services. Many organizations commonly use fax, e-mail, and overnight delivery services as a substitute for the U.S. Postal Service.
13.	True		
14.	False	83	<u>Backward integration</u> is the purchase of one or more of its suppliers by a larger corporation as a cost-cutting or quality enhancement strategy. If McDonald's baked its own bread, grew its own potatoes, and raised its own cattle to get lower prices and better quality, McDonald's would be using backward integration.
15.	False	85	The <u>Equal Credit Opportunity Act</u> entitles the customer to be considered for credit without regard to race, color, age, gender, or marital status. The credit grantor must apply credit worthiness fairly and impartially.
16.	True		
17.	False	87	<u>Representation</u> refers to membership in an outside organization that is intended to serve the interests of the member's organization or group. <u>Socialization</u> is the process by which people learn the values held by an organization and the broader society. It includes formal and informal attempts by organizations to mold new employees to accept certain desired attitudes and ways of dealing with others and their jobs.
18.	True		
19.	True		
20.	False	92	The Information Superhighway will affect every organization in the years ahead.

MULTIPLE CHOICE SOLUTIONS

Question	Answer	Page	Explanation
1.	b	70	The general environment, sometimes called the macroenvironment, includes the external factors that usually affect all or most organizations. Employees would be an internal force impacting an organization.
2.	d	71	The first three statements are true. The economy is not centrally planned, as in North Korea, Cuba, and the People's Republic of China.
3.	c	72	The limitations of geographic borders apply less and less. Firms can increasingly reach customers directly without regard to their physical location or that of their customers. The Internet is revolutionary because it has dramatically reduced the cost of communication and coordination in business and personal transactions.
4.	a	74–75	The number of Hispanic workers is expected to be 13 percent by 2010.
5.	d	75	One consequence of the massive downsizing of organizations has been an increase in the number of contingent workers, employees who are independent contractors, entering the market.
6.	d	75–76	A value is a basic belief about a condition that has considerable importance and meaning to individuals and is relatively stable over time.
7.	c	78	Mexico, France, Malaysia, and the Philippines rank high in power distance. Membership in a particular class or caste is crucial to an individual's opportunity for advancement. In contrast, individuals in the United States, Canada, Sweden, and Austria can achieve prestige, wealth, and social status, regardless of family background.
8.	b	78–79	Uncertainty avoidance is the extent to which members of a culture feel threatened by risky or unknown situations. An organization with high uncertainty avoidance is associated with built-in career stability, numerous rules governing behavior, intolerance of deviant ideas and behavior, belief in absolute truths, and overreliance on expertise.

| 9. | d | 78 | <u>Power distance</u> is the degree to which less powerful members of society accept that influence is unequally divided. |

| 10. | a | 78 | <u>Uncertainty avoidance</u> is the extent to which members of a culture feel threatened by risky or unknown situations. |

| 11. | c | 79 | <u>Collectivism</u> refers to a tight social framework in which group members focus on the common welfare and feel strong loyalty to one another. |

| 12. | d | 81 | The five competitive forces are: competitors, new entrants, substitute goods and services, customers, and suppliers. |

| 13. | b | 82 | <u>Economies of scale</u> refers to decreases in per unit costs as the volume of goods and services produced by a firm increases. <u>Capital requirements</u> are the dollars needed to finance equipment, purchase supplies, purchase or lease land, hire staff, and the like. |

| 14. | b | 82 | <u>Product differentiation</u> is uniqueness in quality, price, design, brand image, or customer service that gives one firm's product an edge over the competition. |

| 15. | a | 83 | <u>Backward integration</u> is the purchase of one or more of its suppliers by a larger organization as a cost-cutting measure. Meijer's food store is going backward on the channel of distribution to reduce costs and ensure a quality supply. |

| 16. | d | 83 | The customer purchases a large volume relative to the supplier's total sales. |

| 17. | c | 85 | The <u>Equal Credit Opportunity Act</u> entitles the customer to be considered for credit without regard to race, color, age, gender or marital status. |

| 18. | d | 85 | <u>Lobbying</u> is an attempt to influence government decisions by providing officials with information on the anticipated effects of legislation or regulatory rulings. Congress and regulatory agencies such as the Securities and Exchange Commission (SEC), the Federal Communications Commission (FCC), and the Interstate Commerce Commission (ICC) are the targets of continuous lobbying efforts by organizations affected by their decisions. |

3. **Language**—serves to bind as well as separate cultures.

    a. Fluency in another language can give an international manager a competitive edge in understanding and gaining the acceptance of people from the host culture.

    b. A manager must also be able to recognize and interpret the nuances of phrases, sayings, and nonverbal gestures.

4. **Value Systems**—differences in cultural values naturally affect how managers and professionals function in international business. A country's cultural values determine how people interact with one another and with companies and institutions.

    a. Cultural Distance—differences in religious beliefs, race, social norms, and language are all capable of creating cultural distance between two countries.

    b. Some cultural differences between countries, such as language, are easily perceived and understood, while others (e.g., social norms) are much more subtle.

    c. Social norms, the deeply rooted system of unspoken principles that guide individuals in their everyday behaviors, are often nearly invisible.

    d. Cultural differences also influence the choices that consumers make.

❖**3**❖   Explain the impact of political-legal forces on international business.

III. **Political–Legal Forces**

1. **Political Risk**—the probability that political decisions or events in a country will negatively affect the long-term profitability of an investment.

2. Political risk factors may be grouped into five principal categories:

    a. Domestic Instability—the amount of subversion, revolution, assassinations, guerrilla warfare, and government crisis in a country.

    b. Foreign Conflict—the degree of hostility that one nation expresses to others.

        1. Such hostility can range from the expulsion of diplomats to outright war.

    c. Political Climate—the likelihood that a government will swing to the far left or far right politically.

        1. Managers may evaluate variables such as the number and size of political parties, the number of factions in the legislature, role of the military in the political process, amount of corruption in government, effectiveness of political leadership, influence of organized religion in politics, extent of racial and nationality tensions, and quality of the governmental bureaucracy.

    d. <u>Economic Climate</u>—reflects the extent of government control of markets and financial investments, as well as government support services and capabilities.

        1. Variables in this category include: government regulatory and economic control policies, government ability to manage its own economic affairs, government provision of support services and facilities (infrastructure), and government capabilities in general.

    e. <u>Corruption</u>—relates to the degree to which institutions, including the government, are perceived to be untrustworthy, are open to bribes, and conduct fraudulent business practices.

3. **Protectionism**—various mechanisms designed to help a home-based industry or firm avoid (or reduce) potential (or actual) competitive or political threats from abroad. Opponents suggest that it works against consumers' interests because it results in higher prices, while advocates claim that it protects home-country industries and jobs against unfair competition. The four widely used protectionism mechanisms are:

    a. <u>Tariff</u>—a government tax on goods or services entering the country.

        1. Its primary purpose is to raise the price of imported goods or services so that domestic goods and services gain a relative price advantage.

    b. <u>Quota</u>—a restriction on the quantity of a country's imports (or sometimes, on its exports).

        1. Import quotas generally are intended to guarantee home-country manufacturers access to a certain percentage of the domestic market.

    c. <u>Subsidy</u>—a direct or indirect payment by a government to its country's firms to make selling or investing abroad cheaper for them—and thus more profitable.

    d. <u>Cartel</u>—an alliance of producers engaged in the same type of business, which is formed to limit or eliminate competition and control production and prices.

        1. International cartels currently exist in oil, copper, aluminum, natural rubber, and other raw materials.

4. **Bribe**—an improper payment made to induce the recipient to do something for the payer.

    a. Bribes are illegal in Canada, the United States, and many other countries, but they are not illegal in some countries.

    b. By offering a bribe, the payer hopes to obtain a special favor in exchange for something of value.

5. **Extortion**—a payment made to ensure that the recipient does not harm the payer in some way.

    a. The purpose of extortion is to obtain something of value by threatening harm to the payer.

b. Bribery and extortion are practiced throughout the world and occur most frequently in Indonesia, Azerbaijan, Honduras, Tanzania, Yugoslavia, and several other countries.

c. U.S. Foreign Corrupt Practices Act of 1977—makes it a crime for U.S. corporations or individuals to offer or make payments to officials of foreign governments or companies for the purpose of obtaining or retaining business.

1. The act established specific record-keeping requirements for publicly held corporations, making difficult the concealment of political payments prohibited by the act.

2. A company may be fined as much as $1 million, and a manager who directly participates in or has knowledge of any violations of the act faces up to five years in prison and/or $100,000 in fines.

6. **Grease Payments**—small payments—almost gratuities—used to get lower level government employees to speed up required paperwork.

a. The Foreign Corrupt Practices Act of 1977 does not prohibit grease payments to employees of foreign governments whose duties are primarily procedural or clerical.

b. Such payments are often required to persuade employees to perform their normal duties.

❖**4**❖ Discuss how three major trade agreements affect global competition.

IV. **Global Trade Agreements**

1. **World Trade Organization**—was established in 1995 as an outgrowth of the General Agreement on Tariffs and Trade (GATT). WTO represents a series of negotiated understandings regarding trade and related issues among the participating countries.

a. The first GATT was signed by twenty-three countries in 1947.

b. The WTO has 144 member countries, which account for about 95 percent of world trade. By 2005, world trade in merchandise and commercial services is forecasted to exceed $8 trillion, or $2 trillion more than in 2000.

c. Key functions of the WTO include:

1. Administering WTO agreements

2. Providing a forum for trade negotiations

3. Handling trade disputes between nations

4. Monitoring national trade policies

5. Providing technical assistance and training for people in developing countries

6. Cooperating with other international organizations (such as the European Union, the Association of South East Asian Nations, and the association formed as a result of the North American Free Trade Agreement).

d. Benefits to member nations include:

1. The agreement promotes peace by handling trade disputes constructively.

2. Rules that make life easier for all organizations to follow.

3. Trade stimulates economic growth and reduces the cost of living.

4. The system encourages good government.

e. Most Favored Nation (MFN) Principle—means that when country A grants a tariff concession to country B, the same concession automatically applies to all other countries that are members of GATT.

f. Reciprocity Principle—ensures each member country that it will not be forced to reduce tariffs unilaterally. A tariff concession is made only in return for comparable concessions from the other countries.

g. Transparency Principle—establishes that tariffs be readily visible to all countries.

2. **North American Free Trade Agreement** (NAFTA)—went into effect in 1994 to increase trade and created a United States, Canadian, and Mexican trade zone of 8.2 million square miles, 400 million consumers, and $600 billion of dollars worth of economic activity.

a. NAFTA essentially created a giant free-trade zone among the US, Canada, and Mexico by removing barriers to trade, such as tariffs, quotas, and licenses.

b. U.S. exports to its NAFTA partners have increased more than 100% between 1993 and 2002, whereas U.S. trade with the rest of the world grew only half as fast. Today the U.S. exports more to Mexico and Canada than to the countries that combine to form the European Union.

c. Although full elimination of certain tariffs will not take place until 2009, more than 70% of goods imported from Mexico may now enter the U.S. without tariffs. At the same time, more than 50% of U.S. exports to Mexico are now tariff free.

d. The agreement also realizes long-held goals of fostering trade in services and liberalizing foreign investment rules. It tightens the protection of intellectual property.

e. Maquiladora Plants—are foreign-owned industrial plants located in Mexico that border the U.S. states of Texas, New Mexico, Arizona, and California.

1. These plants employ over 1 million people and account for 40% of Mexico's manufacturing while paying more than five times that country's minimum wage.

f. Despite much liberalization, NAFTA retains certain protectionist provisions, some of which may persist with no time limit.

3. **European Union** (EU)—called the European Community (EC) until 1994, currently has eighteen members: Austria, Belgium, Denmark, Finland, France, Germany, Greece, Iceland, Ireland, Italy, Liechtenstein, Luxembourg, the Netherlands, Norway, Portugal, Spain, Sweden, and the United Kingdom.

   a. These countries are home to nearly 400 million consumers and have introduced a common currency, the euro, in 2001.

   b. The goals of the EU include: creating a single market among member countries through the removal of trade barriers (such as tariffs) and establishing the free movement of goods, people, services, and investment capital.

   c. International Organization for Standardization (ISO)—issues certification standards for excellence in quality.

   d. The EU is more than an economic union—it is a state of mind and a political force.

   e. A major stage of the EU program is to complete formation of the common internal market by eliminating: physical barriers, technical barriers, fiscal barriers, and financial barriers.

   f. The European Commission is the EU's executive body and sole initiator of legislation. It claims that 95% of the legislative measures set out in the 1992 program have been adopted (although many of the toughest measures have not yet been adopted).

   g. Many non-Europeans are concerned that the free market of Europe will not be "free" to outsiders in the future.

❖**5**❖ Describe six strategies used by organizations in international business

V. **Strategies for International Business**

   1. **Complexity/Resource Commitment**—Complexity refers to the structure of the organization and the amount of coordination required to deliver a product or service to customers. Resource commitment refers to the amount of tangible financial assets and information support systems that the organization dedicates to its global strategy.

   2. **Exporting Strategy**—involves maintaining facilities within a home country and transferring goods and services abroad for sale in foreign markets.

   a. Exporting is a practical means for small or medium-sized organizations with little financial resources to invest but who are facing increased competition in their domestic markets.

   b. Countertrade—an agreement that requires companies from the exporting nation to purchase products of equivalent value from the importing nation.

3. **Licensing Strategy**—involves a firm (the licensor) in one country giving other domestic or foreign firms (licensees) the right to use a patent, trademark, technology, production process, or product in return for the payment of a royalty or fee.

   a. The licensor may provide manufacturing, technical, or marketing expertise to the licensee.

   b. Licensors do not have to worry about making major capital investments abroad or becoming involved in daily production, marketing, or management.

   c. Technological and market forces are combining to stimulate use of the licensing strategy.

4. **Franchising Strategy**—a parent organization (the franchiser) grants other companies or individuals (franchisees) the rights to use its trademarked name and to produce and sell its goods and services.

   a. The franchiser provides franchisees with a complete assortment of materials and services for a fee.

   b. The franchiser usually is actively involved in training, monitoring, and controlling the actions of the franchisee to ensure that it conforms to the franchise agreement.

5. **Alliance Strategy**—involves agreeing with other organizations to pool physical, financial, and human resources to achieve common goals.

   a. Global Strategic Alliances—joint ventures that involve actions taken internationally by two or more companies contributing an agreed upon amount of resources.

   b. The following factors have stimulated the formation of alliances, especially joint ventures:

      1. The need to share and lower the costs of high-risk, technologically intensive development projects, such as computer-based information systems.

      2. The desire to lower costs by sharing the large fixed-cost investments for manufacturing plants in some locations and in industries such as autos, steel, and appliances.

      3. The desire to learn another firm's technology and special processes or to gain access to customers and distribution channels.

      4. The desire to participate in the evolution of competitive activity in growing global industries.

   c. Alliances provide entry into markets that are risky because of strict political requirements or great economic uncertainty.

   d. Domestic partners are likely to have a deeper understanding of how to deal with severe political and economic uncertainty in countries such as China and Russia.

6. **Multidomestic Strategy**—involves adjusting products, services, and practices to individual countries or regions.

   a. It is based on the assumption that the benefits of local response will outweigh the extra costs of customizing. These companies view the world as a whole of unique parts and deal with each part individually.

   b. Each major overseas subsidiary is somewhat independent. Often each is a profit center and contributes earnings and growth in line with its market opportunity.

   c. A profit center is an organizational unit that is accountable for both the revenues generated by its activities and the costs of those activities.

7. **Global Strategy**—stresses operating with worldwide consistency, standardization, and low relative cost.

   a. Subsidiaries in various countries are highly interdependent in terms of goals, practices, and operations.

   b. Top managers focus on coordination and mutual support of the firm's worldwide activities.

   c. The customers of global firms have needs that are basically similar in many countries; thus primary marketing strategies are highly transferable across national boundaries.

MATCHING

Directions: Select the term that best identifies the statement listed below. Place the letter of the correct term in the space provided.

A. Corruption
B. Alliance Strategy
C. Cartel
D. ISO
E. Tariff
F. Protectionism
G. Reciprocity Principle
H. Global Strategy
I. Extortion
J. Domestic Instability

K. Political Climate
L. Exporting Strategy
M. Countertrade
N. Foreign Conflict
O. Economic Climate
P. Multidomestic Strategy
Q. Licensing Strategy
R. Subsidy
S. Grease Payments
T. Franchising Strategy

_____ 1. The mechanisms designed and used to help a home-based industry or firm avoid potential competitive or political threats from abroad.

_____ 2. A parent organization grants other companies or individuals the right to use its trademarked name and to produce and sell its goods or services.

_____ 3. Relates to the degree to which institutions, including the government, are perceived to be untrustworthy, are open to bribes, and conduct fraudulent business practices.

___ 4. Maintaining facilities within a home country and transferring goods and services abroad for sale in foreign markets.

___ 5. A direct or indirect payment by a government to its country's firms to make selling or investing abroad cheaper for them.

___ 6. The amount of subversion, revolution, assassinations, guerrilla warfare, and government crisis in a country.

___ 7. A set of worldwide standards that establish requirements for the management of quality.

___ 8. Adjusting products, services, and practices to individual countries or regions.

___ 9. The likelihood that a government will swing to the far left or far right politically.

___ 10. This stresses operating with worldwide consistency, standardization, and low relative cost.

___ 11. Small payments used to get lower level government employees to speed up required paperwork.

___ 12. Agreeing with other companies to pool physical, financial, and human resources to achieve common goals.

___ 13. An arrangement in which the export sales of goods and services by a producer is linked to an import purchase of other goods and services.

___ 14. A payment made to ensure that the recipient does not harm the payer in some way.

___ 15. A firm in one country gives other domestic or foreign firms the right to use a patent, trademark, technology, production process, or product in return for the payment of a royalty or fee.

___ 16. An alliance of producers engaged in the same type of business, formed to limit or eliminate competition and control production and prices.

___ 17. The degree of hostility that one nation shows toward others.

___ 18. A government tax on goods or services entering the country.

___ 19. Ensures that each member country that it will not be forced to reduce tariffs unilaterally.

___ 20. The extent of government control of markets and financial investments, as well as government support services and capabilities.

TRUE OR FALSE

Directions: Write True or False in the space provided.

❖1❖

___ 1. Exports alone represent approximately 40 percent of the U.S. gross domestic product.

_____ 2. The production of components for products is increasingly scattered around the world.

_____ 3. Since 1995, U.S. exports of goods and services has soared over 40 percent.

_____ 4. Currently, almost ten percent of jobs in the U.S. economy are dependent on international trade.

_____ 5. As domestic policies are becoming more market oriented, governments are restricting their nations from joining regional trade associations.

_____ 6. The prevalence of labor and resources in different parts of the world has fueled the growth of the global economy.

❖2❖

_____ 7. There are four aspects of culture that have direct implications for international management and they include: time orientation, language, cultural distance, and value systems.

_____ 8. Different views of the need for social change and its pace can have a significant impact on an organization's plans for international operations.

_____ 9. Most people in the United States and Canada think of time as an unlimited and unending resource.

_____ 10. The American culture accepts large power distances between people in that they believe that everyone has his or her place in an order of inequality.

❖3❖

_____ 11. Domestic instability is the probability that political decisions or events in a country will negatively affect the long-term profitability of an investment.

_____ 12. Protectionism refers to various mechanisms designed to help a home-based industry or firm avoid potential competitive or political threats from abroad.

_____ 13. A quota's primary purpose is to raise the price of imported goods or services.

_____ 14. A grease payment is considered an exception to the U.S. Foreign Corrupt Practices Act of 1977.

❖4❖

_____ 15. The most favored nation principle means that each member country will not be forced to reduce tariffs unilaterally.

_____ 16. NAFTA is intended to reduce and eliminate all trade and most nontariff barriers between Canada, Mexico, and the United States within the next five years; thus all protectionist elements will be eliminated by the end of the five-year time frame.

_____ 17. The goals of the EU include the creation of a single market among the member countries through the removal of trade barriers and establishing the free movement of goods, people, services, and investment capital.

❖5❖

___ 18. Complexity refers to the amount of tangible assets and information support systems that the organization dedicates to its global strategy.

___ 19. Countertrade continues to grow as a marketing tool for doing business in lesser developed countries.

___ 20. A multidomestic strategy involves adjusting products, services, and practices to individual countries or regions.

MULTIPLE CHOICE

<u>Directions</u>: Select the best answer in the space provided.

❖1❖

___ 1. Since 1995, U.S. exports of goods and services have soared _____ percent, accounting for much of the overall growth in the economy.
   a. 57
   b. 40
   c. 15
   d. 25

___ 2. Which of the following statements is <u>not</u> true?
   a. Exports and imports of goods and services represent about 30 percent of the U.S. gross domestic product.
   b. Today, one in six jobs in the U.S. depends on trade.
   c. Since 1995, U.S. exports of goods and services has soared over 60 percent.
   d. The globalization of business has placed a premium on information.

❖2❖

___ 3. Which of the following countries' people view change as a slow and natural progression where the attitude toward change tends to be passive or reactive?
   a. India
   b. Canada
   c. Australia
   d. United States

___ 4. The _____ attitude toward time could best be summarized by the word *mañana*, meaning "not today"—but not necessarily tomorrow either.
   a. Indian
   b. Mexican
   c. Portuguese
   d. Chinese

_____ 5.   In _____ managers are used to giving only positive feedback to their supervisors and to expressing views that only agree with their bosses.
   a.   China
   b.   Mexico
   c.   Taiwan
   d.   India

_____ 6.   Which of the following statements about the culturally differences between Mexico and the United States is <u>false</u>?
   a.   Americans prefer small power distances and Mexicans are comfortable with large power distances.
   b.   In Mexico, superiors have certain privileges by right and titles are very important and used regularly.
   c.   More than in Mexico, Americans feel threatened by uncertain and ambiguous situations and thus feel the need for written rules and procedures to develop security in their lives.
   d.   The typical American is more individualistic than the typical Mexican.

_____ 7.   Motorola's experience in Malaysia illustrates the impact of which of the following which hindered its ability to develop a team approach to fit that culture?
   a.   uncertainty avoidance
   b.   cultural distance
   c.   power distance
   d.   individualism

❖3❖

_____ 8.   _____ refers to the extent of government control of markets and financial investments as well as government support services and capabilities.
   a.   Political climate
   b.   Infrastructure
   c.   Economic climate
   d.   Domestic instability

_____ 9.   By utilizing _____, the U.S. government has given direct/indirect payments to certain domestic firms to make selling or investing abroad cheaper for them.
   a.   tariffs
   b.   import quotas
   c.   cartels
   d.   subsidies

_____ 10.   The best known example of a cartel is _____.
   a.   GATT
   b.   OPIC
   c.   OPEC
   d.   AT&T

____ 11. Foreign _____ are used to obtain a special favor in exchange for something of value.
  a. bribes
  b. extortion payments
  c. personal residences
  d. None of the above

❖4❖

____ 12. The _____ principle ensures each member country of GATT that it will not be forced to reduce tariffs unilaterally.
  a. most favored nation
  b. transparency
  c. reciprocity
  d. protectionism

____ 13. Which of the following statements about the WTO is false?
  a. One of its functions is to handle trade disputes between nations.
  b. It monitors national trade policies.
  c. It went into effect in 1994 to increase free trade between the United States, Canada, and Mexico
  d. It was established as an outgrowth of GATT.

____ 14. Which of the following countries is not currently a member of the European Union?
  a. Belgium
  b. France
  c. Portugal
  d. Turkey

____ 15. A major stage of the EU program is to complete formation of the common internal market. That involves eliminating _____.
  a. physical barriers
  b. fiscal barriers
  c. technical barriers
  d. All of the above.

❖5❖

____ 16. Is a practical means for small or medium-sized firms with little financial resources to invest but who are facing increased competition in their domestic markets.
  a. Exporting
  b. Franchising
  c. Licensing
  d. Domestic partnering

_____ 17. Marriott and Burger King are examples of organizations employing the _____ strategy.
   a. licensing
   b. alliance
   c. profit center
   d. franchising

_____ 18. Royal Crown Cola Company signed a joint venture agreement with Mexico's Consorico Aga to help RC Cola boost its sales there. In addition to liscensing its brands, RC Cola provides advertising, promotional, and technical support to Consorico Aga. This is an example of the _____ strategy.
   a. alliance
   b. domestic partner
   c. multidomestic
   d. conglomerate

_____ 19. Pressures for local customizing to respond to differences in customer demand, distribution channels, host government demands, and/or employee needs drive this strategy?
   a. strategic alliances
   b. exporting
   c. licensing
   d. multidomestic strategy

_____ 20. Which of the following ingredient(s) is needed for a multinational's global strategy to be successful?
   a. Most new goods and services need to be developed for the whole world.
   b. Profit targets should be based on product lines rather than countries or regions of the world.
   c. Foreign managers need to be promoted into senior ranks at corporate headquarters.
   d. All of the above.

ESSAY QUESTIONS

❖1❖

1. Explain several characteristics of the global economy.

❖2❖

2. Explain the concept of cultural distance, its importance, and whether its components are easily perceived in each country.

❖3❖

3. What is political risk? Discuss the five principal categories of political risk factors.

4. Discuss the U.S. Foreign Corrupt Practices Act of 1977.

❖4❖

5. Identify the members of the EU and its goals.

❖5❖

6. Explain the six strategies used in international business.

CHAPTER 4
MANAGING GLOBALLY

MATCHING SOLUTIONS

1. F - Protectionism
2. T - Franchising Strategy
3. A - Corruption
4. L - Exporting Strategy
5. R - Subsidy
6. J - Domestic Instability
7. D - ISO
8. P - Multidomestic Strategy
9. K - Political Climate
10. H - Global Strategy
11. S - Grease Payments
12. B - Alliance Strategy
13. M - Countertrade
14. I - Extortion
15. Q - Licensing Strategy
16. C - Cartel
17. N - Foreign Conflict
18. E - Tariff
19. G - Reciprocity Principle
20. O - Economic Climate

TRUE/FALSE SOLUTIONS

Question	Answer	Page	Explanation
1.	False	99	Employees and consumers are increasingly affected by the growing global economy. Exports and imports of goods and services represent about 30 percent of the U.S. gross domestic product, up from less than 21 percent in 1992.
2.	True		
3.	True		
4.	False	99	Trade is now so important to the U.S. economy that one job in six (over 16%) depends on it.

5.	False	100	As domestic policies are becoming more market oriented, governments are opening their countries to multinational trade and joining regional trade associations.
6.	True		
7.	False	101	Five aspects of a culture have direct implications for international management: views of social change, time orientation, language, value systems, and cultural distance.
8.	True		
9.	False	101	People in the U.S. and Canada think of time as an extremely scarce commodity. They often say "time is money" or "that there is too little time."
10.	False	102	Americans prefer small power distances and Mexicans are comfortable with large power distances.
11.	False	106	Political risk is the probability that political decisions or events in a country will negatively affect the long-term profitability of the investment.
12.	True		
13.	False	107–108	A <u>quota</u> is a restriction on the quantity of a country's imports. It generally is intended to guarantee home-country manufacturers access to a certain percentage of the domestic market. A <u>tariff</u> is a government tax on goods or services entering the country. Its primary purpose is to raise the price of imported goods or services.
14.	True		
15.	False	111	The <u>most favored nation principle</u> means that when country A grants a tariff concession to country B, the same concession automatically applies to all other countries that are members of WTO. The <u>reciprocity principle</u> means that each member will not be forced to reduce tariffs unilaterally.
16.	False	111	The North American Free Trade Agreement (NAFTA) went into effect in 1994 to increase free trade between the United States, Canada, and Mexico. NAFTA was intended to reduce and eliminate all tariffs and most nontariff barriers among the member countries. However, NAFTA retains some protectionist elements, some of which may persist indefinitely.

17.	True		
18.	False	114–115	Complexity refers to the structure of the organization and the amount of coordination required to deliver a product or service to customers.
19.	True		
20.	True		

MULTIPLE CHOICE SOLUTIONS

Question	**Answer**	**Page**	**Explanation**
1.	b	99	Since 1995, U.S. exports of goods and services have soared 40 percent, accounting for much of the overall growth in the economy. However, imports have been growing more than exports, in part because the economy has expanded, which gave U.S. consumers more money to spend.
2.	c	99	Since 1995, U.S. exports of goods and services has soared 40 percent, accounting for much of the overall growth in the economy.
3.	a	101	The people of many non-Western cultures, such as those of India, Saudi Arabia, and China, view change as a slow and natural progression. Their attitude toward change is passive or reactive.
4.	b	102	The Mexican attitude toward time could best be summed up in the word *mañana*, meaning "not today"—but not necessarily tomorrow either.
5.	b	102	In Mexico, managers are used to giving only positive feedback to their supervisors and to expressing views that only agree with their bosses. Mexican executives would consider it disrespectful of a subordinate to contradict them because they are essentially "people oriented."
6.	c	102–103	Many Mexicans feel threatened by uncertain and ambiguous situations, and they struggle to develop security in their lives. In this regard, they feel a need for written rules and procedures and rely on experts to provide them guidance. They also seek consensus and social harmony.

7.   b   104–105   Cultural distance is created by the differences in religious beliefs, race, social norms, and language between two countries.

8.   c   107   The economic climate reflects the extent of government control of markets and financial investments as well as government support services. Domestic instability is the amount of subversion, revolution, assassinations, guerrilla warfare, and government crisis in a country. Political climate is the likelihood that a government will swing to the far left or far right politically. Infrastructure is the government provision of support services and facilities (roads, airports, electricity, water, and refuse and sewage disposal) and government capabilities in general.

9.   d   108   A quota is a restriction on the quantity of a country's imports. Import quotas generally guarantee home-country manufacturers access to a certain percentage of the domestic market. A tariff is a government tax on goods or services entering the country. A subsidy is a direct or indirect payment by a government to its country's firms to make selling or investing abroad cheaper for them—and thus more profitable. A cartel is an alliance of producers engaged in the same type of business, which is formed to limit or eliminate competition and control production and prices.

10.   c   108   A cartel is an alliance of producers engaged in the same type of business, formed to eliminate competition. OPEC (Organization of Petroleum Exporting Countries) is the best known example of a cartel. OPIC is the Overseas Private Investment Corporation, which is a self-sustaining agency of the U.S. government that helps qualified U.S. investors establish commercial projects in developing countries.

11.   a   108   A bribe is an improper payment made to induce the recipient to do something for the payer. Bribes are illegal in Canada and the United States but not in some countries.

12.   c   111   The reciprocity principle ensures each member country that it will not be forced to reduce tariffs unilaterally. A tariff concession is made only in return for comparable concessions from the other countries. The most favored nation principle means that when country A grants a tariff concession to country B, the

same concession automatically applies to all other countries that are members of GATT. The transparency principle establishes that any tariffs be readily visible to all countries. Protectionism is the use of various mechanisms to help a home-based industry or firm avoid (or reduce) potential (or actual) competitive or political threats from abroad.

13.	c	110	The World Trade Organization was established in 1995 as an outgrowth of GATT. It has 144 members which account for about 95% of the world trade.
14.	d	113	The European Union (EU), called the European Community (EC) until 1994, has eighteen members: Austria, Belgium, Denmark, Finland, France, Germany, Greece, Iceland, Ireland, Italy, Liechtenstein, Luxembourg, the Netherlands, Norway, Portugal, Spain, Sweden, and the United Kingdom.
15.	d	114	A major stage of the EU program is to complete formation of the common internal market. That involves eliminating physical barriers, technical barriers, fiscal barriers, and financial barriers.
16.	a	115–116	The exporting strategy involves maintaining facilities within a home country and transferring goods and services abroad for sale in foreign markets. Exporting is a practical means for small or medium-sized firms with little financial resources to invest but who are facing increased competition in their domestic markets.
17.	d	116–117	These organizations are utilizing the franchising strategy where a parent organization (the franchiser) grants other companies or individuals (franchisees) the rights to use its trademarked name and to produce and sell its goods and services.
18.	a	117	An alliance strategy involves agreeing with other organizations to pool physical, financial, and human resources to achieve common goals. The desire to learn another firm's technology and special processes or to gain access to customers and distribution channels has stimulated the formation of alliances.

19.   d   118   A <u>multidomestic strategy</u> involves adjusting products, services, and practices to individual countries or regions. Companies that have followed a multidomestic strategy successfully include Coca-Cola, General Mills, and Frito-Lay. Frito-Lay, for example, uses this strategy to tailor its snack foods to taste preferences around the world.

20.   d   119–120   A <u>global strategy</u> stresses worldwide consistency, standardization, and low relative cost. All of the statements are true.

ESSAY SOLUTIONS

[Pages 98–100]

1. There are several major characteristics of the global economy.

    a. In a global economy, products are shipped anywhere in the world in a matter of days, communication is instant, and new product introductions and their life cycles are shorter.

    b. Exports and imports of goods and services represent about 30 percent of the U.S. GDP.

    c. Globalization has placed a premium on information.

    d. There is a movement towards increased openness, both economically and politically.

    e. Privatization permits organizations to adapt their strategies to meet the demands of the market.

    f. Governments are opening their countries to multinational trade agreements and joining regional trade associations.

    g. One of the most important factors that has fueled the growth of the global economy is the prevalence of labor and resources in different parts of the world.

[Page 104]

2. A country's cultural values determine how people interact with one another and with companies and institutions. Differences in religious beliefs, race, social norms, and language are call capable of creating <u>cultural distance</u> between two countries. Some cultural differences between countries, such as language, are easily perceived and understood. While others are much more subtle. Social norms, the deeply rooted system of unspoken principals that guide individuals in their everyday behaviors, are often nearly invisible.

[Pages 106–107]

3. <u>Political risk</u> is the probability that political decisions or events in a country will negatively affect the long-term profitability of an investment. <u>Domestic instability</u> is the amount of subversion, revolution, assassinations, guerrilla warfare, and government crisis in a country. <u>Foreign conflict</u> is the degree of hostility one nation shows toward others. <u>Political climate</u> is the likelihood that a government will swing to the far left or far right politically. The <u>economic climate</u> reflects the extent of government control of markets and financial investments, as well as government support services and capabilities. <u>Corruption</u> refers to the degree to which institutions, including the government, are perceived to be untrustworthy, to be open to bribes, and to conduct fraudulent business practices.

[Page 109]

4. The <u>U.S. Foreign Corrupt Practices Act of 1977</u> makes it a crime for U.S. corporations or individuals to offer or make payments to officials of foreign governments or companies for the purpose of obtaining or retaining business. The act established specific record-keeping requirements for publicly held corporations, making difficult the concealment of political payments prohibited by the act. A company may be fined as much as $1 million, and a manager who directly participates in or has knowledge of any violations of the act faces up to five years in prison and/or $100,000 in fines. Furthermore, the act prohibits corporations from paying any fines imposed on their directors, managers, employees, or agents. The act does not prohibit grease payments to employees of foreign governments whose duties are primarily procedural or clerical. <u>Grease payments</u> are small payments—almost gratuities—used to get lower level government employees to speed up required paperwork. It is used to persuade employees to perform their normal duties.

[Pages 113–114]

5. The <u>European Union (EU)</u>, called the European Community (EC) until 1994, has eighteen members: Austria, Belgium, Denmark, Finland, France, Germany, Greece, Iceland, Ireland, Italy, Liechtenstein, Luxembourg, the Netherlands, Norway, Portugal, Spain, Sweden, and the United Kingdom. The goals of the European Union include creating a single market among member countries through the removal of trade barriers (such as tariffs) and establishing the free movement of goods, people, services, and investment capital. The changes go beyond economic interests to include social changes as well. It is more than an economic union: it is a state of mind and a political force. To form a common internal market, the EU must eliminate physical barriers, technical barriers, fiscal barriers, and financial barriers.

[Page 114–118]

6. The six main strategies of international operations are listed below. These strategies are only a sample of the many choices available.

    a.   *Exporting Strategy*—involves maintaining facilities within a home country and transferring goods and services abroad for sale in foreign markets.

    b.   *Licensing Strategy*—involves a firm (the <u>licensor</u>) in one country giving other domestic or foreign firms (<u>licensees</u>) the right to use a patent, trademark, technology, production process, or product in return for the payment of a royalty or fee.

    c.   *Franchising Strategy*—a parent organization (the <u>franchiser</u>) grants other companies or individuals (<u>franchisees</u>) the rights to use its trademarked name and to produce and sell its goods or services.

    d.   *Alliance Strategy*—involves agreeing with other companies to pool physical, financial, and human resources to achieve common goals. International business alliances range from straightforward marketing agreements to joint ventures.

    e.   *Multidomestic Strategy*—involves adjusting products, services, and practices to individual countries or regions. Customizing of products/services is done to respond to the differences in customer desires, distribution channels, host government demands, and/or employee needs.

    f.   *Global Strategy*—stresses operating with worldwide consistency, standardization, and low relative cost. Top managers focus on coordination and mutual support of the organization's worldwide activities.

CHAPTER 5
ENTREPRENEURSHIP

LEARNING OBJECTIVES

After studying this chapter, you should be able to:

❖**1**❖   Explain the role of entrepreneurs and how external factors impact their ventures.

❖**2**❖   Describe the personal attributes that contribute to entrepreneurs' success.

❖**3**❖   Outline the planning essentials for potential entrepreneurs.

❖**4**❖   State the role of intrapreneurs and how organizations can foster intrapreneurship.

OUTLINE

❖**1**❖   Explain the role of entrepreneurs and how external factors impact their ventures.

   I.   **Entrepreneurs and External Factors**

      1. **Entrepreneurs**—create something for the purpose of gain while accepting the risk and uncertainty associated with their ventures.

         a. In launching a new business, entrepreneurs typically incorporate at least one of the following: something new, something better, an underserved or new market, or a new delivery system or distribution channel.

         b. Several key factors that are unique to entrepreneurship:

            1. Relatively open and free markets.

            2. A support system which includes such things as the current availability of investment capital, the availability of loans, tax rates and policies, and the availability of support services.

      2. **Business Incubators**—are organizations designed to accelerate the growth and success of entrepreneurial companies through an array of business support resources and services.

         a. These organizations offer the following features:

            1. An existing building is used that has been renovated to accommodate multiple tenants, as well as varying types of businesses.

        2.   The tenants are offered below-market rent and flexible lease arrangements, including the opportunity to expand within the business incubator location.

        3.   The incubator provides shared services such as telephone answering, access to a fax machine and copier, the use of a conference room or library, and on-site management consulting-business assistance by the incubator manager.

        4. Psychological or moral support that is fostered in the incubator.

3. **Small-Business Owner**—is anyone who owns a major equity stake in a company with fewer than 500 employees.

    a. The <u>Small Business Administration</u> (SBA) aids, counsels, assists, and protects the interests of small-business concerns, and advocates on their behalf within the U.S. government. It also helps small-business victims of disaster.

    b. There are more than 25 million small businesses in the U.S., and most of the employment growth in the U.S. has come from businesses with less than 500 employees.

4. **Family Business**—the term used to describe a business owned and managed mostly by people who are related by blood and/or marriage. Often are passed down one generation to another.

❖**2**❖   Describe the personal attributes that contribute to entrepreneurs' success.

   II.   **Attributes of Successful Entrepreneurs**

      1. **Personal Attributes**—Even with the best business conditions, not everyone becomes an entrepreneur nor do all entrepreneurs become successful. A combination of all of the following attributes increases the probability of entrepreneurial success:

        a. <u>Need for Achievement</u>—a person's desire for excellence or to succeed in competitive situations.

           1. High achievers take responsibility for attaining their goals, set moderately difficult goals, and want immediate feedback on how well they have performed.

           2. David McClelland and others have conducted extensive research into the human needs for power, affiliation, and achievement. Their findings indicate that perhaps a low percentage of the U.S. population is characterized by a predominant need to achieve.

           3. Entrepreneurs learn to set challenging but achievable goals for themselves and for their business and, when they achieve them, to set new goals.

  b. <u>Desire for Independence</u>—entrepreneurs often seek independence from others.

   1. Entrepreneurs aren't motivated to perform well in large, bureaucratic organizations.

   2. They have internal drive, are confident of their own abilities, and possess a great deal of self-respect.

  c. <u>Self-Confidence</u>—because of the risks involved in running an entrepreneurial organization, having an "upbeat" attitude is essential.

   1. Most people want an optimistic and enthusiastic leader—someone they can look up to.

  d. <u>Self-Sacrifice</u>—entrepreneurs recognize that nothing worth having is free.

   1. Success has a high price and they are willing to pay it.

  e. <u>Entrepreneurs: Made, Not Born</u>—Although different from most people, entrepreneurs probably weren't born that way. Instead, they developed personal attributes over the years, but they acquire many of their key attributes early in life.

2. **Technical Proficiency**—entrepreneurs often demonstrate strong technical skills, typically bringing some related experience to their business ventures.

3. **Managerial Competencies**—to succeed, entrepreneurs need to develop and draw upon the following competencies.

  a. <u>Strategic Action Competency</u>—a study of CEOs who were winners of awards in the Ernst & Young LLP Entrepreneur of the Year Program identified these five strategic practices:

   1. Delivering products and services that were perceived as being of the highest quality to expanding market segments,

   2. Using new products and services to expand revenue by about 20 percent annually,

   3. Generating new customers that expand revenue by about 30 percent annually,

   4. Focusing marketing expenditures on a high-quality sales force that can rapidly expand the company's geographic presence, and

   5. Maintaining financial control of the firm.

  b. <u>Planning and Administration Competency</u>—though plans may have to change, planning is important for entrepreneurial companies, and nearly 80 percent of successful entrepreneurs put their plans in writing.

   1. The planning horizon is relatively short, often less than 3 years.

   2. Written monthly plans (12–24 months) are common and as the time frame grows longer, the plans tend to become more general.

3. In the start-up phase, when funds are scarce and the company has no track record, attracting top-notch employees is difficult.

c. Teamwork Competency—successful entrepreneurs are self-starters who usually support subordinates and their programs.

1. The majority of successful companies (of the study previously described) had a particularly effective top management team.

d. Communication Competency—being able to communicate effectively is essential to gaining the cooperation and support needed to turn a vision into reality.

1. Much of communication that occurs in larger companies takes the form of speeches, written reports, formal proposals, and scheduled reviews. In small companies, most communication is direct and less formal.

❖**3**❖   Outline the planning essentials for potential entrepreneurs.

III. **Planning Essentials for Entrepreneurs**

1. **Business Plan**—describes the basic idea that is the foundation for the start-up and outlines how that idea can be turned into reality.

2. **Deciding to Buy, Start, or Franchise a Business**—in deciding whether to start a business, the prospective entrepreneur should weigh the advantages and disadvantages of each strategy.

a. Buy Strategy—if they have the resources, entrepreneurs often find that buying an existing company is a good idea. Buying an existing firm is tricky and may involve considerable risk.

b. Start-Up Strategy—When deciding what types of businesses to own, people should begin by examining their competencies and the contacts they can bring to their possible ventures.

c. Franchise Strategy—a business operated by someone (the franchisee) to whom a franchiser grants the right to market a good or service.

1. The franchisee pays a franchise fee and a percentage of the sales.

2. The franchisee often receives financial help, training, guaranteed supplies, a protected market, and technical assistance in site selection, accounting, and operations management.

3. A franchise agreement means the franchisee obtains a brand name that enjoys recognition among potential customers.

4. Franchisees must conform to standards set by the franchisor, and sometimes they must buy the franchisor's goods and service.

      d. <u>Other Strategic Options</u>—the prospective entrepreneur may consider the following questions:

        1. Is there a way that I can begin the enterprise in stages or with a limited investment?

        2. Can I run the business at first from my home?

        3. Can I continue working for someone else and put in time on my own business after hours?

        4. To what extent can I draw on relatives to help me, perhaps simply by answering the phone while I work at my regular job?

3. **Assessing Affordable Loss**—should be researched and forecasting techniques should be used.

    a. <u>Principle of Affordable Loss</u>—the conscious determination of the amount of resources (money, time, and effort) entrepreneurs are willing to commit to an idea, which, in turn, influences the choice of strategies and methods needed to generate early revenues.

4. **Finding Funds**—the new-venture plan should identify anticipated costs of opening the business (e.g., deposits, fixtures, and incorporation fees).

    a. The business plan should also project, month by month, the expenses that reasonably can be expected for the first 1 to 3 years.

    b. The entrepreneur must plan for obtaining funds to handle expenses, such as those associated with the start-up phase, that revenues can't initially cover.

    c. Common sources of funds include the entrepreneur and other members of the venture team, family and friends, financial institutions such as banks and venture capital firms, and business angels.

    d. <u>Venture Capitalists</u>—provide equity (ownership) financing. In contrast, banks and other financial institutions provide debt (loan) financing. They get their funds and profits back only if their equity stake rises in value and if dividends are paid.

    e. <u>Business Angel</u>—a private individual who invests directly in firms and receives an equity stake in return. Often such a person acts as a business advisor to the founder. They may make less stringent demands than do venture capitalists on controlling the actions of the entrepreneur.

5. **Going Global**—most new ventures begin with a domestic focus, but increasingly entrepreneurs find their firm turning into global enterprises.

    a. Specific considerations for whether to found a domestic or global start-up include the following.

        1. Are the best human resources dispersed among various countries?

        2. Would foreign financing be easier or more suitable?

        3. Do target customers require a venture to be international?

    4. Will worldwide communication lead to quick responses from competitors in other countries?

    5. Will worldwide sales be required to support the venture?

    6. Will changing the government policies, procedures, product designs, and advertising strategies of your established domestic company be more difficult than building a globally effective firm from the beginning?

6. **Managing a Family Business**—family-owned businesses are an integral part of the U.S. economy.

    a. For a family business to succeed, a family should take the following steps:

      1. Settle conflicts as they come up.

      2. Decide who is responsible for what and who has authority.

      3. Agree on the hiring criteria to be used before considering any particular family member.

      4. Use a board of advisers or board of directors to review and recommend key courses of action.

      5. Develop a legal agreement.

❖**4**❖   State the role of intrapreneurs and how organizations can foster intrapreneurship.

  IV. **Corporate Intrapreneurship**

1. **Corporate Intrapreneurship**—refers to the fostering of entrepreneurial behavior within established companies to produce growth and profits.

2. **Intrapreneur**—someone in an existing organization who turns ideas into profitable realities.

    a. Many large organizations now recognize that entrepreneurial behavior can produce growth and profits.

3. **Fostering Intrapreneurship**—top management can foster an intrapreneurial culture by eliminating obstacles and providing incentives for intrapreneurship.

    a. Organizations that redirect themselves through innovation have the following characteristics:

      1. Commitment from senior management.

      2. Flexible organization design.

      3. Autonomy of the venture team.

      4. Competent and talented people who exhibit entrepreneurial behaviors and attitudes.

      5. Incentives and rewards for risk taking.

      6. An appropriately designed control system.

    b. Skunkworks—islands of intrapreneurial activity, where formal rules and procedures are ignored in favor of experimentation and innovation.

MATCHING

<u>Directions</u>: Select the term that best identifies the statement listed below. Place the letter of the correct term in the space provided.

A. Family Business
B. Principle of Affordable Loss
C. Business Plan
D. Intrapreneur
E. Franchise

F. Venture Capitalists
G. Small-Business Owner
H. Skunkworks
I. Business Angel
J. Entrepreneur

_____ 1. This describes the basic idea that is the foundation for the start-up and outlines how that idea can be turned into reality.

_____ 2. Someone who creates a new business activity in the economy.

_____ 3. A business owned and managed mostly by people who are related by blood or marriage.

_____ 4. Get their funds and profits back only if their equity stake rises in value and if dividends are paid.

_____ 5. The conscious determination of the amount of resources entrepreneurs are willing to commit to an idea, which in turn, influences the choice of strategies and methods needed to generate early revenues.

_____ 6. Someone who owns a majority equity stake in a company with fewer than 500 employees.

_____ 7. A business run by an individual to whom a franchisor grants the right to market a certain good or service.

_____ 8. Islands of intrapreneurial activity within an organization.

_____ 9. Someone in an existing organization who turns new ideas into profitable realities.

_____ 10. An individual who invests directly in firms, receiving an equity stake, and often acts as a business adviser to the founder.

TRUE OR FALSE

<u>Directions</u>: Write True or False in the space provided.

❖1❖

_____ 1. Most entrepreneurs succeed because they invent new products or services.

_____ 2. Rates of entrepreneurship are relatively consistent with the U.S. having consistent levels of entrepreneurs since World War II.

_____ 3. New technologies, particularly the Internet, allow companies to reach customers more efficiently.

_____ 4. There are approximately 550 business incubators in the United States.

____   5.   Small business owners refers to anyone who employs fewer than 100 employees.

____   6.   All small-business owners are entrepreneurs.

____   7.   The SBA aids, counsels, assists, and protects the interests of small-business concerns, and advocates on their behalf within the U.S. government.

____   8.   Family businesses may be either small or large.

❖2❖

____   9.   Self-sacrifice enables entrepreneurs to be optimistic in representing their firm to employees and customers alike.

____   10. The need to achieve is consistently strong in successful entrepreneurs.

____   11. Entrepreneurs use the strategic action competency in their daily actions.

____   12. Individuals are born with the key attributes to be successful entrepreneurs, such as willingness to take risks and need for high achievement..

____   13. The teamwork competency is seldom used by entrepreneurs because they do nearly all the work themselves.

❖3❖

____   14. The principle of affordable loss increases a new business's chance of success but may decrease the probability of creating a business in the first place.

____   15. Once a franchise has been purchased the business owner has total discretion on how to run the enterprise.

____   16. Venture capitalists do <u>not</u> invest money in new entrepreneurial firms due to the high failure rate and extreme risk.

____   17. A business angel is a private individual who invests directly in firms and receives an equity stake in return.

____   18. Due to their usually small size, successful family businesses generally do not need the formality of a board of directors.

❖4❖

____   19. An entrepreneur is someone in an organization who turns ideas into profitable realities.

____   20. Islands of intrapreneurial activity have been called skunkworks.

MULTIPLE CHOICE

<u>Directions</u>: Select the best answer in the space provided.

❖1❖

_____ 1. _____ is the label usually given to someone who creates new business activity in the economy.
a. Developer
b. Intrapreneur
c. Entrepreneur
d. Industrialist

_____ 2. _____ are often located in recycled buildings and serve businesses by providing administrative services and management advice.
a. Incubator organizations
b. Start-up organizations
c. New business consultants
d. Small Business Administration offices

_____ 3. Second-Chance Body Armor manufactures bullet-proof vests and other body armor used by police officers and the military. It was established in 1973 and still only employs 70 people. This is a(n) _____.
a. incubator organization
b. small business
c. corporation
d. nonprofit organization

❖2❖

_____ 4. Which of the following is <u>not</u> a key personal attribute of entrepreneurs?
a. desire for dependence
b. high need for achievement
c. self-confidence
d. a and c

_____ 5. Which of the following statements regarding entrepreneurs is <u>false</u>?
a. Entrepreneurs have to be self-sacrificing.
b. Entrepreneurs are different from most people because they were born that way.
c. A successful track record does much to improve an entrepreneur's self-confidence and self-esteem.
d. Entrepreneurs often seek independence from others.

_____ 6. Entrepreneurs who deliver products and services that were perceived as the highest quality to expand market segments and cultivate pace-setting new products and services that are first to market are implementing the _____ competency.
a. self-management
b. strategic action
c. planning and administration
d. teamwork

___   7.   Which of the following is <u>not</u> a managerial competency associated with successful entrepreneurs?
       a.   teamwork competency
       b.   strategic action competency
       c.   communication competency
       d.   innovation competency

❖3❖

___   8.   Which component of business plans describes the advantages of such things as zoning, tax laws, and wage rates?
       a.   marketing
       b.   management
       c.   business description
       d.   location

___   9.   Which of the following statements regarding buy strategies is <u>false</u>?
       a.   Buying an existing firm is relatively easy and involves little risk.
       b.   Often a good idea is to buy an existing company that the current owner is having difficulty managing.
       c.   Purchasing and negotiating a purchase agreement often requires the assistance of experts.
       d.   Attorneys usually prepare or review sale documents.

___   10. A middle ground between starting a business and buying an existing business is to run a _____.
       a.   partnership
       b.   franchise
       c.   conglomerate
       d.   pyramid organization

___   11. Which of the following statements regarding franchisees is true?
       a.   The franchisee pays a franchise fee and a percentage of the sales.
       b.   The franchisee often receives financial help, training, guaranteed supplies, and technical assistance.
       c.   The franchisee must conform to standards set by the franchiser.
       d.   All of the above

___   12. All of the statements below about the principle of affordable loss are true, <u>except</u>:
       a.   analysis increases a new business's chance of success but may decrease the probability of creating a business in the first place.
       b.   a bias toward quick action increases the probability of creating a business but decreases the probability of success.
       c.   this principle increases the entrepreneur's tension between excessive analysis versus quick action.
       d.   too much information and analysis only leads to more uncertainty and doubt about the opportunity.

_____ 13. A(n) _____ is a private individual who invests directly in a firm and receives an equity stake in return.
   a. venture capitalist
   b. business angel
   c. philanthropist
   d. financial intrapreneur

_____ 14. A(n) _____ is like a banker in that they are a formal business, but are freer to take greater risks in making investments.
   a. financial intrapreneur
   b. venture capitalist
   c. angel
   d. philanthropist

_____ 15. All of the following statements regarding venture capitalists are true except:
   a. venture capitalists become part owners of the business by providing funds.
   b. venture capitalists expect their investments to provide returns of 25 to 35 percent annually.
   c. venture capitalists are subject to the same state and federal regulations as banks.
   d. venture capitalists get their funds and profits back only if their equity stake rises in value and if dividends are paid.

❖4❖

_____ 16. A(n) _____ describes someone in an organization who turns ideas into profitable realities.
   a. entrepreneur
   b. intrapreneur
   c. manager
   d. extrapreneur

_____ 17. The introduction of the CNNFN network is an example of _____.
   a. employee autonomy
   b. intrapreneurship
   c. entrepreneurship
   d. matrix collaboration

_____ 18. Organizations that redirect themselves through innovation have all of the following characteristics except:
   a. flexible organization design.
   b. autonomy of the venture team.
   c. bureaucratic controls.
   d. incentives and rewards for risk taking.

_____ 19. _____ are islands of intrapreneurial activity within an organization.
   a. Skunkworks
   b. Corridors
   c. Incubators
   d. Turnkeys

___ 20. Which of the following statements is true regarding skunkworks?
  a. The subculture within skunkworks is similar to those in many incubator organizations.
  b. Formal rules and procedures are ignored in favor of experimentation and innovation.
  c. Tying performance to rewards can keep the skunkworks team focused on its goals.
  d. All of the above

ESSAY QUESTIONS

❖1❖

1. Define and explain who funds *business incubators*.

❖2❖

2. What are the key personal attributes of entrepreneurs?

❖3❖

3. Identify and discuss the steps a family business should take to increase its potential for success.

❖4❖

4. Discuss the ways in which top management can foster an intrapreneurship culture.

CHAPTER 5
ENTREPRENEURSHIP

MATCHING SOLUTIONS

1. C - Business Plan
2. J - Entrepreneur
3. A - Family Business
4. F - Venture Capitalists
5. B - Principle of Affordable Loss
6. G - Small Business Owner
7. E - Franchise
8. H - Skunkworks
9. D - Intrapreneur
10. I - Business Angel

TRUE/FALSE SOLUTIONS

Question	Answer	Page	Explanation
1.	False	127	Most successful entrepreneurs begin by offering a higher quality product or service, rather than by introducing something completely new.
2.	False	127	Rates of entrepreneurship ebb and flow with environmental conditions in the United States.
3.	True		
4.	True		
5.	False	128	A small-business owner is anyone who owns a major stake in a company with fewer than 500 employees.
6.	False	128	Many entrepreneurs are small business owners for awhile, but not all small-business owners become entrepreneurs. That is, not all small-business owners introduce new business activity.
7.	True		
8.	True		
9.	False	130	Self-confidence enables a person to be optimistic in representing the firm to employees and customers alike. Self-sacrifice recognizes that nothing comes for free, these individuals make many sacrifices for their enterprise.

10.	True		
11.	True		
12.	False	131	Entrepreneurs are made, not born. Although they develop personal attributes over many years, entrepreneurs develop many of their key attributes early in life, with the family environment playing an important role.
13.	False	134	Successful entrepreneurs are extremely hard working and task oriented, but they aren't lone wolves—one person can do only so much alone. Many day-to-day problems that entrepreneurs encounter require the application of teamwork competency for effective resolution—both by top management and by lower levels of management.
14.	True		
15.	False	138	A <u>franchise</u> is a business operated by someone (the franchisee) to whom a franchiser grants the right to market a good or service. Whoever enters a franchise agreement obtains a brand name that enjoys recognition among potential customers. However, franchisees are their own bosses only to a degree. They usually must conform to standards set by the franchiser, and sometimes they must buy the franchiser's goods and services.
16.	False	139	Because venture capitalists aren't subject to the same state and federal regulations as banks, they can take greater risks when making investments.
17.	True		
18.	False	141–142	The effective use of a board of directors can assist a family business in forming and implementing all of the recommendations presented. Of course, boards of directors are useful for all private companies, not just family businesses.
19.	False	143	<u>Intrapreneur</u>—is someone in an organization who turns ideas into profitable realities.
20.	True		

MULTIPLE CHOICE SOLUTIONS

Question	Answer	Page	Explanation
1.	c	126	Entrepreneur is the label usually given to someone who creates new business activity in the economy. During the past 10 years, entrepreneurs have created several million new businesses throughout the world.
2.	a	128	The term *incubator organization* applies to organizations that support entrepreneurs. They rent space to new businesses or to people wanting to start businesses. They often are located in recycled buildings, such as warehouses or schools. In addition to making space available, they serve fledgling businesses by offering administration services and providing management advice.
3.	b	128	The U.S. government defines a small business as a company employing fewer than 500 people.
4.	a	129–131	The key personal attributes of entrepreneurs include: need for achievement, desire for independence, self-confidence, and self-sacrificing.
5.	b	131	Although entrepreneurs are different from most people, they probably weren't born that way. They develop personal attributes over the years, but they acquire many of their key attributes early in life, with the family environment playing an important role.
6.	b	132–133	A study of 906 CEOs who were winners of awards in the Ernst & Young LLP Entrepreneur of the Year program revealed several leading strategic practices they had used to sustain rapid growth for their companies. The most common strategic practices were: delivering products and services that were perceived as highest quality to expanding market segments; cultivating pace-setting new products and services that are first to market; delivering products and services that demand average or higher pricing; and others listed in the textbook.
7.	d	132–134	The six managerial competencies are: strategic action competency, planning and administration competency, teamwork competency, communication competency, self-management competency, and global awareness competency.

8.	d	136	A <u>business plan</u> describes the basic idea that is the foundation for the start-up and outlines how that idea can be turned into reality. Location components describe the advantages of your location like zoning, tax laws and wage rates.
9.	a	136–138	Buying an existing firm is tricky and may involve considerable risk. The seller may not reveal some hidden problems and may not even be aware of others. A prospective buyer is wise to specify, in the purchase agreement, restrictions limiting the previous owner's ability or right to compete with the new owner. Such restrictions may limit the types of businesses that the previous owner can operate in a certain area and/or for a stipulated period of time.
10.	b	138	A <u>franchise</u> is operated by someone (the franchisee) to whom a franchiser grants the right to market a good or service. It is a middle ground between starting a business and buying an existing business.
11.	d	138	All of the statements are true. Whoever enters a franchise agreement obtains a brand name that enjoys recognition among potential customers. However, franchisees are their own bosses only to a degree. They can't run their businesses exactly as they please. They usually have to conform to standards set by the franchiser, and sometimes they must buy the franchiser's goods and services.
12.	c	139	The <u>principle of affordable loss</u> refers to the conscious determination of the amount of resources entrepreneurs are willing to commit to an idea, which in turn, influences the choice of strategies and methods needed to generate early revenues. This principle helps potential entrepreneurs resolve the tension between excessive analysis versus quick action.
13.	b	139	A <u>business angel</u> is a private individual who invests directly in a firm and receives an equity stake in return. Often such a person acts as a business adviser to the founder.
14.	b	139	<u>Venture capitalists</u> provide equity (ownership) financing. In contrast, banks and other financial institutions provide debt (loan) financing.
15.	c	139	Because venture capitalists aren't subject to the same state and federal regulations as banks, they can take greater risks when making investments.

16.	b	143	An <u>intrapreneur</u> is someone in an organization who champions turning new ideas into profitable realities.
17.	b	143	CNN's financial news station is an example of intrapreneurship. Lou Dobbs took the lead and championed getting the station up and running.
18.	c	144	Organizations that redirect themselves through innovation have the following characteristics: commitment from senior management, flexible organization design, autonomy of the venture team, competent and talented people who exhibit entrepreneurial behaviors and attitudes, incentives and rewards for risk taking, and an appropriately designed control system. Nothing is more stifling to an intrapreneurial activity than bureaucratic controls.
19.	a	144	<u>Skunkworks</u> are islands of intrapreneurial activity, which often violate formal review and reporting policies. Top management must create subcultures wherein these violations are tolerated, if not rewarded.
20.	d	144–145	All of the statements are true. However, a large organization isn't likely to support a particular skunkworks operation forever.

ESSAY SOLUTIONS

[Page 128]

1. Business incubators are organizations designed to accelerate the growth and success of entrepreneurial companies through an array of business support resources and services. There are approximately 550 business incubators in the United States. Local, regional, or state governments or other nonprofit organizations fund almost half of all incubators to stimulate economic development in their regions. Universities and colleges fund 13 percent of incubators, private investors fund 12 percent, joint efforts of nonprofit and for-profit groups fund 18 percent, and other organizations fund 8 percent.

[Pages 129–132]

2. The many studies of entrepreneurs that have been conducted over the years indicate that those who succeed have several characteristics in common.

   a. *Need for Achievement.* This is a person's desire either for excellence or to succeed in competitive situations. High achievers take responsibility for attaining their goals, set moderately difficult goals, and want immediate feedback on how well they have performed. This need is consistently strong in successful entrepreneurs. Entrepreneurs strive to achieve goals and measure success in terms of what those efforts have accomplished. They learn to set challenging but achievable goals for themselves and for their businesses and, when they achieve them, to set new goals.

   b. *Desire for Independence.* Entrepreneurs often seek independence from others. As a result, they generally aren't motivated to perform well in large, bureaucratic organizations. They have internal drive, are confident of their own abilities, and possess a great deal of self-respect.

   c. *Self-Confidence.* A successful track record of accomplishment does much to improve an entrepreneur's self-confidence and self-esteem. It enables the person to be optimistic in representing the firm to employees and customers alike.

   d. *Self-Sacrificing.* Successful entrepreneurs must be self-sacrificing. They recognize that nothing worth having is free.

   e. *Technical Proficiency.* Entrepreneurs often demonstrate strong technical skills, typically bringing some related experience to their ventures.

[Pages 141–142]

3. Family-owned businesses are an integral part of the U.S. economy, responsible for nearly half of the nation's gross domestic product (GDP). To increase their probability of success a family should take the following steps:

   a. *Decide who is responsible for what and who has authority.* Jobs in companies just starting up should not be too narrowly defined. Families should recognize each other's areas of expertise to determine who is best able to make each decision.

   b. *Draw up a legal agreement specifying how to dispose of, or reallocate, the equity.* Investors and other outsiders have an interest in family member accord on how to handle management transitions in the business when the current head of the business steps down or dies.

   c. *Decide whether the business will employ other family members and, if so, what hiring criteria will be used.* It may be difficult to hire every family member and extended family member. Without specific criteria for hiring determined in advance, a family member who is not hired may have negative feelings and ill-will toward the business.

    d.   *Settle fights as they develop.* If a co-worker/family member does something on the job that makes another angry, correcting the problem requires that it be brought into the open.

    e.   *Use a board of advisers to review and recommend key courses of action.* Sometimes outsiders are needed to mediate a conflict or at least to provide a fresh perspective.

[Pages 143–144]

4.   An intrapreneur is someone in an organization who turns ideas into profitable realities. Top management can foster an intrapreneurial culture by eliminating obstacles and providing incentives for intrapreneurship. Organizations that redirect themselves through innovation have the following characteristics.

    a.   *Commitment from senior management.* This commitment must include a willingness to tolerate failure.

    b.   *Flexible organizational design.* Intrapreneurial organizations are designed for fast action. Management gives information to those best positioned to react to changing market conditions.

    c.   *Autonomy of the venture team.* Successful intrapreneurs usually are allowed considerable leeway in their actions.

    d.   *Competent and talented people who exhibit entrepreneurial behaviors and attitudes.*

    e.   *Incentives and rewards for risk taking.*

    f.   *An appropriately designed control system.*

CHAPTER 6
ETHICS AND STAKEHOLDER SOCIAL RESPONSIBILITY

LEARNING OBJECTIVES

After studying this chapter, you should be able to:

❖**1**❖ State the importance of ethics for individual employees and organizations.

❖**2**❖ Describe four forces that influence the ethical behavior of individuals and organizations.

❖**3**❖ Describe three approaches that people use when making ethical judgments.

❖**4**❖ Explain stakeholder social responsibility and how it influences managers' ethical decisions.

OUTLINE

❖**1**❖ State the importance of ethics for individual employees and organizations.

   I. **Importance of Ethics**

   1. The importance of ethical issues facing managers and employees have been magnified in recent years due to the unethical and illegal conduct of some of the top executives in various major U.S. organizations.

   2. Unethical and often illegal practices by top executives of such organizations have resulted in bankruptcies, massive financial losses for shareholders, and loss of jobs by employees.

   3. This has led to a general loss in trust in business leaders. In one recent poll, 71% of the public felt that the typical CEO is less honest and ethical than the average person and 72% rated the moral and ethical standards of CEOs of major corporations as either fair or poor.

   4. Effective ethics programs and practices help companies achieve: 1) strong financial performance over the long run; 2) greater sales, brand image, and reputation; 3) more employee loyalty and commitment; 4) less vulnerability to activist pressure and boycotts; and 5) fewer or no fines, court-imposed remedies, and criminal charges.

❖**2**❖   Describe four forces that influence the ethical behavior of individuals and
         organizations.

II. **Shaping Ethical Conduct**

1. **Ethics**—is a set of values and rules that defines right and wrong conduct.

    a. Ethics indicates when behavior is acceptable and when it is unacceptable.

    b. Forces that shape ethical conduct include: societal norms and culture; laws
        and regulations; organizational practices and culture; and individual
        perspective.

2. **Cultural Forces**—a large part of any view of what is considered ethical comes
    from the society in which the behavior occurs.

3. **Legal and Regulatory Forces**—what a society interprets as ethical or unethical
    frequently ends up being expressed in laws, government regulations, and court
    decisions.

    a. <u>Laws</u>—are simply society's values and standards that are enforceable in the
        courts.

    b. The legality of actions and decisions doesn't necessarily make them ethical.

    c. <u>Employment-at-Will</u>—a traditional common-law concept holding that
        employers are free to discharge employees for any reason at any time and that
        employees are free to quit their jobs for any reason at any time.

    d. <u>Sarbanes-Oxley Act</u>—imposes rigorous auditing, financial disclosure,
        executive compensation, and corporate governance requirements on publicly
        traded companies. It has also created entirely new employment rights that
        expose both corporations and individual employees to civil and even criminal
        liability.

4. **Organizational Forces**—to provide guidance for employees, an organization
    can define ethical and unethical conduct.

    a. <u>Code of Ethics</u>—states the principles that employees are expected to follow
        when acting on behalf of the organization.

    b. The basic informal source of guidance is top management's behavior, which
        demonstrates the ethical principles that are important to the organization.

    c. One survey of more than 4,000 employees found that 29 percent felt pressure
        to engage in conduct that violates their companies' business standards in
        order to meet business objectives.

        1. About 25 percent reported that their managers looked the other way and
            ignored unethical conduct in order to achieve their business objectives.

     d. <u>Ethics Resource Center</u>—located in Washington, D.C., has as its mission to be a leader in fostering ethical practices in individuals and organizations. It recommends the following:

        1. Create a formal ethics system.

        2. Communicate ethical expectations.

        3. Include ethical conduct as a measure on performance evaluations.

        4. Make it acceptable to talk about ethics.

5. **Individual Forces**—we all have our own values and a sense of what is right and wrong.

     a. <u>Moral Development</u>—Psychological studies of ethical behavior suggest that people develop morally, much as they do physically, from early childhood to adulthood. As they develop, their ethical criteria and patterns of moral reasoning change.

     b. <u>Whistle-Blowers</u>—are employees who report unethical or illegal actions by their employers to people or organizations that are capable of taking corrective action. Anyone thinking about whistle-blowing should consider four important questions:

        1. Is this the only way?

        2. Do I have the evidence?

        3. Why am I doing this?

        4. Am I ready?

❖**3**❖   Describe three approaches that people use when making ethical judgments.

III. **Making Ethical Judgments**

1. Each model provides a different but somewhat related set of principles or standards for judging the right or wrong of managerial and employee decisions and behavior.

2. **Utilitarian Approach**—judges the effect of decisions and behavior on others, with the primary goal of providing the greatest good for the greatest number of people.

     a. A manager or employee guided by this model considers the potential effects of alternative actions from the perspective of the accepted social contract.

     b. Nobel prize-winning economist Milton Friedman is probably the best-known advocate of this approach.

     c. According to classic capitalist theory, the primary managerial obligation is to maximize shareholders' profits and their long-term interests. Friedman argues that using resources in ways that do not clearly maximize shareholder interests amounts to spending the owners' money without their consent—and is equivalent to stealing.

    d. The Utilitarian approach prescribes ethical standards which include:

        1. *Organizational Goals*—providing the greatest good for the greatest number in a competitive market system means focusing on maximizing profits. Achieving high profits is thought to result in the highest quality products and the lowest prices for consumers. No firm should unilaterally go beyond what the law requires.

        2. *Efficiency*—is achieved by both minimizing inputs (labor, land, capital, etc.) and maximizing productive outputs.

        3. *Conflicts of Interest*—managers and employees alike should not have personal interests that conflict with the organization's achievement of its goals.

    e. The utilitarian approach is consistent with strong values of individualism, acceptance of uncertainty, and masculinity.

    f. These values support profit maximization, self-interest, rewards based on abilities and achievements, sacrifice and hard work, and competition.

3. **Moral Rights Approach**—judges decisions and behavior by their consistency with fundamental personal and group liberties and privileges.

    a. This approach holds that decisions should be consistent with fundamental rights and privileges (life, freedom, health, privacy, and property), as set forth in the first ten amendments to the U.S. Constitution—the Bill of Rights—and the United Nations' Declaration of Human Rights.

    b. <u>Life and Safety</u>—employees, customers, and the general public have the right not to have their lives and safety unknowingly and unnecessarily endangered.

    c. <u>Truthfulness</u>—employees, customers, and the general public have the right not to be intentionally deceived on matters about which they should be informed.

        1. Caveat emptor—"let the buyer beware"—used to be the defense for a variety of shady business practices.

        2. Shifting societal attitudes and values concerning appropriate behavior by businesses let to a flood of U.S. consumer legislation.

    d. <u>Privacy</u>—citizens have the right to control access to and use of personal information about themselves and its use by government agencies, employers, and others.

        1. *U.S. Privacy Act of 1974*—restricts the use of certain kinds of information by the federal government and limits those to whom this information can be released.

        2. *The 1988 Video Privacy Protection Act*—forbids retailers from disclosing video rental records without the customer's consent or a court order.

3. With the availability of new information technologies, enormous concern has been expressed about invasions of privacy (e.g., drug testing, monitoring e-mail, confidentiality of medical and psychological counseling records).

e. Freedom of Conscience—individuals have the right to refrain from carrying out orders that violate their moral or religious beliefs.

f. Free Speech—employees have the right to criticize the ethics or legality of their employer's actions.

4. **Justice Approach**—evaluates decisions and behavior with regard to how equitably they distribute benefits and costs among individuals and groups. To ensure just decisions and behavior, the proponents of this approach argue that three principles should be followed when designing management systems and making organizational decisions:

a. Distributive Justice Principle—morally requires that individuals not be treated differently on the basis of arbitrarily defined characteristics.

1. This principle holds that (1) individuals who are similar in relevant respects should be treated similarly, and (2) individuals who differ in relevant respects should be treated differently in proportion to the differences between them.

2. *U.S. Equal Pay Act of 1963*—made illegal the payment of different wages to women and men when their jobs require equal skill, effort, and responsibility and are performed under similar working conditions.

b. Fairness Principle—morally requires employees to support the rules of the organization when two conditions are met: (1) the organization is just (or fair), and (2) employees have voluntarily accepted benefits provided by the organization or have taken advantage of opportunities offered to further their own interests.

c. Natural Duty Principle—morally requires that decisions and behavior be based on universal principles associated with being a responsible member of society. Four universal duties are: (1) to help others who are in need or in jeopardy, provided that the help can be given without excessive personal risk or loss; (2) not to harm or injure another; (3) not to cause unnecessary suffering; and (4) to support and comply with just institutions.

5. Combining Ethical Approaches

a. No approach to ethical decisions can be said to be the "best" approach. Each one has strengths and weaknesses.

b. Utilitarian views are most compatible with the goals of efficiency, productivity, and profit maximization—all strong managerial values in the United States.

      c. The moral rights and justice approaches emphasize individuals' rights and obligations and the need to distribute benefits and burdens fairly among individuals. These approaches give greater weight to long-term employee welfare than to quarterly profits.

❖**4**❖   Explain stakeholder social responsibility and how it influences managers' ethical decisions.

   IV. **Stakeholder Social Responsibility**

     1. **Stakeholder Social Responsibility**—holds that managers and other employees have obligations to identifiable groups that are affected by or can affect the achievement of an organization's goals.

       a. Three reasons are suggested for embracing stakeholder social responsibility: 1) enlightened self-interest, 2) sound investment, and 3) interference avoidance.

       b. The general idea is that a better society creates a better environment for business.

     2. **Stakeholders**—are individuals or groups that have interests, rights, or ownership in an organization and its activities.

       a. Stakeholders who have similar interests and rights are said to belong to the same stakeholder groups.

       b. Customers, suppliers, employees, and strategic partners are examples of primary stakeholder groups.

       c. Stakeholder groups can benefit from a company's successes and can be harmed by its failures and mistakes. Also, stakeholder groups are important to the general well-being and effectiveness of organizations.

     3. **Primary Stakeholders**—are those whose concerns the organization must address in order to ensure its own survival.

       a. <u>Secondary Stakeholders</u>—are also important because they can take actions that can damage—but not destroy—the organizations.

         1. Public opinion leaders, political action groups, and the media are secondary stakeholders for many organizations.

     4. **Stakeholder Pressures**—each group of stakeholders has somewhat different concerns; each cares more about some aspects of an organization's activities and less about others.

     5. **Protecting the Natural Environment**

       a. <u>Sustainable Development</u>—conducting business in a way that protects the natural environment while making economic progress.

       b. The European Union's Eco-Management and Audit Scheme (EMAS) and the International Organization for Standardization's (ISO 14000) standards are examples of environmental policy statements designed to provide guidance to multinational businesses.

6. **Finding Win-Win Solutions**—the primary pressures from various stakeholder groups differ, as do their views about the appropriate role of business in society.

7. **Evaluating Social Performance**—many companies are discovering that they can't avoid having people evaluate how well they perform in corporate social responsibility.

   a. Proactive Responsibility—a proactive stakeholder social responsibility approach involves five categories of initiatives:

      1. *Broad Performance Criteria*—managers and employees must consider and accept broader criteria for measuring the organization's performance and social role than those required by law and the marketplace.

      2. *Ethical Norms*—managers and employees must take definite stands on issues of public concern and advocate ethical norms for the organization, the industry, and business in general.

      3. *Operating Strategy*—managers and employees should maintain or improve the current standards of the physical and social environments.

      4. *Response to Social Pressures*—managers and employees should accept responsibility for solving current problems. They also need to be receptive to formal and informal inputs from outside stakeholders in decision making.

      5. *Legislative and Political Activities*—managers must show a willingness to work with outside stakeholders; and promote honesty and openness in government and in their own organization's lobbying activities.

8. **Social Audit**—is an attempt to identify, measure, evaluate, report on, and monitor the effects that the organization is having on its stakeholders and society as a whole.

   a. A social audit focuses on indicators, measurements, and goals relevant to key primary and secondary stakeholders.

MATCHING

Directions: Select the term that best identifies the statement listed below. Place the letter of the correct term in the space provided.

A. Laws
B. Equal Pay Act
C. Justice Approach
D. Distributive Justice Principle
E. *Caveat Emptor*
F. Social Audit
G. Sabranes-Oxley Act
H. Ethics
I. Natural Duty Principle
J. Ethics Resource Center

K. Secondary Stakeholders
L. Fairness Principle
M. Primary Stakeholders
N. Utilitarian Approach
O. Code of Ethics
P. Stakeholder Social Responsibility
Q. Whistle-blowers
R. Stakeholders
S. Sustainable Development
T. Employment-at-Will

_____ 1. States the principles that employees are expected to follow when acting on behalf of the organization.

_____ 2. Public opinion leaders, political action groups, and the media for many organizations.

_____ 3. Makes illegal the payment of different wages to women and men when their jobs require equal skill, effort, and responsibility and are performed under similar working conditions.

_____ 4. A traditional common-law concept holding that employers are free to discharge employees for any reason at any time, and that employees are free to quit their jobs for any reason at any time.

_____ 5. A set of rules and values that defines right and wrong conduct.

_____ 6. To conduct business in a way that protects the natural environment while making economic progress.

_____ 7. "Let the buyer beware"—a defense in the past for a variety of shady business practices.

_____ 8. The mission of this organization is be a leader in fostering ethical practices in individuals and organizations.

_____ 9. Individuals or groups that have interests, rights, or ownership in an organization or its activities.

_____ 10. A moral requirement that employees support the rules of the organization when certain conditions are met.

_____ 11. Judging the effect of decisions and behavior on others, with the primary goal of providing the greatest good for the greatest number of people.

_____ 12. Came about as a response to the numerous corporate scandals, such as those of Enron, WorldCom, Tyco, and Adelphia.

_____ 13. Individuals' or groups' concerns that the organization must address in order to ensure its own survival.

_____ 14. Society's values and standards that are enforceable in the courts.

_____ 15. This holds that managers and other employees have obligations to identifiable groups that are affected by or can affect the achievement of an organization's goals.

_____ 16. An attempt to identify, measure, evaluate, report on, and monitor the effects the organization is having on its stakeholders and society.

_____ 17. Judging decisions and behavior by their consistency with an equitable, fair, and impartial distribution of benefits (rewards) and costs among individuals and groups.

_____ 18. A moral requirement that decisions and behaviors be based on a variety of universal obligations.

_____ 19. Employees who report unethical or illegal actions of their employers to management, external stakeholders, or the public.

_____ 20. A moral requirement that individuals not be treated differently because of arbitrarily defined characteristics.

TRUE OR FALSE

<u>Directions</u>: Write True or False in the space provided.

❖1❖

_____ 1. Due to higher morale standards and training, the ethical issues faced by managers is declining.

_____ 2. Recent polls indicate that the public has generally lost trust in today's business leaders.

❖2❖

_____ 3. Moral principles are a set of values and rules that define right and wrong conduct.

_____ 4. What is considered ethical in a society never changes because ethics are important cultural components.

_____ 5. A legal action or activity is always ethical.

_____ 6. A large part of any view of what is ethical comes from the society in which the behavior occurs.

_____ 7. An important source of ethical guidance is top management's behavior in an organization.

_____ 8. A code of ethics states the principles that employees are expected to follow when acting on behalf of the organization.

_____ 9. Psychological studies of ethical behavior suggest that individuals' morals are set at birth.

_____ 10. An individual's view of what is ethical always converges with the views of the organization and the larger society.

_____ 11. Whistle-blowers are employees who report unethical or illegal actions by their employers to other people or organizations that are capable of taking corrective action.

❖3❖

_____ 12. According to Friedman, firms should often go beyond what the law requires.

_____ 13. Efficiency is achieved by minimizing inputs and maximizing productive outputs.

_____ 14. The utilitarian approach prescribes ethical standards for managers and employees in the areas of organizational goals, efficiency, and freedom of speech.

_____ 15. The utilitarian approach holds that decisions should be consistent with fundamental rights and privileges.

_____   16.   With the development of new technologies, concern for privacy issues has decreased.

❖4❖

_____   17.   Stakeholder groups can benefit from a company's successes and can be harmed by its failures and mistakes.

_____   18.   Secondary stakeholders are those whose concerns the organization must address to ensure its own survival.

_____   19.   Each group of stakeholders has somewhat different expectations.

_____   20.   Proactive responsibility involves conducting business in a way that protects the natural environment while making economic progress.

MULTIPLE CHOICE

<u>Directions</u>: Select the best answer in the space provided.

❖1❖

_____   1.   In a recent poll, _____ percent of the respondents felt that the typical CEO is less honest and ethical than the average person.
a. 31
b. 51
c. 61
d. 71

❖2❖

_____   2.   _____ prescribe general rules of acceptable behavior that are intended to be impartial.
a. Ethics
b. Values
c. Moral principles
d. Social norms

_____   3.   Forces which shape ethical conduct include all of the following <u>except</u>
a. laws and regulations.
b. individual perspective.
c. societal norms and culture.
d. all of the above.

_____   4.   Which of the following concerns the ability of employers to discharge employees at any time and that employees are free to quit their jobs at any time?
a. employment-at-will
b. Sarbanes-Oxley Act
c. Civil Rights Act
d. OSHA

❖**3**❖

_____ 5. Which of the following is <u>not</u> one of the ethical approaches for judging the right or wrong of managerial and employee decisions and behavior?
  a. utilitarian approach
  b. moral rights approach
  c. universal principles approach
  d. justice approach

_____ 6. This approach is most consistent with Milton Friedman's views.
  a. moral rights
  b. traditional
  c. utilitarian
  d. justice

_____ 7. The Douglas Company manufactures and sells customized sail boats. It rewards its employees with a merit pay system for effective work performance. The ethical aspect of this system is justified under the _____ approach.
  a. justice
  b. affirmative
  c. moral rights
  d. utilitarian

_____ 8. General Motors chose to use a higher standard than required for its operations in Mexico. General Motors voluntarily installed sewage treatment systems in towns throughout the country. The company was operating under the _____ approach.
  a. moral rights
  b. justice
  c. affirmative
  d. utilitarian

_____ 9. The _____ approach justifies OSHA.
  a. justice
  b. fairness
  c. moral rights
  d. utilitarianism

_____ 10. The _____ and _____ approaches give greater weight to long-term employee welfare than to quarterly profits.
  a. moral rights; justice
  b. justice; utilitarianism
  c. moral rights; utilitarianism
  d. natural duty; justice

_____ 11. The pre-1950's statement "let the buyer beware" is termed:
  a. *bustarella.*
  b. *caveat venditor.*
  c. *caveat emptor.*
  d. *resipsa loquitor.*

_____ 12. This approach's principles include fairness and natural duty.
   a. utilitarian
   b. moral rights
   c. justice
   d. none of the above

_____ 13. Which of the following is a <u>false</u> statement of the fairness principle?
   a. Employees are expected to follow the organization's rules, even if the rules restrict their individual choices.
   b. Both the organization and its employees have obligations and both should accept their responsibilities.
   c. The mutual obligations can be considered fair if they result from voluntary acts.
   d. It is a responsibility that is accepted in exchange for certain rights.

_____ 14. The _____ principle complements the moral rights approach.
   a. fairness
   b. justice
   c. distributive
   d. natural duty

❖4❖

_____ 15. The Mead Paper Corporation located in Escanaba, Michigan, wanted to add an expansion to its pulp mill in the 1960s. At that time, Escanaba had the cleanest air in the country. Local citizens formed a group called Save Our Air (SOA) to stop the expansion. This group is referred to as a(n) _____.
   a. lobby group
   b. trade group
   c. stakeholder
   d. environment informist

_____ 16. _____ refers to conducting business in a way that protects the natural environment while making economic progress.
   a. Strategic action
   b. Sustainable development
   c. Planning and administration
   d. Sustainable competitive advantage

_____ 17. Norm Thompson, Inc. has a specific environmental policy and is considered a leader in _____.
   a. sustainable development
   b. employment-at-will
   c. the utilitarian approach
   d. the moral rights approach.

_____ 18. Chrysler Chairman Robert Eaton's views would be most consistent with which of the following?
   a. moral rights approach
   b. utilitarian approach
   c. justice approach
   d. stakeholder social responsibility

❖**5**❖

_____ 19. Which of the following initiatives typifies a proactive stakeholder?
   a. ethical norms
   b. broad performance criteria
   c. operating strategy
   d. all of the above

_____ 20. A(n) _____ is an attempt to identify, measure, evaluate, report on, and monitor the effects that an organization is having on its stakeholders and society as a whole.
   a. environmental scanning
   b. code of ethics
   c. annual report
   d. social audit

ESSAY QUESTIONS

❖**1**❖

1. Why has there been in increase recently in the emphasis of ethics in business?

❖**2**❖

2. Define and contrast ethics with laws.

❖**3**❖

3. Explain the three ethical approaches: utilitarianism, moral rights, and justice approach.

4.   Discuss the distributive justice principle, fairness principle, and natural duty principle.

❖4❖

5.   What is a social audit?

CHAPTER 6
ETHICS AND STAKEHOLDER SOCIAL RESPONSIBILITY

MATCHING SOLUTIONS

1.   O - Code of Ethics
2.   K - Secondary Stakeholders
3.   B - Equal Pay Act
4.   T - Employment-at-Will
5.   H - Ethics
6.   S - Sustainable Development
7.   E - *Caveat Emptor*
8.   J - Ethics Resource Center
9.   R - Stakeholders
10.   L - Fairness Principle
11.   N - Utilitarian Approach
12.   G - Sabranes-Oxley Act
13.   M - Primary Stakeholders
14.   A - Laws
15.   P - Stakeholder Social Responsibility
16.   F - Social Audit
17.   C - Justice Approach
18.   I   - Natural Duty Principle
19.   Q - Whistle-blowers
20.   D - Distributive Justice Principle

TRUE/FALSE SOLUTIONS

Question	Answer	Page	Explanation
1.	False	150	The importance of ethical issues facing managers and employees have been magnified in recent years due to the unethical and illegal conduct of some of the top executives in various major U.S. organizations.
2.	True		
3.	False	151	Ethics is a set of values and rules that defines right and wrong conduct. They indicate when behavior is acceptable and when it is unacceptable. Moral principles prescribe general rules of acceptable behavior that are intended to be impartial.
4.	False	152–153	Even in the same society the view of what is ethical and legal changes over time. Changing societal views of ethical behavior eventually result in new legal requirements.
5.	False	152	Laws are simply society's values and standards that are enforceable in the courts. The legality of actions and decisions does not necessarily make them ethical. For example, at one time U.S. organizations could legally discriminate against women and minorities in hiring and promotions. As a consensus developed that such discriminatory practices were unethical, laws such as the Civil Rights Act of 1964 were passed to stop the practices and ensure equal employment opportunities for all citizens.
6.	True		
7.	True		
8.	True		
9.	False	156	Psychological studies of ethical behavior suggest that people develop morally, much as they do physically, from early childhood to adulthood.
10.	False	156	Individuals have their own values and a sense of what is right or wrong. Sometimes an individual's view of what is ethical converges with the views of their organization and the larger society, but not always.
11.	True		
12.	False	158	According to Friedman, no firm unilaterally should go beyond what the law requires.

13.	True		
14.	False	159–160	The utilitarian approach prescribes ethical standards for managers and employees in the areas of organizational goals, efficiency, and conflicts of interest.
15.	False	161	The moral rights approach holds that decisions should be consistent with fundamental rights and privileges (e.g., life, freedom, health, and privacy).
16.	False	161	With the availability of new information technologies (especially computers and surveillance equipment), enormous concern has been expressed about invasions of privacy.
17.	True		
18.	False	165	Primary stakeholders are those whose concerns the organization must address to ensure its own survival.
19.	True		
20.	False	167	Sustainable development involves conducting business in a way that protects the natural environment while making economic progress, thus meeting the needs of the present generation without compromising the ability of future generations to meet their own needs.

MULTIPLE CHOICE SOLUTIONS

Question	**Answer**	**Page**	**Explanation**
1.	d	151	The losses in individual firms have spilled over to a general loss of trust in business leaders. In one recent poll, 71 percent of the public felt that the typical CEO is less honest and ethical than the average person. Seventy-two percent of those polled rated the moral and ethical standards of CEOs of major corporations as either fair or poor.
2.	a	151	Ethics is a set of values and rules that define right and wrong conduct.

3.	d	151–152	All the statements are true. Forces that shape ethical conduct include: societal norms and culture; laws and regulations; organizational practices and culture; and individual perspective.
4.	a	153	Employment-at-will is a traditional common-law concept holding that employers are free to discharge employees for any reason at any time and that employees are free to quit their jobs for any reason at any time.
5.	c	158–163	The three ethical approaches are: utilitarian approach, moral rights approach, and justice model.
6.	c	158	Nobel Prize-winning economist Milton Friedman is probably the best known advocate of the utilitarian approach.
7.	d	160	The ethical aspect of the merit pay system (which rewards different employees with different rates of pay based on their performance) is justified under the utilitarian approach. The utilitarian approach is consistent with strong values of individualism, acceptance of uncertainty, and masculinity. These values support profit maximization, self-interest, rewards based on abilities and achievement, sacrifice and hard work, and competition.
8.	a	161	The moral rights approach holds that decisions should be consistent with fundamental rights and privileges. Businesses operating in other countries often find that laws are less restrictive there, so they must choose whether to meet only the standards of the host country or exceed those legal requirements. General Motors chose the higher standard.
9.	c	161	The life and safety moral right (under the moral rights model) justifies the U.S. Occupational Safety and Health Act (OSHA) of 1970. It contains many requirements designed to increase the safety and healthfulness of work environments that organizations must meet.
10.	a	164	The moral rights and justice approaches emphasize individual rights and obligations and the need to distribute benefits and burdens fairly among individuals. These approaches give greater weight to long-term employee welfare than to quarterly profits.

11.	c	161	*Caveat emptor* means "let the buyer beware." *Caveat venditor* means "let the seller beware." *Bustarella* is a bribe in Italy. *Resipsa loquitor* is a legal term that means "the thing speaks for itself."
12.	c	163–164	The justice approach consists of three principles that should be followed when designing management systems and making organizational decisions: the distributive justice principle, the procedural fairness principle, and the natural duty principle.
13.	d	163–164	The <u>fairness principle</u> morally requires employees to support the rules of the organization when two conditions are met (1) the organization is just (or fair), and (2) employees have voluntarily accepted benefits provided by the organization or has taken advantage of opportunities offered in order to further their own interests. The <u>natural duty principle</u> morally requires that decisions and behavior be based on universal principles associated with being a responsible member of society. The first three statements are true.
14.	d	164	One way to think of a natural duty is as a responsibility that is accepted in exchange for certain rights. For example, if you have a right to safety, as suggested by the moral rights approach, this right can best be assured if members of society also agree that they have a duty not to harm others. Thus the natural duty principle complements the moral rights approach.
15.	c	165	<u>Stakeholders</u> are individuals or groups that have interests, rights, or ownership in an organization and its activities. Stakeholders who have similar interests and rights are said to belong to the same stakeholder group. Customers, suppliers, employees, and strategic partners are examples of stakeholder groups.
16.	b	167	<u>Sustainable development</u> involves conducting business in a way that protects the environment while making economic progress, thus meeting the needs of the present generation without compromising the ability of future generations to meet their own needs.
17.	a	167	Norm Thompson, Inc., has a specific environmental policy and is recognized as a leader in sustainable development.

18.	b	169	Chrysler Chairman Robert Eaton said, "The idea of corporations taking on social responsibility is ridiculous. You'll simply burden industry to a point where it is no longer competitive." This viewpoint is most consistent with the utilitarian perspective which advocates maximizing shareholder wealth.
19.	d	169	A proactive stakeholder social responsibility approach involves five categories of initiatives: broad performance criteria, ethical norms, operating strategy, response to social pressures, and legislative and political activities.
20.	d	170	Managers concerned about their company's social performance may undertake a social audit. In contrast to a financial audit, a social audit focuses on social actions rather than fiscal accountability and measures achievement under the affirmative social responsibility concept.

ESSAY SOLUTIONS

[Pages 150–151]

1. The importance of ethical issues facing managers and employees have been magnified in recent years due to the unethical and illegal conduct of some of the top executives in various major U.S. corporations (e.g., Enron, Arthur Anderson, WorldCom). These notorious unethical and often illegal practices of such organizations have resulted in bankruptcies, massive financial losses for shareholders, and loss of jobs by employees.

[Page 151]

2. Ethics is a sense of values and rules that define right and wrong conduct. These values and rules indicate when behavior is acceptable and when it is unacceptable. Laws are society's values and standards that are enforceable in the courts. The legality of actions and decisions doesn't necessarily make them ethical, however.

[Pages 158–164]

3. The utilitarian approach focuses on actions (behaviors), not on the motives for such actions. A manager or employee guided by this approach considers the potential effects of alternative actions from the perspective of the accepted social contract. The alternative chosen is supposed to benefit the greatest number of people, although such benefit may come at the expense of the few or those with little power.

The <u>moral rights approach</u> holds that decisions should be consistent with fundamental rights and privileges (e.g., life, freedom, health, privacy, and property), as set forth in documents such as the first ten amendments to the U.S. Constitution (the Bill of Rights) and the United Nations' Declaration of Human Rights.

The <u>justice approach</u> evaluates decisions and behaviors with regard to how equitably they distribute benefits and costs among individuals and groups. To ensure just decisions and behavior, the proponents of this approach argue that three principles should be followed when designing management systems and making organizational decisions: the distributive justice principle, the fairness principle, and the natural duty principle.

[Pages 163–164]

4. The <u>distributive justice principle</u> morally requires that individuals not be treated differently on the basis of arbitrarily defined characteristics. It holds that: (1) individuals who are similar in relevant aspects should be treated similarly, and (2) individuals who differ in relevant respects should be treated differently in proportion to the differences between them. The <u>fairness principle</u> morally requires employees to support the rules of the organization when two conditions are met: (1) the organization is just (or fair), and (2) employees have voluntarily accepted benefits provided by the organization or have taken advantage of opportunities offered to further their own interests. The <u>natural duty principle</u> morally requires that decisions and behavior be based on universal principles associated with being a responsible member of society. Four universal duties are: (1) to help others who are in need or in jeopardy, provided that the help can be given without excessive personal risk or loss; (2) not to harm or injure another; (3) not to cause unnecessary suffering; and (4) to support and comply with just institutions.

[Page 170]

5. A <u>social audit</u> is an attempt to identify, measure, evaluate, report on, and monitor the effects the organization is having on its stakeholders and society as a whole. A social audit focuses on indicators, measurements, and goals relevant to key primary and secondary stakeholders.

CHAPTER 7
PLANNING AND STRATEGY

LEARNING OBJECTIVES

After studying this chapter, you should be able to:

❖**1**❖   Explain the importance of the planning function.

❖**2**❖   Describe the core components of strategic and tactical planning.

❖**3**❖   Discuss the effects of degree of diversification on planning.

❖**4**❖   Describe the three basic levels of strategy and planning.

❖**5**❖   State the eight primary phases of the planning process.

❖**6**❖   Explain the generic competitive strategies model.

OUTLINE

❖**1**❖   Explain the importance of the planning function.

    I.   **The Planning Function**

       1. **Planning**—is determining organization goals and developing ways to reach them.

          a. Planning is a basic managerial function because it sets the framework and the direction for the organizing, leading, and controlling functions.

       2. When used by competent leaders and managers it should assist in: (1) identifying future opportunities, (2) anticipating and avoiding future problems, (3) developing courses of action (strategies and tactics), and (4) understanding the risks and uncertainties associated with various options.

          a. Thus the organization will have a better chance of achieving its general goals. These goals include adapting and innovating in order to create desirable change, improving productivity, and maintaining organizational stability.

          b. Achieving these goals should enable the organization to achieve long-term growth, profitability, and survival.

❖**2**❖   Describe the core components of strategic and tactical planning.

II.   Two Types of Planning

1. **Strategic Planning**—is the process of (1) diagnosing the organization's external and internal environments, (2) deciding on a vision and mission, (3) developing overall goals, (4) creating and selecting general strategies to be pursued, and (5) allocating resources to achieve the organization's goals.

   a. The focus is on developing strategies that deal effectively with environmental opportunities and threats as they relate to the organization's strengths and weaknesses.

   b. Contingency Planning—is the preparation for unexpected and quick changes (positive and negative) in the environment that will have a significant impact on the organization and require immediate responses.

      1. Contingency planning forces managers to be aware of possibilities and prethink strategies to respond to them.

      2. This process begins with managers developing scenarios of major environmental events that could occur.

2. **Vision**—expresses an organization's fundamental aspirations and purpose, usually by appealing to its members' hearts and minds.

   a. A vision statement adds "soul" to a mission statement if it lacks one.

   b. Over time, traditional statements of mission may change, but the organization's vision may endure for generations.

3. **Mission**—is the organization's purpose or reason for existing.

   a. A statement of mission may answer basic questions such as: (1) What business are we in? (2) Who are we? and (3) What are we about?

   b. It describes the organization in terms of the customer needs it aims to satisfy, the goods or services it supplies, and the markets it is currently pursuing or intends to pursue in the future.

   c. A mission statement has meaning only if it serves as a unifying and driving force for guiding strategic planning and achieving the organization's long-term goals.

4. **Organizational Goals**—are the results that the managers and others have selected and are committed to achieving for the long-term survival and growth of the firm.

   a. Goals may be expressed both qualitatively and quantitatively (what is to be achieved, how much is to be achieved, and by when is it to be achieved).

5. **Strategies**—are the major courses of action (choices) selected and implemented to achieve one or more goals.

   a. A key challenge is to develop strategies that are at least partially unique relative to competitors or to pursue strategies similar to those of competitors but in different ways.

6. **Resource Allocation**—involves assigning money, people, facilities and equipment, land and other resources among various current and new business opportunities, functions, projects, and tasks.

   a. As part of the strategic planning process, resource allocation generally boils down to earmarking money, through budgets for various purposes.

7. **Tactical Planning**—is the process of making concrete decisions about what to do, who will do it, and how to do it with a normal time horizon of one year or less.

   a. Middle and first-line managers and teams often are heavily involved in tactical planning.

   b. The process generally includes the following tasks: choosing specific goals and the means of implementing the organization's strategic plan; deciding on courses of action for improving current operations; and developing budgets for each department, division, and project.

   c. Departmental managers and employee teams develop tactical plans to anticipate or cope with the actions of competitors, to coordinate with other departments, customers, and suppliers, and to implement strategic plans.

   d. Tactical planning differs from strategic planning primarily in terms of shorter time frames, size of resource allocations, and level of detail.

❖**3**❖   Discuss the effects of degree of diversification on planning.

III.   Degree of Diversification and Planning

1. **Diversification**—refers to the variety of goods or services produced and the number of different markets it serves.

   a. The degree of diversification directly affects the complexity of an organization's strategic planning.

   b. Strategic changes in the amount of diversification should be guided by answers to the following questions that help managers identify the potential risks—and opportunities—that diversification presents.

      1. What can we do better than any of our competitors if we enter a new market?

      2. What strategic assets are needed to succeed in the new market?

         a. *Downscoping*—a divestiture, spin-off, or some means of eliminating divisions and business lines that are unrelated to a firm's core business.

      3. Will we be simply a player in the new market or will we emerge a winner?

      4. What can we learn by diversifying, and are we sufficiently organized to learn it?

2. **Types of Business Firms**

    a. <u>Single-Business Firm</u>—provides a limited number of goods or services to one segment of a particular market.

    b. <u>Dominant-Business Firm</u>—serves various segments of a particular market.

        1. *Market*—refers collectively to the various users of a particular product line.

    c. <u>Related-Business Firm</u>—provides a variety of similar goods and/or services.

        1. Its divisions generally compete in the same markets, use similar technologies, share common distribution channels, or benefit from common strategic assets.

    d. <u>Unrelated-Business Firm</u>—provides diverse products (goods and/or services) to many different markets.

        1. Often referred to as a *conglomerate*, such a firm usually consists of distinct companies that have no relation to each other.

❖**4**❖   Describe the three basic levels of strategy and planning.

IV. **Strategic Levels and Planning**

1. **Corporate-Level Strategy**—focuses on the types of businesses the firm wants to be in, ways to acquire or divest businesses, allocation of resources among the businesses, and ways to develop learning and synergy among those business.

    a. Top corporate managers determine the role of each separate business within the organization.

    b. <u>Strategic Business Unit (SBU)</u>—is a division or subsidiary of a firm that provides a distinct product or service and often has its own mission and goals.

        1. An SBU is usually evaluated on the basis of its own income statement and balance sheet.

        2. Top corporate management is heavily involved in determining which SBUs to form, acquire, or divest.

    c. <u>Growth Strategies</u>—the five common corporate-level growth strategies are:

        1. *Forward Integration Strategy*—occurs when a company enters the businesses of its customers, moving it closer to the ultimate consumer.

        2. *Backward Integration Strategy*—occurs when a company enters the businesses of its suppliers, usually to control component quality, ensure on-time delivery, or stabilize prices.

            a. This strategy is implemented by acquiring suppliers or by creating new businesses that provide the same goods or services as the organization's suppliers.

            b. Sometimes called an *upstream strategy*.

3. *Horizontal Integration Strategy*—occurs when a company acquires one or more competitors to consolidate and extend its market share.

    a. The alliance strategy, as through joint ventures, is an alternative to traditional forms of backward, forward, and horizontal integration.

4. *Concentric Diversification Strategy*—also known as related diversification, occurs when a firm acquires or starts a business related to the organization's existing business in terms of technology, markets, or products.

    a. Frequently, a related-business enterprise acquires another company or starts a new venture.

    b. Some common thread must link the two firms, such as the same general set of customers, similar technology, overlapping distribution channels, compatible managerial competencies, or similar goods or services.

5. *Conglomerate Diversification Strategy*—occurs when a firm adds unrelated goods or services to its line of businesses.

    a. Generally, one company acquires another company or starts a venture in a totally new field.

    b. Diversified enterprises operating unrelated businesses most often purchase established companies.

2. **Business-Level Strategy**—refers to the resources allocated and actions taken to achieve desired goals in serving a specific market with a highly interrelated set of goods and/or services.

    a. Top managers of an enterprise or SBU are constantly involved with planning and formulating strategies for: (1) maintaining or gaining a competitive edge in serving its customers, (2) determining how each functional area can best contribute to its overall effectiveness, and (3) allocating resources among its functions.

    b. A focus on customers is the foundation of successful business-level plans and strategies. Management must address three basic questions: Who will be served? What customer needs will be satisfied? and How will customers' needs be satisfied?

3. **Functional-Level Strategy**—refers to the actions and resource commitments established for operations, marketing, human resources, finance, legal services, accounting, and the organization's other functional areas.

    a. Functional-level plans and strategies should be designed to complement business-level strategies and plans.

    b. Functional-level strategies often involve a combination of tactical and strategic planning.

    c. Operations strategies—specify how the firm will develop and utilize its production capabilities to support the firm's business-level strategies.

    d. <u>Marketing strategies</u>—address how the firm will distribute and sell its goods and services.

    e. <u>Finance strategies</u>—identify how best to obtain and allocate the firm's financial resources.

❖**5**❖   State the eight primary phases of the planning process.

V.   **Tasks of Planning**

1. Involves eight core tasks: (1) develop vision, mission, and goals, (2) diagnose threats and opportunities, (3) diagnose strengths and weaknesses, (4) develop strategies, (5) prepare a strategic plan, (6) prepare tactical plans, (7) control and diagnose results, and (8) continue planning.

    a. <u>Task 1: Develop Vision, Mission, and Goals</u>—answers questions such as: What business are we in? What are we committed to? and What results do we want to achieve?

        1. General goals provide broad direction for decision making and may not change from year to year.

        2. The mission and goals are not developed in isolation. They are influenced by diagnosis of environmental threats and opportunities and diagnosis of the organization's strengths and weaknesses.

    b. <u>Task 2: Diagnose Opportunities and Threats</u>—environmental forces—internal and external, domestic and global—that can affect an organization. These forces represent both opportunities and threats for an organization.

        1. *Competitors*—the rivalry among existing competitors in an industry varies with top management's view of threats and opportunities, the strategies a firm pursues, and competitor's reactions to those strategies.

        2. *New Entrants*—the entry of new competitors often is a response to high profits earned by established firms and/or rapid growth in an industry.

        3. *Customers*—the bargaining power of customers depends on their relative ability to play one firm off against another in order to force down prices, obtain higher quality, or buy more goods and services for the same price.

        4. *Suppliers*—the bargaining power of suppliers increases when they can increase or protect market share, raise prices, or eliminate certain features of their goods or services with little fear of losing customers.

        5. *Substitute Goods or Services*—the threat of substitute goods or services depends on the ability and willingness of customers to change their buying habits. They limit the price that firms in a particular industry can charge for their products without risking a loss in sales.

    c. <u>Task 3: Diagnose Strengths and Weaknesses</u>—enables managers to identify an organization's core competencies and to determine which need to improved.

1. *Core Competencies*—are the strengths that make an organization distinctive and more competitive by providing goods or services that have unique value to its customers.

2. From a business-level strategy perspective, core competencies fall into three broad groups: superior technological know-how, reliable processes, and close relationships with external stakeholders.

3. A reliable process involves delivering an expected result quickly, consistently, and efficiently with the least inconvenience to customers.

4. *Outsourcing* means letting other organizations perform a needed service and/or manufacture needed parts or products.

d. <u>Task 4: Develop Strategies</u>—potential strategies must be evaluated in terms of (1) external opportunities and threats, (2) internal strengths and weaknesses, and (3) the likelihood that the strategies will help the organization achieve its mission and goals.

1. *Market Penetration Strategy*—involves seeking growth in current markets with current products. This may be accomplished by:

   a. encouraging greater use of its goods or services

   b. attracting competitiors customers

   c. buying a competitor

2. *Market Development Strategy*—involves seeking new markets for current products. This may be accomplished by:

   a. entering new geographic markets

   b. entering target markets

   c. expanding uses for current products and facilities

3. *Product Development Strategy*—involves developing new or improved goods or services for current markets. This may be accomplished by:

   a. improving features

   b. increasing quality in terms of reliability, speed, efficiency, or durability   b.

   c. enhancing the aesthetic appeal

   d. introducing new models

e. <u>Task 5: Prepare Strategic Plan</u>—a strategic plan should specify the primary actions (strategies) to be taken to achieve the organization's mission and goals.

1. Contains: (1) organizational vision, mission, and goals; (2) strategies for obtaining and utilizing the necessary technological, marketing, financial, and human resources to achieve those goals; (3) goods and/or services offered, including what makes them unique; (4) strategies for developing and utilizing organizational and employee competencies; (5) financial statements, including profit-and-loss, cash flow, and break-even projections; and (6) market analysis and strategies, including opportunities and threats and contingency plans if things don't go as expected.

f. <u>Task 6: Prepare Tactical Plans</u>—the purpose of tactical plans is to help implement strategic plans.

1. Middle and first-line managers and employee teams normally base tactical plans on the organization's strategic plans.

g. <u>Task 7: Control and Diagnose Results</u>—strategic and tactical planning must be accompanied by controls to ensure implementation of the plans and evaluation of their results.

1. If the plans haven't produced the desired results, managers and teams may need to change the controls, mission, goals, or strategies, or the plans themselves.

h. <u>Task 8: Continue Planning</u>—planning is a continuing and ongoing process.

1. Sometimes these changes are gradual and foreseeable; at other times they are abrupt and unpredictable.

❖**6**❖   Explain the generic competitive strategies model.

VI. **Generic Competitive Strategies Model**—comprises a framework of four basic business-level strategies that can be applied to a variety of organizations in diverse industries.

1. This model is called generic because all types of organizations can use it, whether they are involved in manufacturing, distribution, or services.

2. *Strategic Target* dimension (vertical axis) indicates how widely the good or service is intended to compete—throughout the industry or within a particular market segment of the industry.

3. *Source of Advantage* dimension (horizontal axis) indicates the basis on which the good or service is intended to compete—uniqueness as perceived by the customer or low cost (price) to the customer.

4. *Differentiation Strategy*—involves competing by offering goods or services that customers perceive to be unique in ways that are important to them.

   a. This strategy is dominant in the auto industry.

   b. Various approaches are associated with this strategy such as: innovative product design, high quality, unique brand image, technological leadership, customer service leadership, an extensive dealer network, and product warranty.

   c. The long-term effectiveness of the differentiation strategy depends on how easily competitors can imitate the unique benefits provided by the firm. Once competitors imitate the offering, it no longer is an effective means of differentiation.

   d. A few of the requirements for implementing this strategy include: 1) strong marketing, 2) effective integration among functions, 3) creative and innovative employees, 4) continuous development of new or improved products and services, and 5) reputation for quality and a commitment to continuous improvement in it.

5. *Focused Differentiation Strategy*—emphasizes competing in a specific industry niche by serving the unique needs of certain customers or a specific geographic market.

   a. *Niche*—is a specialized group of customers or a narrowly defined market segment that competitors may overlook, ignore, or have difficulty serving.

   b. Organizations attempt to create a unique image for their products by catering to the specific demands of the selected niche, ignoring other potential customers.

6. *Cost Leadership Strategy*—means competing by providing goods or services at a price as low or lower than competitors' prices.

   a. This strategy requires a constant concern with efficiency.

   b. Essential actions associated with this strategy include: (1) utilizing facilities or equipment that yield high economies of scale; (2) constantly striving to reduce per unit overhead, manufacturing, marketing, and follow-up service costs; (3) minimizing labor-intensive personal services and sales forces; and (4) avoiding customers whose demands would result in high personal selling or service costs.

   c. High volume and/or rapid growth often are needed for profitability with the cost leadership strategy.

7. **Focused Cost Leadership Strategy**—refers to competing in a specific consumer or geographic niche by providing goods and services at a price low or lower than competitors prices.

   a. The requirements implementing this strategy are aligned with those of cost leadership, but the focus is on serving a subset of customers in an industry or set of customers in a particular geographic area.

MATCHING

Directions: Select the term that best identifies the statement listed below. Place the letter of the correct term in the space provided.

A. Resource Allocation
B. Mission
C. Backward Integration
D. Generic Competitive Strategies Model
E. Concentric Diversification
F. Diversification
G. Business-Level Strategy
H. Outsourcing
I. Unrelated-Businesses Firm

J. Strategic Planning
K. Related-Business Firm
L. Market Penetration Strategy
M. Core Competencies
N. Differentiation Strategy
O. Tactical Planning
P. Functional-Level Strategy
Q. Horizontal Integration
R. Vision

_____ 1.   Occurs when a company enters the businesses of its suppliers, usually to control component quality, on-time delivery, or stabilize prices.

_____ 2.   The strengths that make an organization distinctive and more competitive by providing goods or services that have unique value to its customers.

_____ 3.   Means letting other organizations perform a needed service and/or manufacture needed parts or products.

_____ 4.   The process of making detailed decisions about what to do, who will do it, and how to do it—with a normal time horizon of one year or less.

_____ 5.   Occurs when a firm acquires or starts a business related to an organization's existing business in terms of technology, markets, or products.

_____ 6.   An organization's fundamental aspirations and purpose that usually appeals to its members' hearts and minds.

_____ 7.   The process of analyzing the organization's external and internal environments, developing the appropriate mission, vision, and overall goals; identifying the general strategies to be pursued; and allocating resources.

_____ 8.   The earmarking of money, through budgets, for various purposes.

_____ 9.   Occurs when a company acquires one or more competitors to consolidate and extend its market share.

_____ 10. The interconnected set of key commitments and actions intended to provide value to customers and gain a competitive advantage for an organization by using its core competencies (abilities) in specific markets.

_____ 11. Seeking growth in current markets with current products.

_____ 12. Emphasizes competing with all other firms in the industry by offering a product that customers perceive to be unique.

_____ 13. An organization's current purpose or reason for existing.

_____ 14. A framework of three basic business-level strategies that can be applied to a variety of organizations in diverse industries.

_____ 15. The variety of goods and/or services produced and the number of different markets served by an organization.

_____ 16. Provides a variety of similar goods and/or services.

_____ 17. The set of highly related commitments and actions intended to provide value and help an organization gain a competitive advantage through its operations, marketing, human resources, and finance.

_____ 18. Provides diverse products (goods and/or services) to many different markets.

TRUE OR FALSE

Directions: Write True or False in the space provided.

❖1❖

_____ 1. Planning sets the framework and direction for the organizing, leading, and controlling functions.

_____ 2. Controlling is the most basic managerial function.

❖2❖

_____ 3. Managers and others must take an organizationwide or divisionwide approach in the process of strategic planning.

_____ 4. Contingency planning forces managers to be aware of possibilities and outline strategies to respond to them.

_____ 5. A vision is the organization's purpose or reason for existing.

_____ 6. Strategies are the results that the managers and others have selected and are committed to achieving for the long-term survival and growth of the firm.

_____ 7. One task of strategic planning is to develop budgets for each department, division, or project.

_____ 8. Tactical planning differs from strategic planning primarily in terms of shorter time frames, size of resource allocations, and level of detail.

❖3❖

_____ 9. A firm involved in a single product line or service needs more elaborate planning to ensure success of the business than would a firm with multiple product lines and services.

_____ 10. A related-business firm is often referred to as a conglomerate.

❖4❖

_____ 11. Business-level strategy focuses on the types of businesses the firm wants to be in, ways to acquire or divest businesses, allocation of resources among the businesses, and ways to develop learning and synergy among those businesses.

_____ 12. National Funeral Services purchases funeral homes in small towns to extend its market share. This is an example of forward integration.

_____ 13. A focus on customers is the foundation of successful business-level plans and strategies.

_____ 14. The strategic action competency requires that managers stay informed of the actions of competitors and understand the strengths and limitations of various business strategies.

❖5❖

_____ 15. A market development strategy requires seeking growth in current markets with current products.

_____ 16. A product development strategy involves developing new or improved goods or services for current markets.

_____ 17. The last phase in planning is the tasks of control and diagnosing results.

❖6❖

_____ 18. The focus strategy involves competing in the industry by providing a product at a price as low as or lower than competitors' prices.

_____ 19. The differentiation strategy involves competing with all other firms in the industry by offering a product that customers perceive to be unique.

_____ 20. The source of advantage dimension indicates the how widely the good or service is intended to compete.

MULTIPLE CHOICE

<u>Directions</u>: Select the best answer in the space provided.

❖1❖

_____ 1. _____ sets the direction for the other functions of management.
  a. Leading
  b. Organizing
  c. Planning
  d. Controlling

_____ 2. Which of the following statements is true regarding planning?
   a. Planning assists in anticipating and avoiding future problems.
   b. Planning creates a process for organizationwide learning.
   c. Planning involves devising divisional, departmental, and even individual goals based on organizational goals.
   d. All of the above

❖2❖

_____ 3. The UPS (United Parcel Service) strike in 1997 crippled many businesses that needed package delivery. Businesses that continued operations despite the strike had a(n) _____ plan.
   a. contingency
   b. strategic
   c. emergency
   d. logistics

_____ 4. It answers basic questions such as: What business are we in? Who are we? What are we about?
   a. corporate vision
   b. tactical plan
   c. mission statement
   d. long-term goals

_____ 5. The major courses of action that an organization takes to achieve its goals are called _____.
   a. strategies
   b. initiatives
   c. strategic plans
   d. competencies

_____ 6. Which statement below is <u>false</u> regarding tactical planning?
   a. It includes developing budgets for each department, division, and project.
   b. Top managers are heavily involved in tactical planning.
   c. It involves making detailed decisions about what to do and how to do it.
   d. Tactical planning differs from strategic planning in terms of the size of resource allocations.

❖3❖

_____ 7. Southwest Airlines provides one type of transportation service to travelers seeking high value for a low price. This is an example of a(n) _____ firm.
   a. dominant-business
   b. related-businesses
   c. single-business
   d. unrelated-businesses

_____ 8. Often referred to as a conglomerate, a(n) _____ firm usually consists of distinct companies that have no relation to each other.
   a. dominant-business
   b. related-businesses
   c. unrelated-businesses
   d. single-business

❖4❖

_____ 9. All of the following statements about SBUs are true, <u>except</u>:
   a. an SBU may have a well-defined set of customers and/or cover a specific geographic area.
   b. it is usually evaluated on the basis of its own income statement and balance sheet.
   c. an SBU is a division or subsidiary of a firm that provides a distinct product or service and often has its own mission and goals.
   d. first-line managers of each SBU are responsible for developing plans and strategies for their unit.

_____ 10. Dan Fenton owned and operated a septic company that installed many concrete septic tanks and concrete drains. To ensure a steady supply of concrete products at a reasonable price, Fenton purchased the local concrete production company. This is known as _____ integration.
   a. horizontal
   b. forward
   c. concentric
   d. backward

_____ 11. Boeing's recent acquisition of McDonnell Douglas for about $13 billion is an example of _____.
   a. global diversification
   b. concentric diversification
   c. forward integration
   d. backward integration

_____ 12. Diversified enterprises operating unrelated businesses most often use the _____ strategy.
   a. concentric diversification
   b. horizontal integration
   c. conglomerate diversification
   d. alliance

_____ 13. In the _____ strategy, a focus on customers is the foundation of successful plans and strategies.
   a. business-level
   b. product-level
   c. corporate-level
   d. functional-level

_____ 14. Which of the following statements reflects a key issue in developing functional strategies?
a. What is the desired mixture of borrowed funds and equity funds?
b. How should products be distributed?
c. What should be the level of commitment to total quality?
d. All of the above

❖5❖

_____ 15. Which of the following is <u>not</u> a step in the strategic planning process?
a. developing operational budgets
b. developing the mission statement
c. developing strategies
d. diagnosing threats and opportunities

_____ 16. The bargaining power of suppliers is likely to be great in which of the following situations?
a. A small number of suppliers sell to a large number of customers in an industry.
b. Suppliers don't have to worry about substitute goods or services that their customers can readily buy.
c. Suppliers' goods or services are differentiated.
d. All of the above

_____ 17. _____ are the strengths that make an organization distinctive and more competitive by providing goods or services that have unique value to its customers.
a. Focus strategies
b. Trade names
c. Core competencies
d. Generic strategies

_____ 18. If the Meltzer Computer Company introduces a talking computer to be utilized by the business clients it already serves, it would be implementing the _____ strategy.
a. diversification
b. market development
c. product development
d. market penetration

❖6❖

_____ 19. High volume and/or rapid growth are often needed for profitability with the _____ strategy.
a. focus
b. differentiation
c. cost leadership
d. generic

___   20.   A _____ is a specialized group of customers or a narrowly defined market segment that competitors may overlook, ignore, or have difficulty serving.
   a. segment
   b. niche
   c. core group
   d. focus group

ESSAY QUESTIONS

❖1❖

1.   Define *planning* and explain why managers should employ it.

❖2❖

2.   Define *contingency planning*. Why is this an important concept?

3.   What is the link between goals and strategies?

❖3❖

4.   Discuss the four types of diversified businesses presented in your text.

❖4❖

5. Discuss the five common corporate-level growth strategies.

❖5❖

6. Identify and discuss the eight tasks/steps in the strategic planning process.

❖6❖

7. Explain the four competitive generic strategies: differentiation strategy, cost leadership strategy, and focused differentiation strategy and focused cost leadership strategy.

CHAPTER 7
PLANNING AND STRATEGY

MATCHING SOLUTIONS

1. C - Backward Integration
2. M - Core Competencies
3. H - Outsourcing
4. O - Tactical Planning
5. E - Concentric Diversification
6. R - Vision
7. J   - Strategic Planning
8. A - Resource Allocation
9. Q - Horizontal Integration
10. G - Business-Level Strategy
11. L - Market Penetration Strategy
12. N - Differentiation Strategy
13. B - Mission
14. D - Generic Competitive Strategies Model
15. F   - Diversification
16. K - Related-Business Firm
17. P - Functional-Level Strategy
18. I   - Unrelated-Business Firm

TRUE/FALSE SOLUTIONS

Question	Answer	Page	Explanation
1.	True		
2.	False	178	Planning is the most basic managerial function. When done properly, it sets the direction for the organizing, leading, and controlling functions.
3.	True		
4.	True		

5.   False   181   The <u>mission</u> is the organization's purpose or reason for existing. A statement of mission may answer basic questions such as: (1) What business are we in? (2) Who are we? and (3) What are we about? A <u>vision</u> expresses an organization's fundamental aspirations and purpose, usually by appealing to its members' hearts and minds. A vision statement adds "soul" to a mission statement, if it lacks one.

6.   False   181   <u>Organizational goals</u> are the results that the managers and others have selected and are committed to achieving for the long-term survival and growth of the firm.

7.   False   183   <u>Tactical planning</u> is the process of making detailed decisions about what to do, who will do it, and how to do it—with a normal time horizon of one year or less. The process generally includes: choosing specific goals and the means of implementing the organization's strategic plan, deciding on courses of action for improving current operations, and developing budgets for each department, division, and project.

8.   True

9.   False   185–186   Diversification and scope of strategic planning are directly related (see Figure 7.1 in textbook). A firm that produces varied goods or services for unrelated markets often must have a broadly based planning process. A firm involved in a single product line or service needs a less elaborate planning process.

10.   False   186   A <u>related-business firm</u> provides a variety of similar goods and/or services. Its divisions generally operate in the same or similar markets, use similar technologies, share common distribution channels, or benefit from common strategic assets. An <u>unrelated-business firm</u> provides diverse products (goods and/or services) to many different markets. Often referred to as a conglomerate, such a firm usually consists of distinct companies that have no relation to each other.

11.   False   187–188   <u>Corporate-level strategy</u> focuses on the types of businesses the firm wants to be in, ways to acquire or divest businesses, allocation of resources among the businesses, and ways to develop learning and synergy among those businesses.

12.	False	189	Horizontal integration occurs when a company acquires one or more competitors to consolidate and extend its market share. This is National Funeral Services' strategy. Whereas, forward integration occurs when a company enters the businesses of its customers, moving it closer to the ultimate consumer.
13.	True		
14.	True		
15.	False	196	A market penetration strategy involves seeking growth in current markets with current products.
16.	True		
17.	False	199	The last phase of the planning process is to continue planning.
18.	False	200	The cost leadership strategy means competing in the industry by providing a product at a price as low as or lower than competitors' prices.
19.	True		
20.	False	199	The strategic target dimension indicates how widely the good or service is intended to compete. The source of advantage dimension indicates the basis on which the good or service is intended to compete.

MULTIPLE CHOICE SOLUTIONS

Question	Answer	Page	Explanation
1.	c	178	Planning is the most basic managerial function. If done properly, it sets the direction for the functions of organizing, leading, and controlling.
2.	d	179	If undertaken properly, planning should assist in: identifying future opportunities, anticipating and avoiding future problems; developing courses of action; and understanding the risks and uncertainties associated with various options. It also creates a process for organization-wide learning, including the discovery of key issues and options for their resolution.

3.   a   179   A <u>contingency plan</u> is a plan that prepares for unexpected and rapid changes in the environment that will have a significant impact on the organization and that will require a quick response. When the UPS strike occurred, some organizations implemented their contingency plan to use FedEx, the U.S. Postal Services, and other sources.

4.   c   181   The <u>mission statement</u> is the organization's purpose or reason for existing. It answers basic questions such as: (1) What business are we in? (2) Who are we? and (3) What are we about? It may describe the organization in terms of the customer needs it aims to satisfy, the goods or services it supplies, or the markets that it is currently pursuing or intends to pursue in the future.

5.   a   182   The major courses of action that an organization takes to achieve its goals are called <u>strategies</u>. A key challenge is to develop strategies that are at least partially unique relative to competitors or to pursue strategies similar to those of competitors but in different ways.

6.   b   183   <u>Tactical planning</u> is the process of making detailed decisions about what to do, who will do it, and how to do it—with a normal time horizon of one year or less. Middle and first-line managers and teams often are heavily involved in tactical planning. The other statements are true.

7.   c   186   A <u>single-business firm</u> provides a limited number of goods or services to one segment of a particular market.

8.   c   186   An <u>unrelated-business firm</u> provides diverse products (goods and/or services) to many different markets. Often referred to as a conglomerate, such a firm usually consists of distinct companies that have no relation to each other. During the past ten years, many North American firms have backed away from such diversification by selling off unrelated businesses.

9.   d   188   A <u>strategic business unit</u> (SBU) is a division or subsidiary of a firm that provides a distinct product or service and often has its own mission and goals. Corporate-level management provides guidance and reviews the performance of strategic business units. The top managers of each SBU are responsible for developing plans and strategies for their unit. The other statements are true.

10.   d   189   <u>Backward integration</u> occurs when a company enters the businesses of its suppliers, usually to control component quality, ensure on-time delivery, or stabilize prices. Fenton is using backward integration by purchasing the concrete company (former supplier), which should help to ensure timely delivery and stable prices.

11.   b   190   <u>Concentric diversification</u>, sometimes called related diversification, occurs when a firm acquires or starts a business related to the firm's existing business in terms of technology, markets, or products. Boeing's recent acquisition of McDonnell Douglas is a good example of concentric diversification.

12.   c   190   <u>Conglomerate diversification</u> occurs when a firm adds unrelated goods or services to its line of business. Generally one company acquires another company or starts a venture in a totally new field. Diversification enterprises operating unrelated businesses most often use this strategy.

13.   a   191   <u>Business-level strategy</u> refers to the resources allocated and actions taken to achieved desired goals in serving a specific market with a highly interrelated set of goods and/or services.

14.   d   192   <u>Functional-level strategy</u> refers to the actions and resource commitments established for operations, marketing, human resources, finance, legal services, accounting, and the organization's other functional areas. Table 7.2 provides examples of the issues that management in various types of firms usually address in developing functional-level plans and strategies.

15.   a   193–199 The steps in the strategic planning process include: develop vision, mission, and goals, diagnose threats and opportunities, diagnose strengths and weaknesses, develop strategies, prepare a strategic plan, prepare tactical plans, control and diagnose results, and continue planning.

16.	d	195	The bargaining power of suppliers increases when they can increase or protect market share, raise prices, or eliminate certain features of their goods or services with little fear of losing customers. The statements listed are all true.
17.	c	195	<u>Core competencies</u> are the strengths that make an organization distinctive and more competitive by providing goods or services that have unique value to its customers. Core competencies may strengthen the competitiveness of an enterprise.
18.	c	197	A <u>product development strategy</u> involves developing new or improved goods or services for current markets. Approaches that can be used to develop enhanced products include improving features; improving quality in terms of reliability, speed, efficiency, or durability; enhancing aesthetic appeal; or introducing new models.
19.	c	200	The <u>cost leadership strategy</u> emphasizes competing in the industry by providing a product at a price as low as or lower than competitors. This strategy requires a constant concern with efficiency (reduction in per unit costs). High volume and/or rapid growth often are needed for profitability with this strategy.
20.	b	200	A <u>niche</u> is a specialized group of customers (e.g., teenagers, physicians, or retirees) or a narrowly defined market segment that competitors may overlook, ignore, or have difficulty serving (e.g., a specific geographic area).

ESSAY SOLUTIONS

[Pages 178–179]

1. <u>Planning</u> is the determination of organizational goals and the means to reach them. We consider planning a basic general managerial function because it sets the framework and direction for the organizing, leading, and controlling functions. Managers should use planning to assist them to 1) discover new opportunities, 2) anticipate and avoid future problems, 3) develop effective courses of action (strategies and tactics), and 4) comprehend the uncertainties and risks with various options.

[Page 179]

2. <u>Contingency planning</u> is the preparation for unexpected and rapid changes (positive or negative) in the environment that will have a large impact on the organization and require a quick response. This process begins with managers developing scenarios of major environmental events that could occur. Contingency planning forces managers to be aware of possibilities and to outline strategies to respond to them. It supports orderly and speedy adaptation, in contrast to panic-like reactions, to external events beyond the organization's direct control.

[Pages 181–182]

3. <u>Goals</u> are what an organization is committed to achieving for the long-term survival and growth of the firm. Goals may be expressed both qualitatively and quantitatively (what is to be achieved, how much is to be achieved, and by when it is to be achieved). There is a direct link between goals and strategies. <u>Strategies</u> are the major courses of action that an organization takes to achieve its goals.

[Pages 186]

4. A <u>single-business firm</u> provides a limited number of goods or services to one segment of a particular market. A <u>dominant-business firm</u> serves various segments of a particular market. A <u>related-business firm</u> provides a variety of similar goods and/or services. An <u>unrelated-business firm</u> provides diverse products (goods and/or services) to many different markets.

[Pages 189–190]

5. <u>Forward integration</u> occurs when a company enters the businesses of its customers, moving it closer to the ultimate consumer. <u>Backward integration</u> occurs when a company enters the businesses of its suppliers, usually to control component quality, ensure on-time delivery, or stabilize prices. This strategy is implemented by acquiring suppliers or by creating new businesses that provide the same goods or services as the organization's suppliers. <u>Horizontal integration</u> occurs when a company acquires one or more competitors to consolidate and extend its market share. <u>Concentric diversification,</u> sometimes called related diversification, occurs when a firm acquires or starts a business related to the organization's existing business in terms of technology, markets, or products. Generally, a related-businesses enterprise acquires another company or starts a new venture. Some common tread must link the two firms, such as the same general set of customers, similar technology, overlapping distribution channels, compatible managerial competencies, or similar goods or services. <u>Conglomerate diversification</u> occurs when a firm adds unrelated goods or services to its line of business. Diversified enterprises operating unrelated businesses most often use this strategy.

[Pages 179, 193–199]

6. <u>Strategic planning</u> is the process of analyzing the organization's external and internal environments; developing the appropriate mission, vision, and overall goals, identifying the general strategies; and allocating resources. The process includes the following tasks:

   Task 1: Develop vision mission, and goals
   Task 2: Diagnose opportunities and threats
   Task 3: Diagnose strengths and weaknesses
   Task 4: Develop strategies
   Task 5: Prepare strategic plan
   Task 6: Prepare tactical plans
   Task 7: Control and diagnose results
   Task 8: Continue planning

[Pages 200–201]

7. The <u>differentiation strategy</u> emphasizes competing with all other firms in the industry by offering a product that customers perceive to be unique in ways that are important to them. This strategy is dominant in the auto industry. It may include: innovative product design, high quality, unique brand image, technological leadership, customer service leadership, an extensive dealer network, and product warranty. The long-term effectiveness of the differentiation strategy depends on how easily competitors can imitate the unique benefits provided by the firm.

   The <u>cost leadership strategy</u> emphasizes competing in the industry by providing a product at a price as low as or lower than competitors' prices. This strategy requires a constant concern with efficiency (reduction in per unit costs). High volume and/or rapid growth are needed for profitability with the cost leadership strategy.

   The <u>focused differentiation strategy</u> emphasizes competing in a specific industry niche by serving the unique needs of certain customers or a specific geographic market. Organizations attempt to create a unique image for their products by catering to the specific demands of the selected niche, ignoring other potential customers.

   The <u>focused cost leadership strategy</u> refers to competing in a specific customer or geographic niche by providing goods and services at a price as low or lower than competitors' prices. The requirements implementing this strategy are aligned with those of cost leadership, but the focus is on serving a subset of customers in an industry or set of customers in a particular geographic area.

CHAPTER 8
FUNDAMENTALS OF DECISION MAKING

LEARNING OBJECTIVES

After studying this chapter, you should be able to:

❖1❖   State the conditions under which individuals make decisions.

❖2❖   Describe the characteristics of routine, adaptive, and innovative decisions.

❖3❖   Explain the three basic models of decision making.

OUTLINE

❖1❖   State the conditions under which individuals make decisions.

I.   Role of Decision Making

1. **Decision Making**—is the process of defining problems, gathering information, generating alternatives, and choosing a course of action.

2. An effective manager relies on several managerial competencies to make and implement decisions. In turn, decision making underlies most managerial competencies.

II.   Decision-Making Conditions

1. Numerous developments and events—often outside of the control of individuals—influence the results of individuals' decision making.

2. The conditions under which decisions are made can be classified as:

    a. Certainty—is the condition under which individuals are fully informed about a problem, alternative solutions are obvious, and the likely results of each solution are clear.

        1. Certainty means that both the problem and alternative solutions are known and well defined.

        2. Decision making under the condition of certainty is the exception for most middle and top managers and various professionals.

        3. First-line managers make day-to-day decisions under conditions of certainty or near certainty.

   b. **Risk**—is the condition under which individuals can define a problem, specify the probability of certain events, identify alternative solutions, and state the probability of each solution leading to the desired results.

   1. Risk—generally means that the problem and the alternative solutions fall somewhere between the extremes of being certain and being unusual and ambiguous.

   2. Probability—is the percentage of times that a specific outcome would occur if an individual were to make a particular decision a large number of times.

   3. Objective Probability—the likelihood that a specific outcome will occur, based on hard facts and numbers.

   4. Subjective Probability—the likelihood that a specific outcome will occur, based on personal judgment and beliefs.

      a. Such judgments vary among individuals, depending on their intuition, previous experience with similar situations, expertise, and personality traits (e.g., preference for risk taking or risk avoidance).

   c. **Uncertainty**—is the condition under which an individual doesn't have the necessary information to assign probabilities to the outcomes of alternative solutions.

   1. Uncertainty often suggests that the problem and the alternative solutions are both ambiguous and highly unusual.

   2. Dealing with uncertainty is an important facet of the jobs of many managers and various professionals, such as research and development engineers, market researchers, and strategic planners.

   3. Managers, teams, and other professionals often need to resolve uncertainty by using their intuition, creativity, and all available information to make a judgment regarding the course of action (decision) to take.

❖**2**❖   Describe the characteristics of routine, adaptive, and innovative decisions.

III. Basic Types of Decisions

   1. **Problem Types**—range from the relatively common and well-defined problem to the unusual and ambiguous. When the number of such problems escalates with short time frames for resolution, a pattern of *fire fighting* may occur with linked elements, creating unsatisfactory results, such as the following:

   a. Solutions are incomplete.

   b. Problems recur and cascade.

   c. Urgency supersedes importance.

   d. Some problems become crises.

2. **Solution Types**—also range from the known and well-defined problem to the untried and ambiguous.

3. **Routine Decisions**—are standard choices made in response to relatively well-defined and common problems and alternative solutions.

   a. A solution is often available in established rules or standard operating procedures or, increasingly, in computer software, such as computerized airline reservation systems.

   b. Cleaning buildings, processing payroll vouchers, packing and shipping customers' orders, and making travel arrangements are but a few examples of tasks requiring routine decisions.

   c. Managers and employees need to guard against the tendency to make routine decisions when a problem actually calls for an adaptive or innovative decision.

      1. *Active Inertia*—the rigid devotion to the status quo by attempting to do more of the same old thing better.

4. **Adaptive Decisions**—are choices made in response to a combination of moderately unusual and only fairly known problems and alternative solutions.

   a. Adaptive decisions often involve modifying and improving on past routine decisions and practices.

      1. *Convergence*—a business shift in which two connections with the customer that were previously viewed as competing come to be seen as complementary.

   b. Continuous Improvement—refers to a management philosophy that approaches the challenge of product and process enhancements as an ongoing effort to increase the levels of quality and excellence.

      1. It involves streams of adaptive organizational decisions made over time that result in a large number of small incremental improvements year after year.

      2. It is driven by the goals of providing better quality, improving efficiency, and being responsive to customers.

5. **Innovative Decisions**—are choices based on the discovery, identification, and diagnosis of unusual and ambiguous problems and/or the development of unique or creative alternative solutions.

   a. The solutions frequently involve a series of small, interrelated decisions made over a period of months or even years.

   b. Innovative decisions are often based on incomplete and rapidly changing information and, in fact, may be made before problems are fully defined and understood.

   c. To be effective, decision makers must be especially careful to define the right problem and recognize that earlier actions can significantly affect later decisions.

d. <u>Radical innovators</u>—are those individuals or organizations who do one or more of the following: change customer expectations, change the bases for competition in an industry, or change the economic efficiency of an industry.

❖**3**❖   Explain the features of three basic models of decision making.

IV.   **Models of Decision Making**

1. **Rational Model**—prescribes a set of phases that individuals or teams should follow to increase the likelihood that their decisions will be logical and sound.

    a. A <u>rational decision</u> permits the maximum achievement of goals within the limitations of the situation. It usually focuses on means—how best to achieve one or more goals.

    b. The rational model includes the following steps:

        1. Define and diagnose the problem—this step involves three skills that are part of a managers planning and administration competency: noticing, interpreting, and incorporating.

            a. <u>Noticing</u>—involves identifying and monitoring numerous external and internal environmental forces and deciding which ones are contributing to the problem(s).

            b. <u>Interpreting</u>—involves assessing the forces noticed and determining which are causes, not merely symptoms, of the real problem(s).

            c. <u>Incorporating</u>—involves relating those interpretations to the current or desired goals of the department or organization.

        2. Set goals

            a. <u>Goals</u> – are results to be attained and thus indicate the direction toward which decisions and actions should be aimed.

            b. <u>General goals</u>—provide broad direction for decision making in qualitative terms.

            c. <u>Operational goals</u>—state what is to be achieved in quantitative terms, for whom and within what time period.

            d. <u>Hierarchy of goals</u>—represents the formal linking of goals between organizational levels.

        3. Search for alternative solutions—this step involves seeking additional information, thinking creatively, consulting experts, undertaking research, and taking similar actions.

        4. Compare and evaluate alternative solutions—this step emphasizes expected results and determining the relative cost of each alternative.

        5. Choose among alternative solutions

        6. Implement the solution selected—a technically correct decision has to be accepted and supported by those responsible for implementing it if the decision is to be acted on effectively.

7. Follow up and control—individuals or teams must control implementation activities and follow up by evaluating results.

    a. If implementation isn't producing satisfactory results, corrective action will be needed.

2. **Bounded Rationality Model**—contends that the capacity of the human mind for formulating and solving complex problems is small compared with what is needed for objectively rational behavior.

   a. Herbert Simon, a management scholar, introduced this model in the mid-1950s.

   b. It emphasizes the limitations of rationality and provides a better picture of the day-to-day decision-making processes used by most people.

   c. <u>Decision Biases</u>—individuals often fall prey to some information processing biases when they engage in decision making, including:

      1. *Availability Bias*—refers to easy recall of specific instances of an event that may lead individuals to overestimate how frequently the event occurs and, thus, become a problem.

      2. *Selective Perception Bias*—means that what people expect to see often is what they do see. People seek information consistent with their own views and downplay conflicting information.

      3. *Concrete Information Bias*—refers to the recollection of a vivid, direct experience usually prevailing over more objective and complete information. A single personal experience can outweigh statistical evidence.

      4. *Law of Small Numbers Bias*—means that people may view a few incidents or cases as representative of a larger population (i.e., a few cases "prove the rule") even when they are not representative.

      5. *Gambler's Fallacy Bias*—means that seeing an unexpected number of similar events can lead people to the conviction that an event not seen will occur.

   d. <u>Limited Search for Alternatives</u>—individuals usually do not make an exhaustive search for possible goals or alternative solutions to a problem. They tend to consider options until they find one that seems adequate.

   e. <u>Limited Information</u>—recognizes that individuals frequently have inadequate information about the precise nature of the problems facing them and the consequences of each alternative.

      1. *Ignorance*—the lack of relevant information or the correct interpretation of the information that is available.

   f. <u>Satisficing</u>—is the practice of selecting an acceptable goal or alternative solution rather than searching extensively for the best goal or solution.

3. **Political Model**—describes the decision-making process in terms of the particular interests and goals of powerful stakeholders.

    a. Power—is the ability to influence or control individual, departmental, team, or organizational decisions and goals. To have power is to be able to influence or control the (1) definition of the problem, (2) choice of goals, (3) consideration of alternative solutions, (4) selection of the alternative to be implemented, and (5) actions and success of the organization.

    b. Divergence in Problem Definition—external and internal stakeholders try to define problems for their own advantage. Conflicts occur when various stakeholders have different perceptions about the nature and sources of problems.

        1. *Scapegoating*—the process of casting blame for problems or shortcomings on an innocent or only partially responsible individual, team, or department.

    c. Divergence in Goals—is influenced strongly by the relative power of stakeholders. A balance of power among several stakeholders may lead to negotiation and compromise in the decision-making process.

    d. Divergence in Solutions—some goals or the means to achieve them may be perceived as win–lose situations; that is, my gain is your loss, and your gain is my loss. In such a situation, stakeholders often distort and selectively withhold information to further their own interests.

        1. Stakeholders within the organization often view information as a major source of power and use it accordingly.

        2. *Co-optation*—involves bringing new stakeholder representatives into the strategic decision-making process as a means of averting threats to an organization's stability or existence.

MATCHING

Directions: Select the term that best identifies the statement listed below. Place the letter of the correct term in the space provided.

A. Risk	K. Certainty
B. Objective Probability	L. Noticing
C. Innovative Decisions	M. Availability Bias
D. Adaptive Decisions	N. Continuous Improvement
E. Active Inertia	O. Political Model
F. Concrete Information Bias	P. Scapegoating
G. Decision Making	Q. Selective Perception Bias
H. Co-optation	R. Bounded Rationality Model
I. Satisficing	S. Power
J. Law of Small Numbers Bias	T. Convergence

_____ 1. A business shift in which two connections with the customer that were previously viewed as competing come to be seen as complementary.

_____ 2. Involves identifying and monitoring numerous external and internal environmental forces and deciding which ones are contributing to the problem(s).

_____ 3. The practice of selecting an acceptable goal or alternative solution.

_____ 4. A description of the decision-making process in terms of the particular interests and goals of powerful external and internal stakeholders.

_____ 5. The condition under which individuals can define a problem, specify the probability of certain events, identify alternative solutions, and state the probability of each solution leading to the desired results.

_____ 6. Involves bringing new stakeholder representatives into the strategic decision-making process as a means of averting threats to an organization's stability or existence.

_____ 7. The ability to influence or control individual, departmental, team, or organizational decisions and goals.

_____ 8. The condition under which individuals are fully informed about a problem, alternative solutions are obvious, and the possible results of each solution are clear.

_____ 9. The rigid devotion to the status quo by attempting to do more of the same old thing better.

_____ 10. Viewing a few incidents or cases as representatives of a larger population even when they are not.

_____ 11. An individual's tendency to select less than the best goal or alternative solution; to engage in a limited search for alternative solutions; and to have inadequate information and control over external and internal environmental forces influencing the outcomes of decisions.

_____ 12. The likelihood that a specific outcome will occur, based on hard facts and numbers.

_____ 13. Seeing what a person expects to see.

_____ 14. The process of defining problems, gathering information, generating alternatives, and choosing a course of action.

_____ 15. Choices made in response to a combination of moderately unusual and only partially known problems and alternative solutions.

_____ 16. Recall of specific instances of an event, which may overestimate how frequently the event occurs.

_____ 17. Choices based on the discovery, identification, and diagnosis of unusual and ambiguous problems and the development of unique or creative alternative solutions.

_____ 18. The process of casting blame for problems or shortcomings on an innocent or only partially responsible individual, team, or department.

_____ 19. Vivid, direct experience dominating abstract information.

_____ 20. Streams of adaptive decisions made over time in an organization that result in a large number of small, incremental improvements year after year.

TRUE OR FALSE

<u>Directions</u>: Write True or False in the space provided.

❖1❖

_____ 1. Decision making includes defining problems, gathering information, generating alternatives, and choosing a course of action.

_____ 2. Prevo's decision and recommendation to implement the ERP planning project demonstrated his strategic action competency.

_____ 3. To make a decision effectively managers rely on several managerial competencies.

_____ 4. The amount of accuracy of information and the depth of individual's managerial competencies are crucial to sound decision making.

_____ 5. Decision making under the condition of certainty is the norm for most managers.

_____ 6. Objective probability states that judgments will vary among individuals, depending on their intuition and expertise.

_____ 7. The condition of uncertainty is present even when organizations do considerable research and planning before committing resources to projects.

_____ 8. Under the condition of uncertainty, the individual may not be able to define the problem, much less identify alternative solutions and possible outcomes.

❖2❖

_____ 9. Innovative decisions often involve modifying and improving on past routine decisions and practices.

_____ 10. The concept of continuous improvement is a key to total quality management.

_____ 11. Active inertia is what characterizes many of our leading innovative and creative decision making firms.

_____ 12. Adaptive decisions refer to choices made in response to a combination of moderately unusual problems and alternative solutions.

_____ 13. Continuous improvement results in a business shift where customers that were previously competitors are now viewed as complementary.

_____ 14. Innovative decisions are choices based on discovery, identification, and diagnosis of unusual and ambiguous problems and/or the development of unique or creative alternative solutions.

❖3❖

_____ 15. The bounded rational model prescribes a set of phrases that individuals or teams should follow to increase the likelihood that their decisions will be logical and optimal.

_____ 16. A rational decision permits the maximum achievement of goals within the limitations of the situation.

_____ 17. Herbert Simon, a management scholar, introduced the rational model of decision making in the 1970s.

_____ 18. The selective perception bias means that vivid, direct experience usually prevails over abstract information.

_____ 19. The political model recognizes that the likelihood of conflicting goals among stakeholders and the choice of goals will be influenced strongly by the relative power of the stakeholders.

_____ 20. Co-optation refers to brining new stakeholder representatives into the strategic decision-making process as a way to avert threats to an organization's stability or existence.

MULTIPLE CHOICE

Directions: Select the best answer in the space provided.

❖1❖

_____ 1. Which of the following is part of the decision-making process?
   a. defining problems
   b. gathering information
   c. generating alternatives
   d. all of the above

_____ 2. The decision-making process is basic to which managerial competency?
   a. teamwork competency
   b. self-management competency
   c. communication competency
   d. all of the above

_____ 3. Purchasing agents at the Roland Consulting Corporation are expected to order standard-grade paper from the supplier who offers the lowest price and the best service. This is an example of making a decision under the condition of _____.
   a. risk
   b. subjectivity
   c. certainty
   d. uncertainty

_____   4.   First-line managers make most day-to-day decisions under conditions of _____.
             a. certainty
             b. risk
             c. objectivity
             d. uncertainty

_____   5.   _____ is the percentage of times that a specific outcome would occur if an individual were to make a particular decision a large number of times.
             a. Repetition
             b. Large number bias
             c. Probability
             d. Gambler's fallacy

_____   6.   The condition of _____ occurs when individuals have little or no information about developments and events on which to base a decision.
             a. risk
             b. uncertainty
             c. objective probability
             d. certainty

_____   7.   Which of the following professionals would deal with uncertainty as an important part of their jobs?
             a. development engineers
             b. market researchers
             c. strategic planners
             d. all of the above

❖**2**❖

_____   8.   Which of the following terms represents the rigid devotion to the status quo by attempting to do more of the same old thing better?
             a. active inertia
             b. passive inertia
             c. adaptive inertia
             d. convergence

_____   9.   Jackie Westin, a shipping clerk for Creative Looks Cosmetic Company, received a request for a large order of cosmetics from John Molson, a sales representative. Processing the order is considered a task requiring _____ decisions.
             a. routine
             b. adaptive
             c. innovative
             d. creative

_____ 10.   _____ is a cornerstone of Rubbermaid's approach to planning and administration.
             a. Benchmarking
             b. Continuous improvement
             c. Global adaptation
             d. Co-optation

____ 11. Which of the following statements about innovative decisions is true?
   a. The decisions often involve modifying and improving on past routine decisions and practices.
   b. The decisions are often based on incomplete and rapidly changing information and may be made before problems are fully defined and understood.
   c. The choices made are in response to relatively well-defined and common problems and alternative solutions.
   d. The choices are made in response to a combination of moderately unusual and only fairly uncommon problems and alternative solutions.

____ 12. _____ refers to a business shift in which two connections with the customer that were previously viewed as competing come to be seen as complementary.
   a. Active inertia
   b. Rational decision making
   c. Convergence
   d. Innovation

❖3❖

____ 13. The _____ model prescribes a series of steps that individuals or teams should follow to increase the likelihood that their decisions will be logical and sound.
   a. rational
   b. political
   c. incremental
   d. bounded rationality

____ 14. _____ involves identifying and monitoring numerous external and internal environmental forces and deciding which ones are contributing to the problems(s).
   a. Noticing
   b. Interpreting
   c. Incorporating
   d. Scanning

____ 15. Which of the following is not a step in the rational decision-making model?
   a. define and diagnose the problem
   b. determine objective probabilities
   c. compare and evaluate alternative solutions
   d. follow-up and control results

____ 16. The _____ model is particularly useful because it emphasizes the limitations of rationality and provides a better picture of the day-to-day decision-making processes used by most people.
   a. political
   b. adaptive
   c. bounded rationality
   d. probability

____ 17. _____ is the practice of selecting an acceptable goal or alternative solution.
a. Satisficing
b. Co-optating
c. Incorporating
d. Scapegoating

____ 18. A number of Arab-Americans experienced hostility from some non-Arabs after the invasion of Kuwait by Iraqi forces. The Arab-Americans were experiencing a _____ bias.
a. selective perception
b. concrete information
c. cultural fallacy
d. law of small numbers

____ 19. Which of the following information processes would be characterized by people being an unexpected number of similar events that lead them to believe that an event not seen will occur?
a. gambler's fallacy bias
b. law of small numbers bias
c. availability perception bias
d. concrete information bias

____ 20. Meltzer University needed additional money for its endowment fund to support the university's longevity. Therefore, the university placed several new, wealthy professionals, such as a banker, a small-business owner of a zipper company, and a real estate tycoon, on its board of directors. This strategy is known as _____.
a. scapegoating
b. board stacking
c. capital injection
d. co-optation

ESSAY QUESTIONS

❖1❖

1. Define *decision making*. How does the decision-making process relate to the managerial competencies?

2.   Explain the role of probability in making decisions under the condition of risk.

❖2❖

3.   Give an example of and define routine, adaptive, and innovative decisions.

4.   Discuss the concept of continuous improvement.

❖3❖

5.   Differentiate between general and operational goals and explain the reasons for setting goals.

6.   What is co-optation?

CHAPTER 8
FUNDAMENTALS OF DECISION MAKING

MATCHING SOLUTIONS

1. T - Convergence
2. L - Noticing
3. I - Satisficing
4. O - Political Model
5. A - Risk
6. H - Co-optation
7. S - Power
8. K - Certainty
9. E - Active Inertia
10. J - Law of Small Numbers Bias
11. R - Bounded Rationality Model
12. B - Objective Probability
13. Q - Selective Perception Bias
14. G - Decision Making
15. D - Adaptive Decisions
16. M - Availability Bias
17. C - Innovative Decisions
18. P - Scapegoating
19. F - Concrete Information Bias
20. N - Continuous Improvement

TRUE/FALSE SOLUTIONS

Question	Answer	Page	Explanation
1.	True		
2.	True		
3.	True		
4.	True		
5.	True		

6.	False	210–211	The likelihood that a specific outcome will occur, based on hard facts and numbers, is known as <u>objective probability</u>. Sometimes an individual can determine the likely outcome of a decision by examining past records. The likelihood that a specific outcome will occur, based on personal judgment and beliefs, is known as <u>subjective probability</u>. Such judgments vary among individuals, depending on their intuitions, previous experience with similar situations, expertise, and personality traits.
7.	True		
8.	True		
9.	False	216	<u>Adaptive decisions</u> are choices made in response to a combination of moderately unusual and only fairly uncommon problems and alternative solutions. Adaptive decisions often involve modifying and improving on past routine decisions and practices. <u>Innovative decisions</u> are choices based on the discovery, identification, and diagnosis of unusual and ambiguous problems and/or the development of unique or creative alternative solutions.
10.	True		
11.	False	215	<u>Active inertia</u> is the rigid devotion to the status quo by attempting to do more of the same old thing better.
12.	True		
13.	False	216	<u>Convergence</u> represents a business shift in which two connections with the customer that were previously viewed as competing come to be seen as complementary.
14.	True		
15.	False	219	The rational model prescribes a set of phases that individuals or teams should follow to increase the likelihood that their decisions will be logical and optimal.
16.	True		
17.	False	226	Herbert Simon, a management scholar, introduced the <u>bounded rationality model</u> in the mid-1950s.

| 18. | False | 226 | The <u>selective perception bias</u> means that what people expect to see is often what they do see. People seek information consistent with their own views and downplay conflicting information. The <u>concrete information bias</u> means that vivid, direct experience usually prevails over abstract information. A single personal experience can outweigh statistical evidence. |

19.   True

20.   True

MULTIPLE CHOICE SOLUTIONS

<u>Question</u>	<u>Answer</u>	<u>Page</u>	<u>Explanation</u>
1.	d	208	<u>Decision making</u> includes: defining problems, gathering information, generating alternatives, and choosing a course of action.
2.	d	208–209	An effective manager relies on several managerial competencies to make a decision, including the teamwork, self-management, and communication competencies.
3.	c	210	<u>Certainty</u> is the condition under which individuals are fully informed about a problem, alternative solutions are obvious, and the likely results of each solution are clear. The condition of certainty at least allows anticipation (if not control) of events and their outcomes. Once an individual identifies alternative solutions and their expected results, making the decision is relatively easy. The decision maker at the Roland Consulting Corporation simply chooses the solution with the best potential outcome.
4.	a	210	Decision making under the condition of certainty is the exception for most middle and top managers and various professionals. However, first-line managers make most day-to-day decisions under conditions of certainty or near certainty.
5.	c	210	<u>Probability</u> is the percentage of times that a specific outcome would occur if an individual were to make a particular decision a large number of times. The most commonly used example is that of a coin toss: With enough tosses of the coin, heads will show up 50 percent of the time and tails the other 50 percent.

6.	b	211	Uncertainty is the condition under which an individual does not have the necessary information to assign probabilities to the outcomes of alternative solutions. Because of that uncertainty, the decision makers may be able to make only a reasonable guess rather than an informed decision.
7.	d	211	Uncertainty means that individuals may not even be able to define the problem, much less identify alternative solutions and possible outcomes. Uncertainty often suggests that the problem and the alternative solutions are both ambiguous and highly unusual. Dealing with uncertainty is the job of the professionals listed.
8.	a	215	Active inertia is the rigid devotion to the status quo by attempting to do more of the same old thing better.
9.	a	215	Routine decisions are standard choices made in response to relatively well-defined and common problems and alternative solutions. Often a solution is available in established rules or standard operating procedures. Cleaning buildings, processing payroll vouchers, packing and shipping customers' orders, and making travel arrangements are but a few examples of tasks requiring routine decisions.
10.	b	217	Continuous improvement involves streams of adaptive organizational decisions made over time that result in a large number of small incremental improvements year after year. It is driven by the goals of providing better quality, improving efficiency, and being responsive to customers. Continuous improvement is a cornerstone of Rubbermaid's approach to planning and administration.
11.	b	218	Innovative decisions are choices based on the discovery, identification, and diagnosis of unusual and ambiguous problems and/or the development of unique or creative alternative solutions. Because innovative decisions normally represent a sharp break with the past, they normally do not happen in a logical, orderly sequence.
12.	c	216	Convergence is a business shift in which two connections with the customer that were previously viewed as competing come to be seen as complementary.

| 13. | a | 219 | The <u>rational model</u> prescribes a series of steps that individuals or teams should follow to increase the likelihood that their decisions will be logical and sound. A rational decision permits the maximum achievement of goals within the limitations of the situation. |

14.   a   219   In the rational decision-making model, problem definition and diagnosis involves three skills that are part of a manager's planning and administration competency: noticing, interpreting, and incorporating. (1) <u>Noticing</u> involves identifying and monitoring numerous external and internal environmental forces and deciding which ones are contributing to the problem(s). (2) <u>Interpreting</u> involves assessing the forces noticed and determining which are causes, not merely symptoms, of the real problem(s). (3) <u>Incorporating</u> involves relating those interpretations to the current or desired goals of the department or organization.

15.   b   220   The rational decision-making model includes these steps: (1) define and diagnose the problem, (2) set goals, (3) search for alternative solutions, (4) compare and evaluate alternative solutions, (5) choose among alternative solutions, (6) implement the solution selected, and (7) follow-up and control results.

16.   c   226   The <u>bounded rationality model</u> emphasizes the limitations of rationality and thus provides a better picture of the day-to-day decision-making process used by most people. This model partially explains why different individuals make different decisions when they have exactly the same information.

17.   a   228   The practice of selecting an acceptable goal or alternative solution is called <u>satisficing</u>. An acceptable goal might be easier to identify and achieve, less controversial, or otherwise safer than the best available goal.

18.   d   227   The <u>law of small numbers bias</u> means that people may view a few incidents or cases as representative of a larger population even when they are not representative. Apparently, the non-Arabs incorrectly attributed the unsavory characteristics of Saddam Hussein (sample of 1) to Arab-Americans in general.

| 19. | a | 227 | The <u>gambler's fallacy bias</u> refers to people seeing an unexpected number of similar events that lead them to the conviction that an event not seen will occur. |
| 20. | d | 230 | <u>Co-optation</u> involves bringing new stakeholder representatives into the strategic decision-making process as a way to avert threats to an organization's stability or existence. |

ESSAY SOLUTIONS

[Pages 208–209]

1. <u>Decision making</u> is the process of defining problems, gathering information, generating alternatives, and choosing a course of action. An effective manager relies on several managerial competencies to make a decision. Also, decision-making processes are basic to most managerial competencies.

[Pages 210–211]

2. <u>Risk</u> is the condition under which individuals can define a problem, specify the probability of certain events, identify alternative solutions, and state the probability of each solution leading to the desired result. Risk generally means that the problem and the alternative solutions fall somewhere between the extremes of being certain and being unusual and ambiguous.

   <u>Probability</u> is the percentage of times that a specific outcome would occur if an individual were to make a particular decision a larger number of times. The likelihood that a specific outcome will occur, based on hard facts and numbers, is known as <u>objective probability</u>. The likelihood that a specific outcome will occur, based on personal judgment and beliefs, is known as <u>subjective probability</u>.

[Pages 215–218]

3. <u>Routine decisions</u> are standard choices made in response to relatively well-defined and common problems and alternative solutions. Cleaning buildings, processing payroll vouchers, packing and shipping customers' orders, and making travel arrangements are a few examples of tasks requiring routine decisions. <u>Adaptive decisions</u> are choices made in response to a combination of moderately unusual and only fairly uncommon problems and alternative solutions; for example, a company that is considering building a new production plant, or a corporation like GM enhancing its computer system. <u>Innovative decisions</u> are choices based on the discovery, identification, and diagnosis of unusual and ambiguous problems and/or the development of unique or creative alternative solutions. Innovative decisions are often based on incomplete and rapidly changing information and may be made before problems are fully defined and understood. Whirlpool's decision to go global is an example of an innovative decision.

[Page 217]

4. <u>Continuous improvement</u> involves streams of adaptive organizational decisions made over time that result in a large number of small incremental improvements year after year. This concept is a key to total quality management. Continuous improvement is driven by the goals of providing better quality, improving efficiency, and being responsive to customers. Improvements typically enhance value to the customer through improved and new products and services; reduce errors, defects, and waste; increase responsiveness to customer changes and expectations; and elevate productivity and effectiveness in the use of all resources.

[Page 221]

5. <u>General goals</u> provide broad direction for decision making in qualitative terms. <u>Operational goals</u> state what is to be achieved in quantitative terms, for whom, and within what time period.

Setting goals can yield several benefits, which are the same whether the goals apply to an entire organization, a specific department or division, a team, or an individual employer. People set goals for the following reasons: Goals serve to (1) focus individual and organizational decisions and efforts, (2) aid the planning process, (3) motivate people and stimulate better performance, and (4) assist in performance evaluation and control.

[Page 230]

6. <u>Co-optation</u> involves bringing new stakeholder representatives into the strategic decision-making process as a way to avert threats to an organization's stability or existence. An example is placing a banker on a firm's board of directors when the firm needs to borrow money. Co-optation is one of the common political strategies used by stakeholders to achieve their goals.

CHAPTER 9
PLANNING AND DECISION AIDS

LEARNING OBJECTIVES

After studying this chapter, you should be able to:

❖**1**❖ Explain knowledge management and how it creates value for organizations.

❖**2**❖ Describe the basic features of the Delphi technique, simulation, and scenario forecasting aids.

❖**3**❖ Use Osborn's creativity model to stimulate adaptive and innovative decisions.

❖**4**❖ Apply three quality management decision and planning aids: benchmarking, the Deming Cycle, and the balanced scorecard model.

OUTLINE

❖**1**❖ Explain knowledge management and how it creates value for organizations.

   I. Fostering Knowledge Management

      1. **Knowledge Management**—involves recognizing, generating, documenting, distributing, and transferring between persons useful information to improve organizational effectiveness. Knowledge management consists of three main components:

         a. <u>Explicit Knowledge</u>—published and internally generated reports and manuals, books, magazines and journals, government data and reports, online services, newsfeeds, and the like.

         b. <u>Tacit Knowledge</u>—the information, competencies, and experience possessed by employees, including professional contacts and cultural and interpersonal dimensions—openness, the lessons to be gleaned from successes or failures, anecdotal fables, and information sharing.

         c. <u>Enabling Technologies</u>—intranets, Internet, search engines, and work-flow software.

      2. **Knowledge Management Drivers**

         a. The Information Age has replaced the Industrial Age. Knowledge is becoming more valuable than physical or financial assets, or even natural resources.

     b. Common shortcomings in knowledge strategies as a result of not managing knowledge assets and processes include:

         1. Productivity and opportunity loss.

         2. Information overload.

         3. Knowledge attrition.

         4. Reinventing the wheel.

3. **Knowledge Management Targets**—the application of KM has three natural targets: an organization's teams, customers, and workforce.

     a. <u>Teams</u>—collaboration is often crucial to ensuring that goods and services are designed to meet customer needs. KM provides both a method of sharing ideas and identifying best practices in design and development.

     b. <u>Customers</u>—satisfied customers are the foundation of a company's continuing success. KM can facilitate the tracing of ongoing contacts with customers which is essential in developing and improving those relationships.

     c. <u>Workforce</u>—KM can track employees' skills and abilities, facilitate performance reviews, deliver training, provide up-to-date company information, manage benefits, and improve employee knowledge and morale.

4. **Enabling Technology**—It provides the foundation for solutions that automate and centralize the sharing of knowledge and fostering innovation.

     a. <u>Expert system</u>—is a computer program based on the decision-making processes of human experts that stores, retrieves, and manipulates data, diagnoses problems, and makes limited decisions based on detailed information about a particular problem.

     b. Expert systems have problem-solving capabilities within a specific area of knowledge. They vary in complexity, both in terms of knowledge and technology.

5. **Enabling Culture**—Organizations consistently identify cultural issues as the greatest barriers to the successful implementation of KM.

❖**2**❖   Describe the basic features of the Delphi technique, simulation, and scenario forecasting aids.

  II. **Fostering Forecasts**

1. **Forecasting**—involves projecting, or estimating future events or conditions in an organization's environment.

     a. Forecasting is concerned primarily with external events or conditions beyond the organization's control that are important to its survival and growth.

     b. Much forecasting is based on extrapolation.

         1. *Extrapolation*—is the projection of some trend or tendency from the past or present into the future.

    c. Four forecasting pitfalls:

        1. *Listening to the Media*—tracking trends through the headlines can be trouble.

        2. Assuming that things are going to return to the way they used to be.

        3. *Hearsay*.

        4. *Tunnel Vision*—the business media provide only a narrow view of what's going on in the world.

2. **Delphi technique**—is a forecasting aid based on a consensus of a panel of experts—that refine their opinions, phase by phase, until they reach a consensus.

    a. It replaces face-to-face communication and debate with a carefully planned, orderly program of sequential impersonal exchanges.

    b. The Delphi questionnaire may initially be broadly worded. In later rounds, the questions become more specific because they are built on responses to the preceding questionnaires.

    c. The Delphi technique involves three basic steps: (1) a questionnaire is sent to a group of experts, (2) a summary of the first phase is prepared, and (3) a summary of the second phase is prepared.

    d. Three rounds of questionnaires generally are recommended and a range of 15 to 30 experts is suggested for a very focused issue.

3. **Simulation**—is a representation of a real system.

    a. A simulation imitates something real, but is not real itself, and can be altered by its users.

    b. A simulation model usually describes the behavior of the real system in quantitative and/or qualitative terms.

    c. It is often used to forecast the effects of environmental changes and internal management decisions on an organization, department, or SBU.

    d. The goal of simulation is to reproduce or test reality without actually experiencing it.

    e. Most simulations are intended to let management ask numerous "what if" questions.

    f. Spreadsheet Simulations—are often used to create hypothetical financial reports so that planners can experiment with how the future might look based on different sets of assumptions.

        1. They are simulations when used to create pro forma income statements and balance sheets, instead of real income statements and balance sheets.

4. **Scenarios**—are stories that help people recognize and adapt to changing features of their environments.

   a. Scenarios provide a way to identify alternative paths that may exist for an organization in the future and the actions that are likely are involved in going down each of those paths.

   b. Competitor scenario—presents a discussion that considers what a competitor (or set of competitors) might do over some specified time period, how the competitors would do it, and why they would choose to do so.

   c. The three most common categories used in organizations include: (1) the company's worst nightmare, (2) a fundamentally different but better world, and (3) more of the same.

   d. Scenarios are quite useful in forcing those involved in planning to evaluate preliminary plans against future possibilities.

❖3❖   Use Osborn's creativity model to stimulate adaptive and innovative decisions.

III.   Fostering Creativity

1. **Creativity**—is the ability to visualize, foresee, generate, and implement new ideas.

   a. Creative thinking increases the quality of solutions to many types of problems, helps stimulate innovation, revitalizes motivation and commitment by challenging individual competencies, and serves as a catalyst for effective team performance.

   b. The creative process comprises the five following interconnected stages:

      1. *Preparation*—involves a thorough investigation to ensure that all parts of an issue or problem are identified or understood.

      2. *Concentration*—occurs when energies and resources are focused on identifying and solving an issue or problem.

      3. *Incubation*—involves an internal and unconscious ordering of gathered information.

      4. *Illumination*—is the moment of discovery, the instant of recognition, as when a light seems to be turned on mentally.

      5. *Verification*—is the testing of the created solution or idea.

2. **Osborn's creativity model**—is a three-phase decision-making process that involves fact finding, idea finding, and solution finding.

   a. It is designed to help overcome blockages to creativity and innovation, which may occur for a variety of reasons.

   b. Sufficient time and freedom must be allowed for the model to work well, and some degree of external pressure and self-generated tension are helpful.

   c. The model has three phases:

1. *Fact-Finding Phase*—involves defining the issue or problem and gathering and analyzing important data.

2. *Idea-Finding Phase*—starts by generating tentative ideas and possible leads. The most likely of these ideas are modified, combined, and added to, if necessary.

   a. Brainstorming—is an unrestrained flow of ideas in a group with all critical judgments suspended.

   b. A brainstorming session should follow four basic rules.

      1. *Criticism is ruled out.* Participants must withhold critical judgment of ideas until later.

      2. *Freewheeling is welcomed.* The wilder the idea, the better; taming down an idea is easier than thinking up new ones.

      3. *Quantity is wanted.* The greater the number of ideas, the greater is the likelihood that some will be useful.

      4. *Combination and improvement are sought.* In addition to contributing ideas of their own, participants should suggest how ideas of others can be turned into better ideas, or how two or more ideas can be merged into still another idea.

   c. A brainstorming session should have from 5 to 12 or so participants in order to generate diverse ideas. This size range permits each member to maintain a sense of identification and involvement with the group.

   d. A session should normally run not less than 20 minutes nor more than an hour. However, brainstorming could consist of several idea-generating sessions.

3. *Solution-Finding Phase*—involves generating and evaluating possible courses of action and deciding how to implement the chosen course of action.

d. **Effectiveness**—the Osborn creativity model is based on the assumption that most people have the potential for greater creativity and innovation in decision making than they use.

   1. *Electronic Brainstorming*—makes use of personal computers that are networked to input and automatically disseminate ideas in real time to all team members, each of whom may be stimulated to generate additional ideas.

❖**4**❖   Apply three quality management decision and planning aids: benchmarking, the Deming Cycle, and the balanced scorecard model.

IV.   **Fostering Quality**

1.   **Quality**—is defined as how well a good or service does what it is supposed to do—that is, how closely and reliably it satisfies the specifications to which it is built or provided.

   a.   The most common meaning of quality is the extent to which a good or service meets and/or exceeds customers' expectations.

   b.   Consumers often apply the value definition of quality when making purchasing decisions.

2.   **Benchmarking**—is a systematic and continuous process of measuring and comparing an organization's goods and services, and practices against industry leaders anywhere in the world to gain information that will help the organization improve performance.

   a.   Benchmarking helps managers and employees learn from others.

   b.   The steps of benchmarking are: (1) define the domain, (2) identify the best performers, (3) collect and analyze data to identify gaps, (4) set improvement goals, (5) develop and implement plans to close gaps, (6) evaluate results, and (7) repeat the evaluations.

   c.   Effectiveness—benchmarking should be linked to other sources of information, such as changing customer expectations and preferences.

3.   **Deming Cycle**—comprises four stages (plan, do, check, and act) that should be repeated over time to ensure continuous improvements in a function, product, or process.

   a.   It is also referred to as the PDCA cycle, because it involves the four stages of plan (P), do (D), check (C), and act (A).

   b.   The four stages of the Deming cycle are:

      1.   *Plan Stage*—involves analyzing the current situation, gathering data, and developing ways to make improvements.

      2.   *Do Stage*—involves testing alternatives experimentally in a laboratory, establishing a pilot production process, or trying it out with a small number of customers.

      3.   *Check Stage*—requires determining whether the trial or process is working as intended, any revisions are needed, or it should be scrapped.

      4.   *Act Stage*—focuses on implementing the process within the organization or with its customers and suppliers.

4. **Balanced Scorecard Model**—provides a way for an organization to gain a wider perspective on its strategic decisions, which have an impact on quality, by considering the role of finances, customers, internal processes, and innovation/learning.

   a. It attempts to measure and provide feedback to organizations in order to help in implementing overall goals and strategies.

   b. The model contends that long-term organizational excellence and quality can be achieved only by taking a broad approach, not by focusing solely on financials.

   c. Four perspectives: focused on outcomes or activities

      1. Financial perspective

      2. Customer perspective

      3. Internal perspective

      4. Innovation/learning perspective

   d. Benefits of Balanced Scorecard Model:

      1. It helps align key performance goals and measures with strategy at all levels of an organization.

      2. It provides management with a comprehensive picture of business operations.

      3. It facilitates communication and understanding of business goals and strategies at all levels of an organization.

      4. It provides strategic feedback and learning.

   e. Criticisms of Balanced Scorecard Model:

      1. The innovation/learning perspective is internal, so why does it warrant a box separate from the internal process method?

      2. Why aren't other stakeholders represented?

      3. Goals must be set for each of the four perspectives, but managers are not provided any specific methodology or rationale on how to do it.

MATCHING

<u>Directions</u>: Select the term that best identifies the statement listed below. Place the letter of the correct term in the space provided.

A. Simulation
B. Electronic Brainstorming
C. Extrapolation
D. Knowledge Management
E. Competitor Scenarios
F. Brainstorming
G. Concentration
H. Creativity
I. Quality

K. Forecasting
L. Osborn's Creativity Model
M. Illumination
N. Delphi Technique
O. Expert System
P. Benchmarking
Q. Deming Cycle
R. Balanced Scorecard Model
J. Preparation

_____   1.   Is the moment of discovery, the instant of recognition, as when a light bulb seems to be turned on mentally.

_____   2.   Use of technology to input and automatically disseminate ideas in real time over a computer network to all team members, each of whom may be stimulated to generate other ideas.

_____   3.   Predicting, projecting, or estimating future events or conditions in an organization's environment.

_____   4.   Involves focusing energies and resources on identifying and solving an issue or problem.

_____   5.   The continuous process of comparing an organization's strategies, products, or processes with those of *best-in-class* organizations.

_____   6.   A representation of a real system.

_____   7.   The ability to visualize, foresee, generate, and implement new ideas.

_____   8.   An unrestrained flow of ideas in a group with all critical judgments suspended.

_____   9.   A forecasting aid based on a consensus of a panel of experts.

_____   10. Involves thoroughly investigating an issue or problem to ensure that all its aspects have been identified and understood.

_____   11. The four stages of improving quality: planning, doing, checking, and acting.

_____   12. Is the art and science of creating, measuring, distributing, enhancing, evaluating, and integrating the information base of an organization and building on its intellectual assets.

_____   13. A three-phase decision-making process that involves fact finding, idea finding, and solution finding.

_____   14. The projection of some tendency from the past or present into the future.

_____ 15. Value, conformance to specifications or standards, excellence, and meeting or exceeding customers' expectations.

_____ 16. These have problem-solving capabilities within a specific area of knowledge and vary in complexity in terms of both knowledge and technology.

_____ 17. This presents a discussion that considers what a competitor might do over some specified time period, how they will do it, and why they would choose to do so.

_____ 18. This model contends that long-term organizational excellence and quality can be achieved only by taking a broad approach, not by focusing solely on financials.

TRUE OR FALSE

Directions: Write True or False in the space provided.

❖1❖

_____ 1. Knowledge management is the art and science of creating, measuring, distributing, enhancing, evaluating, and integrating the information base of an organization and building on its intellectual assets.

_____ 2. Explicit knowledge is the information, competencies, and experience possessed by employees.

❖2❖

_____ 3. Extrapolation involves predicting, projecting, or estimating future events or conditions in an organization's environment.

_____ 4. Forecasts related to electronic commerce will soon become fundamental to planning and decision making by traditional retailers.

_____ 5. Competitor scenarios are predictions of what the competitor or set of competitors will do.

_____ 6. The Delphi technique is a helpful forecasting aid, that typically consists of four phases.

_____ 7. The goal of simulation is to reproduce or test reality without actually experiencing it.

_____ 8. A simulation imitates something real, is real itself, and can be altered by its users.

❖3❖

_____ 9. The concentration stage of the creative process is where the mind instantly connects an issue or a problem to a solution through a remembered observation or occurrence.

_____ 10. The incubation stage is described as the amount of discovery, the instant of recognition.

_____ 11. Verification is the testing of the created solution or idea.

_____ 12. A brainstorming session normally has 15 to 25 participants.

_____ 13. The Osborn creativity model is based on the assumption that most people have the potential for greater creativity and innovation in decision making than they use.

_____ 14. Electronic brainstorming makes use of technology to input and automatically disseminate ideas in real time over a computer network to all team members.

❖4❖

_____ 15. Benchmarking is the process of planning, doing, checking, and acting on quality improvements of products or services.

_____ 16. It is impossible to benchmark functional areas such as finance, accounting, legal services, and human resources.

_____ 17. Benchmarking may be one of the aids used in the plan stage of the Deming cycle.

_____ 18. The "do" stage of the Deming cycle requires determining whether the trial plan is working as intended or if it should be scrapped.

_____ 19. The Deming Cycle comprises three stages—plan, do, and act.

_____ 20. The act stage focuses on implementing the process within the organization or with its customers and suppliers.

MULTIPLE CHOICE

Directions: Select the best answer in the space provided.

❖1❖

_____ 1. _____ refers to such things as intranets, Internet, search engines, and work-flow software.
a. Enabling technologies
b. Tacit knowledge
c. Explicit knowledge
d. Implicit knowledge

_____ 2. According to some estimates, the average organization loses half its knowledge base every 5 to 10 years. This is an example of which of the following?

a. productivity and opportunity loss
b. information overload
c. knowledge attrition
d. reinventing the wheel

❖2❖

_____ 3. _____ involves the projection of some trend or tendency from the past or present into the future.
a. Electronic brainstorming
b. Extrapolation
c. Delphi technique
d. Electronic imaging

_____ 4. Which of the following is <u>not</u> a commonly used forecasting technique?
  a. scenarios
  b. simulation
  c. benchmarking
  d. Delphi technique

_____ 5. _____ is concerned primarily with external events or conditions beyond the organization's control that are important to its survival and growth.
  a. Project management
  b. PERT
  c. Deming cycle
  d. Forecasting

_____ 6. A _____ presents a discussion that considers what a competitor (or set of competitors) might do over some specified time period, how the competitor would do it, and why they would choose to do so.
  a. competitor scenario
  b. Delphi technique
  c. Pareto analysis
  d. simulation

_____ 7. Scenarios are intended to
  a. answer "what if" questions.
  b. identify alternative paths that may exist for an organization in the future.
  c. help people recognize and adapt to changing features of their environments.
  d. all of the above

_____ 8. Which of the following is <u>not</u> a step in the Delphi technique?
  a. A questionnaire is sent to a group of experts.
  b. No ideas should be criticized.
  c. A summary of the first round is prepared.
  d. A summary of the second round is prepared.

_____ 9. In the Delphi technique, a range of _____ of participating experts is recommended for a very focused issue.
  a. 5 to 10
  b. 10 to 15
  c. 15 to 30
  d. 30 to 40

_____ 10. Which of the following is a true statement regarding a simulation?
  a. Advanced business simulations are relatively expensive, complex, custom-designed, and often require the use of computers to perform calculations.
  b. Simulation is often used to forecast the effects of environmental changes and internal management decisions on an organization, department, or SBU.
  c. The goal of simulation is to reproduce or test reality without actually experiencing it.
  d. All of the above.

_____ 11. Which of the following is one of the typical questions that are used in developing a "what if" competitor scenario?
   a. What if the competitor suddenly divests a number of its product lines?
   b. What if the competitor launches a series of new products?
   c. What if the competitor launches a sequence of extensions to its current product lines?
   d. all of the above

_____ 12. The three most common categories of _____ used in organizational planning are (1) the company's worst nightmare, (2) a fundamentally different but better world, and (3) more of the same but better.
   a. virtual reality
   b. PERT
   c. scenarios
   d. simulations

❖3❖

_____ 13. Which of the following is <u>not</u> a stage in the creative process?
   a. incubation
   b. concentration
   c. brainstorming
   d. verification

_____ 14. The _____ stage of the creative process involves an unconscious personal conflict between what is currently accepted as reality and what may be possible.
   a. illumination
   b. incubation
   c. preparation
   d. verification

_____ 15. Which of the following is <u>not</u> a phase in Osborn's creativity model?
   a. fact-finding phase
   b. solution-finding phase
   c. cause-and-effect phase
   d. idea-finding phase

_____ 16. All of the following are rules to follow in a brainstorming session, <u>except</u>:
   a. participants must withhold critical judgment of ideas until later.
   b. a distinction must be made between a symptom of a problem and an actual problem.
   c. the wilder the idea, the better; taming down an idea is easier than thinking up new ones.
   d. the greater the number of ideas, the greater is the likelihood that some will be useful.

❖4❖

_____ 17. Which of the following statements regarding benchmarking is <u>false</u>?
   a. Functional areas such as manufacturing, finance, and marketing may be benchmarked.
   b. Benchmarking always looks at the past in terms of how some process (logistics) or quality dimension is being performed by others.
   c. The data collected in benchmarking need to focus on specific methods utilized, not simply on the results obtained.
   d. Benchmarking can be expensive and time consuming.

_____ 18. The _____ stage of the Deming cycle involves analyzing the current situation, gathering data, and developing ways to make improvements.
   a. act
   b. check
   c. do
   d. plan

_____ 19. The _____ stage of the Deming cycle involves testing alternatives experimentally in a laboratory, establishing a pilot production process, or trying it out with a small number of customers.
   a. act
   b. check
   c. do
   d. plan

_____ 20. The owner of the Deluxe Diner, Billie Boyd, used _____ to solve the problem of customers having to wait too long to be seated at his restaurant.
   a. PERT
   b. Osborn's creativity model
   c. the Pareto diagram
   d. the Deming cycle

ESSAY QUESTIONS

❖1❖

1. Define the three main components of knowledge management.

❖2❖

2.   Explain the Delphi technique.

❖3❖

3.   Identify and discuss the stages of the creative process.

4.   State the rules of brainstorming and discuss why these rules are important.

❖4❖

5.   What is benchmarking and what are its limitations?

6.   Explain the stages of the Deming cycle.

CHAPTER 9
PLANNING AND DECISION AIDS

MATCHING SOLUTIONS

1. M - Illumination
2. B - Electronic Brainstorming
3. K - Forecasting
4. G - Concentration
5. P - Benchmarking
6. A - Simulation
7. H - Creativity
8. F - Brainstorming
9. N - Delphi Technique
10. J - Preparation
11. L - Osborn's Creativity Model
12. D - Knowledge Management
13. Q - Deming Cycle
14. C - Extrapolation
15. I - Quality
16. O - Expert System
17. E - Competitor Scenarios
18. R - Balanced Scorecard Model

TRUE/FALSE SOLUTIONS

Question	Answer	Page	Explanation
1.	True		
2.	False	239	Tacit knowledge refers to the information, competencies, and experience possessed by employees. Explicit knowledge is published and internally generated reports, books, and magazines.
3.	False	242	Forecasting involves predicting, projecting, or estimating future events or conditions in an organization's environment. Extrapolation is the projection of some tendency from the past or present into the future.
4.	True		

5.   False   246   A competitor scenario presents a discussion that considers what a competitor (or set of competitors) might do over some specified time period, how the competitors would do it, and why they would choose to do so. It is not a prediction of what the competitor or set of competitors will do.

6.   False   243–244   The <u>Delphi technique</u> is a forecasting aid based on a consensus of a panel of experts. It typically involves three phases.

7.   True

8.   False   245   A simulation imitates something real, but is real itself, and can be altered by its users.

9.   False   248–249   The <u>creative process</u> comprises five interconnected stages: preparation, concentration, incubation, illumination, and verification. The <u>concentration stage</u> occurs when energies and resources are focused on identifying and solving an issue or problem. The <u>illumination stage</u> is the moment of discovery, the instant of recognition, as when a light seems to be turned on mentally. The mind instantly connects an issue or a problem to a solution through a remembered observation or occurrence.

10.   False   249   The <u>illumination stage</u> is the moment of discovery, the instant of recognition. The mind instantly connects an issue or a problem to a solution through a remembered observation or occurrence.

11.   True

12.   False   250   <u>Brainstorming</u> is an unrestrained flow of ideas in a group with all critical judgments suspended. A brainstorming session should have from 5 to 12 or so participants in order to generate diverse ideas. This size range permits each member to maintain a sense of identification and involvement with the group.

13.   True

14.   True

15.	False	253–254	Benchmarking is the continuous process of comparing an organization's strategies, products, or processes with those of *best-in-class* organizations. It helps employees learn how such organizations achieved excellence and then set out to match or exceed them. The Deming cycle comprises four stages—plan, do, check, and act—that should be repeated over time to ensure continuous improvements in a function, product, or process.
16.	False	253	Functions such as manufacturing, finance, marketing, inventory management, transportation, accounting, legal services, human resources, and marketing may be benchmarked. Also, various functional processes may be benchmarked.
17.	True		
18.	False	254–255	The do stage involves testing alternatives experimentally in a laboratory, establishing a pilot production process, or trying it out with a small number of customers. The check stage requires determining whether the trial or process is working as intended, if any revisions are needed, or if it should be scrapped.
19.	False	254–255	The Deming cycle comprises four stages—plan, do, check, and act—that should be repeated over time to ensure continuos learning and improvements in a function, product, or process.
20.	True		

MULTIPLE CHOICE SOLUTIONS

Question	Answer	Page	Explanation
1.	a	239	Enabling technologies include such things as the Internet, intranets, search engines, and work-flow software.
2.	c	239	Knowledge attrition—according to some estimates, the average organization loses half its knowledge base every 5 to 10 years through obsolescence and employee and customer turnover.
3.	b	242	Extrapolation is the projection of some trend or tendency from the past or present into the future.

| 4. | c | 243 | Scenarios, the Delphi technique, and simulations are commonly used forecasting techniques. Benchmarking is an aid designed to improve quality. |

| 5. | d | 242 | <u>Forecasting</u> involves predicting, projecting, or estimating future events or conditions in an organization's environment. It is concerned primarily with external events or conditions beyond the organization's control that are important to its survival and growth. |

| 6. | a | 246 | A <u>competitor scenario</u> presents a discussion that considers what a competitor (or set of competitors) might do over some specified time period, how the competitor would do it, and why they would choose to do so. |

| 7. | d | 246 | A <u>scenario</u> is a written description of a possible future. All the statements are true. |

| 8. | b | 244 | The concept that no ideas should be criticized is part of the <u>brainstorming</u> technique. |

| 9. | c | 243 | The <u>Delphi technique</u> is a forecasting aid based on a consensus of a panel of experts. The number of participating experts may range from only a few to more than 100, depending on the scope of the study. A range of 15 to 30 is recommended for a very focused issue. As the sample size (number of experts) increases, the amount of coordination required also increases, as do costs. |

| 10. | d | 245 | A <u>simulation</u> is a representation of a real system. A simulation model usually describes the behavior of the real systems (or some aspect of it) in quantitative and/or qualitative terms. The other statements are all true. |

| 11. | d | 247 | Some typical questions that are used in developing a "what if" competitor scenario include: (1) What if the competitor commits to a diversification of its product line through a combination of current and new technologies? (2) What if the competitor launches a new series of products? (3) What if the competitor launches a sequence extensions to its current product lines? (4) What if the competitor suddenly divests a number of its product lines? (5) What if the competitor moves rapidly to a focused differentiation strategy? (6) What if the competitor fundamentally changes how it competes to win customers in the marketplace? (7) What if the |

competitor commits to gaining significant market share without apparent regard to long-term consequences?

12.	c	247	The three most common categories of scenarios used in organizational planning are (1) the company's worst nightmare; (2) a fundamentally different but better world; and (3) more of the same but better.
13.	c	248	Creativity is the ability to visualize, foresee, generate, and implement new ideas. The creative process comprises five interconnected stages: preparation, concentration, incubation, illumination, and verification.
14.	b	248–249	Preparation involves a thorough investigation to ensure that all parts of an issue or problem are identified or understood. Concentration occurs when energies and resources are focused on identifying and solving an issue or problem. Incubation involves an internal and unconscious ordering of gathered information. This stage may involve an unconscious personal conflict between what is currently accepted as reality and what may be possible. The illumination stage is the moment of discovery, the instant of recognition, as when a light seems to be turned on mentally. Verification is the testing of the created solution or idea.
15.	c	249	Osborn's creativity model is a three-phase decision-making process that involves fact finding, idea finding, and solution finding. It is designed to help overcome blockages to creativity and innovation, which may occur for a variety of reasons.
16.	b	250	A brainstorming session should follow four basic rules: (1) criticism is ruled out, (2) freewheeling is welcomed, (3) quantity is wanted, and (4) combination and improvement are sought.
17.	b	253	Benchmarking always looks at the present in terms of how some process (logistics) or quality dimension is being performed by others. The other statements are true.

18.   d   254–255   The <u>Deming cycle</u> comprises the following four stages that should be repeated over time to ensure continuous improvements in a function, product, or process. The <u>plan stage</u> involves analyzing the current situation, gathering data, and developing ways to make improvements. The <u>do stage</u> involves testing alternatives experimentally in a laboratory, establishing a pilot production process, or trying it out with a small number of customers. The <u>check stage</u> requires determining whether the trial or process is working as intended, any revisions are needed, or if it should be scrapped. The <u>act stage</u> focuses on implementing the process within the organization or with its customers and suppliers.

19.   c   254   The <u>Deming cycle</u> comprises the following four stages that should be repeated over time to ensure continuous improvements in a function, product, or process. The <u>plan stage</u> involves analyzing the current situation, gathering data, and developing ways to make improvements. The <u>do stage</u> involves testing alternatives experimentally in a laboratory, establishing a pilot production process, or trying it out with a small number of customers. The <u>check stage</u> requires determining whether the trial or process is working as intended, any revisions are needed, or if it should be scrapped. The <u>act stage</u> focuses on implementing the process within the organization or with its customers and suppliers.

20.   d   255   The owner of the Deluxe Diner applied the Deming cycle to solve the problem of customers having to wait too long to be seated.

ESSAY SOLUTIONS

[Page 238]

1.   <u>Knowledge management</u> is generally viewed as consisting of three main components. Explicit knowledge, which comprises published and internally generated reports and manuals, books, magazines and journals, government data and reports, online services, newsfeeds, and the like. Tacit knowledge is the information, competencies, and experience possessed by employees. Finally, the enabling technologies include intranets, Internet, search engines, and workflow software.

[Pages 243–244]

2. Named after an ancient Greek oracle, the <u>Delphi technique</u> is a forecasting aid based on a consensus of a panel of experts. The experts refine their opinions, step by step, until they reach a consensus. The consensus arrived at tends to be much more accurate than a single expert's opinion.

   The Delphi technique involves three basic steps: (1) A questionnaire is sent to a group of experts. The experts answer specific technological or marketing questions and the experts remain unknown to one another. (2) A summary of the first round is prepared. The report, along with a revised questionnaire, is sent to those who completed the first questionnaire. They are asked to revise their earlier estimates, if appropriate, or to justify their original opinions. (3) A summary of the second round is prepared. This report often shows that a consensus is developing. The experts are then asked in a third questionnaire to indicate whether they support this emerging consensus and the explanations that accompany it.

   Three rounds generally are recommended. The number of participating experts may range from only a few to more than 100, depending on the scope of the study. A range of 15 to 30 experts is recommended for a very focused issue. As the sample size (number of experts) increases, the amount of coordination required also increases, as do costs.

[Pages 248–249]

3. <u>Creativity</u> is the ability to visualize, foresee, generate, and implement new ideas. The creative process comprises the following interconnected stages.

   a. *Preparation* involves a thorough investigation to ensure that all parts of an issue or problem are identified or understood. This stage involves searching for and collecting facts and ideas.

   b. *Concentration* occurs when energies and resources are focused on identifying and solving an issue or problem. A commitment must be made in this stage to implementing a solution.

   c. *Incubation* involves an internal and unconscious ordering of gathered information. This stage may involve an unconscious personal conflict between what is currently accepted as reality and what may be possible. A successful incubation stage yields fresh ideas and new ways of thinking about the nature of an issue or a problem and alternative solutions.

   d. *Illumination* is the moment of discovery, the instant of recognition, as when a light seems to be turned on mentally. The mind instantly connects an issue or a problem to a solution through a remembered observation or occurrence.

   e. *Verification* is the testing of the created solution or idea. At this stage, confirmation and acceptance of the new approach is sought.

[Page 250]

4. <u>Brainstorming</u> is an unrestrained flow of ideas in a group with all critical judgments suspended. A brainstorming session should follow four basic rules.

   a. *Criticism is ruled out.* Participants must withhold critical judgment of ideas until later.

   b. *Freewheeling is welcomed.* The wilder the idea, the better; taming down an idea is easier than thinking up new ones.

   c. *Quantity is wanted.* The greater the number of ideas, the greater is the likelihood that some will be useful.

   d. *Combination and improvement are sought.* In addition to contributing ideas of their own, participants should suggest how ideas of others can be turned into better ideas, or how two or more ideas can be merged into still another idea.

   These rules are intended to separate creative imagination from judgment.

[Pages 253–254]

5. <u>Benchmarking</u> is the continuous process of comparing an organization's strategies, products, or processes with those of *best-in-class* organizations. It helps employees learn how such organizations achieved excellence and then set out to match or exceed them. Benchmarking has been used to assess most aspects of organizations' operations. It identifies the "best" that is occurring elsewhere and helps organizations determine how to develop their own strategic or tactical plans and processes to reach that level.

   Benchmarking is very useful, but it has limitations. It should be linked to other sources of information, such as changing customer expectations and preferences. Benchmarking always looks at the present in terms of how some process (logistics) or quality dimension is being performed by others. Also, when used to copy the *best-in-class* competitors, benchmarking may lead only to short-term competitive advantage. Finally, benchmarking needs to be used to complement and aid, not to substitute for, the creative and innovative efforts of the organization's own employees.

[Pages 254–255]

6. The <u>Deming cycle</u> comprises four stages—plan, do, check, and act—that should be repeated over time to ensure continuous improvements in a function, product, or process. The <u>plan stage</u> involves analyzing the current situation, gathering data, and developing ways to make improvements. The <u>do stage</u> involves testing alternatives experimentally in a laboratory, establishing a pilot production process or trying it out with a small number of customers. The <u>check stage</u> requires determining whether the trial or process is working as intended, any revisions are needed, or if it should be scrapped. The <u>act stage</u> focuses on implementing the process within the organization or with its customers and suppliers.

CHAPTER 10
CONTROLLING IN ORGANIZATIONS

LEARNING OBJECTIVES

After studying this chapter, you should be able to:

❖1❖   Explain the foundations of control.

❖2❖   Identify the six phases of the corrective control model.

❖3❖   Describe the primary methods of organizational control.

❖4❖   Explain several key corporate governance issues and control mechanisms.

OUTLINE

❖1❖   Explain the foundations of control.

I.   **Foundations of Control**

1. **Control**—involves the use of mechanisms to ensure that behaviors and performance conform to an organization's standards, including rules, procedures, and goals.

   a. Controls are measures that help ensure that decisions, actions, and results are consistent with the formulated plans.

   b. Controls help maintain or redirect actual behaviors and results.

   c. Controls provide some of the essential information managers need in order to plan effectively.

   d. Controls help ensure that plans are implemented as intended. Thus, planning and control complement and support each other.

2. **Preventive Controls**—are mechanisms intended to reduce errors and thereby minimize the need for corrective action.

   a. Rules and regulations, standards, recruitment and selection procedures, and training and development programs function primarily as preventive controls.

3. **Corrective Controls**—are mechanisms intended to reduce or eliminate unwanted behaviors or results and thereby achieve conformity with the organization's regulations and standards.

   a. For example, air traffic controls exercise corrective control by instructing a pilot to change altitude and direction to avoid another plane.

4. **Sources of Control**—the four primary sources of control in most organizations are stakeholders, the organization itself, groups, and individuals.

    a. <u>Stakeholder Control</u>—refers to pressures from outside sources on organizations to change their behaviors.

        1. *Stakeholders*—include unions, government agencies, customers, shareholders, and others who have direct interests in the well-being of an organization.

        2. Many consumers are demanding that companies provide environmentally safe products and often are willing to pay extra for these "green marketed" products.

        3. *Green Marketing*—is the name for marketing of products and services considered environmentally friendly that make their organizations "environmentally responsible."

    b. <u>Organizational Control</u>—comprises the formal rules and procedures for preventing or correcting deviations from plans and for achieving desired goals.

        1. Examples of organizational controls include rules, standards, budgets, and audits.

    c. <u>Group Control</u>—refers to the norms and values that group members share and maintain through rewards and punishments.

        1. Examples include acceptance by the group and punishments, such as giving a group member the silent treatment.

    d. <u>Individual Self-Control</u>—consists of the guiding mechanisms that operate consciously and unconsciously within each person.

        1. Standards of professionalism are becoming an increasingly important aspect of individual self-control.

        2. Becoming a professional involves acquiring detailed knowledge, specialized skills, and specific attitudes and ways of behaving.

5. **Linkage to Desired Goals**—control or control systems should be linked to the desired goals of the organization.

    a. These goals often include improving customer service, protecting the organization's assets, and improving the quality of its goods and/or services.

    b. <u>Objective</u>—an objective control or control system is impartial and cannot be manipulated by employees for personal gain.

        1. In the United States, the Financial Accounting Standards Board (FASB) and several government agencies devote a great deal of effort to developing and monitoring principles and practices to ensure that financial statements objectively and as accurately as possible reflect reality.

    c. <u>Complete</u>—a complete control or control system encompasses all the desired behaviors and goals.

        1. Balancing quantitative (measurable) and qualitative (subjective) controls is necessary.

    d. <u>Timely</u>—a timely control or control system provides information when it is needed most.

        1. Computer-based information systems have played a major role in increasing the timely flow of information.

    e. <u>Acceptable</u>—an acceptable control or control system is recognized as necessary and appropriate.

        1. If a control system is widely ignored, managers need to find out why.

❖**2**❖   Identify the six phases of the corrective control model.

II. Corrective Control Model

  1. **Corrective Control Model**—is a process for detecting and eliminating or reducing deviations from an organization's established standards.

    a. This process relies heavily on information feedback and responses to it.

    b. The corrective control model has six interconnected steps: define the system, identify the key characteristics to be measured, set standards, collect information, make comparisons, and diagnose problems and make corrections.

  2. **Define the System**—a formal control system might be created and maintained for an employee, a department, or an entire organization.

    a. The control mechanisms could focus on specific inputs, transformation processes, or outputs.

    b. Input controls often limit the amount by which raw materials used in the transformation process can vary from the organization's standards.

  3. **Identify Key Characteristics**—the key types of information to be obtained about a person, team, department, or organization must be identified.

    a. Establishing a formal corrective control requires early determination of the characteristics that can be measured, the costs and benefits of obtaining information about each characteristic, and whether variations in each characteristic are likely to affect performance.

    b. <u>Principle of Selectivity</u> (also known as Pareto's law)—holds that a small number of characteristics always account for a large number of effects.

  4. **Set Standards**—are criteria for evaluating qualitative and quantitative characteristics and should be set for each characteristic measured.

    a. One of the most difficult, but important, aspects of doing business in a foreign country is to understand the differences in standards.

       1. Owing to the difficulties that they face in setting standards that apply in widely differing cultures and markets, many global organizations have adopted the strategy of *thinking globally, but acting locally*.

    b. Cultural and cross-cultural differences also are apparent in various human interactions, including language, nonverbal communication, religion, time, space, color, numbers, materialism, customs, status symbols, and food preferences.

       1. U.S. and Canadian executives expect meetings to begin and end at certain times, but Latins typically arrive later than the stated times and are not concerned about ending meetings at the specified time.

       2. In Nigeria, a starting time for a meeting is only an approximation, and tardiness is readily accepted.

    c. Increasingly, control systems are being based on performance standards (performance goals).

5. **Collect Information**—information on each of the standards can be collected manually or automatically.

    a. If information is collected by the individual or group whose performance is to be controlled, its validity must be checked.

       1. Employees and managers have an incentive to distort or conceal information if negative results will be used to criticize or punish them.

    b. When formal controls emphasize punishment, strong group controls often emerge to distort the information that is reported to management.

       1. Such reporting often obscures responsibility for failure to achieve goals or meet standards.

6. **Make Comparisons**—comparisons are needed to determine whether what is happening is what should be happening.

    a. Information about actual results must be compared with performance standards.

    b. Making these comparisons allows managers and team members to concentrate on controlling deviations or exceptions.

7. **Diagnose and Correct Problems**—diagnosis involves assessing the types, amounts, and causes of deviations from standards.

    a. Action is needed to eliminate those deviations and correct problems.

    b. Computer-based management information systems often assist in overcoming inadequacies in corrective controls.

❖**3**❖ Describe the primary methods of organizational control.

III. **Primary Methods of Controls**

1. **Mechanistic Controls**—involve the use of extensive rules and procedures, top-down authority, tightly written job descriptions, and other formal methods for preventing and correcting deviations from desired behaviors and results.

   a. Mechanistic controls are an important part of bureaucratic management.

2. **Organic Controls**—involve the use of flexible authority, relatively loose job descriptions, individual self-controls, and other informal methods for preventing and correcting deviations from desired behaviors and results.

   a. Organic controls reflect organic management.

   b. Organic controls are consistent with a clan culture.

   c. Detailed rules and procedures are used only when necessary as an organic control method.

3. **Market Controls**—involve the use of data to monitor sales, prices, costs, and profits, to guide decisions and evaluate results.

   a. Market controls generally require that the costs of the resources used in producing outputs be measured monetarily, the value of the goods and services produced be defined clearly and monetarily priced, and the prices of the goods and services be set competitively.

   b. Profit-Sharing Plans—provide employees with supplemental income based on the profitability of an entire organization or a selected unit.

      1. The unit may be a strategic business unit, a division, a store in a chain, or other organizational entity.

      2. Profit-sharing plans generally have four goals: (1) to increase employee identification with the organization's profit goals, allowing greater reliance on individual self-control and group controls; (2) to achieve a more flexible wage structure, reflecting the company's actual economic position and controlling labor costs; (3) to attract and retain workers more easily, improving control of selection, and lowering turnover costs; and (4) to establish a more equitable reward system, helping to develop an organizational culture that recognizes achievement and performance.

   c. Customer Monitoring—consists of ongoing efforts to obtain feedback from customers concerning the quality of goods and services.

      1. Customer monitoring is being used increasingly in corrective control, in an attempt to assess or measure customers' perceptions.

      2. Based on such assessments, management may take action to prevent the loss of further business because of customer dissatisfaction.

4. **Financial Control**—refers to the wide range of methods, techniques, and procedures intended to prevent or correct the misallocation of resources.

   a. External auditors, usually certified public accounting firms and/or internal auditing departments, monitor the effectiveness of financial controls.

      1. The primary responsibility of external auditors is to the shareholder.

      2. The auditors' role is to assure shareholders that the firm's financial statements present its true financial position and are in conformity with generally accepted accounting principles.

   b. The evaluation of a firm's financial condition for two or more time periods is called <u>comparative financial analysis</u>.

      1. The most common method of comparison is ratio analysis. *Ratio Analysis*—involves selecting two significant figures, expressing their relationship as a proportion or fraction, and comparing its value for two periods of time or with the same ratio of similar organizations.

         a. <u>Return on Investment</u> (ROI)—generally is considered to be the most important profitability ratio because it indicates how efficiently the organization is using its resources.

            1. A ratio value greater than 1.0 indicates that the organization is using its resources effectively.

         b. <u>Current Ratio</u>—indicates an organization's ability to pay bills on time.

            1. A current ratio should be well above 1:1 and if a firm has a ratio of 2:1, it should be financially sound.

         c. <u>Inventory Turnover</u>—includes the average number of times that inventory is sold and restocked during the year.

            1. A high ratio means efficient operations—a relatively small amount of money is tied up in inventory—enabling the organization to use its resources elsewhere.

         d. <u>Debt Ratio</u>—is computed to assess an organization's ability to meet its long-term financial commitments.

            1. The higher this ratio, the poorer credit risk the organization is perceived to be by financial institutions.

   c. <u>Budgeting</u>—is the process of categorizing proposed expenditures and linking them to goals.

      1. Budgeting has three primary purposes: to help in planning work effectively, to assist in allocating resources, and to assist in controlling and monitoring resource utilization during the budget period.

      2. The control aspect of budgeting may be either corrective or preventive. When budgeting is used as a corrective control, the emphasis is on identifying deviations from the budget. Deviations indicate the need to identify and correct their causes or to change the budget itself.

3. The following are the most common types of budgets used in business.

   a. Sales Budget—a forecast of expected revenues, generally stated by product line on a monthly basis and revised at least annually.

   b. Materials Budget—expected purchases, generally stated by specific categories, which may vary from month to month because of seasonal variations and inventory levels.

   c. Labor Budget—expected staffing, generally stated by number of individuals and dollars for each job category.

   d. Capital Budget—targeted spending for major tangible assets, often requiring a time horizon beyond one year.

   e. Research and Development Budget—targeted spending for the development or refinement of products, materials, and processes.

   f. Cash Budget—expected flow of monetary receipts and expenditures (cash flow), generally developed at least once a year for each month of the year.

4. An organization having a functional structure usually has a budget for each function (e.g., marketing, production, finance, and human resources). However, an organization having a product structure usually has a budget for each product line.

5. **Activity-Based Costing (ABC)**—is a system that focuses on activities as the fundamental cost centers.

   a. An activity is any event that drives costs, including energy consumed, miles driven, computer hours logged, quality inspections made, shipments made, and scrap/rework orders filled.

   b. The more complex the organization's operations, the more cost-driving activities it is likely to have.

   c. The cost view reflects the flow of costs from resources to activities and from activities to products and services.

      1. This cost view is the key concept underlying activity-based costing: Resources are consumed by activities, and activities are consumed by products and services.

   d. The process view reflects the lateral flow from costs of input information to activities and from activities to performance evaluation, or the observed transactions associated with an activity.

   e. The benefits of an activity-based accounting control include: (1) costs are pinpointed by activity instead of being charged to overhead, (2) cost allocations are based on the portion of activities that can be directly traced to a product or job itself, as opposed to the volume of production, (3) costs associated with an activity for a particular product can be traced, and (4) the use of ABC shifts managers' thinking from accounting to managerial decision making.

f.   The limitations of activity-based accounting are: (1) managers must still make some arbitrary cost allocations based on volume, and (2) high measurement costs are associated with multiple activity centers and cost drivers.

6.   **Automation-Based Control**—automation usually involves linking machines with other machines to perform tasks.

a.   <u>Automation</u>—involves the use of devices and process that are self-regulating and operate independently of people.

b.   <u>Machine Controls</u>—utilize self-regulating instruments or devices to prevent and correct deviations from present standards.

1.   Machine control of other machines takes over part of the managerial control function.

2.   There has been a steady shift toward machine controls in production operations.

❖**4**❖   Explain several key corporate governance issues and control mechanisms.

IV.   **Corporate Governance**

1.   **Corporation**—a government-approved form of organization that allows different parties to contribute capital, expertise, and labor for the benefit of all of them.

2.   **Corporate Governance**—is the pattern of relations and controls between the stockholders, the board of directors, and the top management of a company.

a.   <u>Annual Meeting</u>—a company gathering at which shareholders and management discuss the previous year and the outlook for the future, directors are elected and other shareholder concerns are addressed.

b.   <u>Annual Report</u>—an audited document issued annually by all publicly listed corporations to their shareholders in accordance with SEC regulations.

c.   <u>Board of Directors</u>—the collective group of individuals elected by the shareholders of a corporation to oversee the management of the corporation.

d.   <u>Bylaws</u>—a document stating the rules of internal governance for a corporation as adopted by its board of directors.

e.   <u>Disclosure</u>—the public dissemination of material, market-influencing information.

f.   <u>Proxy Statement</u>—a document sent by publicly listed corporations to their shareholders providing material information on corporate matters subject to vote at the general shareholders' meeting.

3. Corporate governance includes a wide variety of issues and activities, such as (1) strategic business planning, (2) risk management associated with major capital investments and the purchase of another firm or sale of a company/division, (3) performance assessment of the top executive and the firm as a whole, (4) compensation and benefits paid to executives and higher level managers, (5) CEO/management succession and appointment, (6) disclosure and reporting to stockholders and government agencies, (7) corporate values and corporate culture, (8) independent inputs from members of the board of directors, and (9) organization design.

4. **Sarbanes-Oxley Act** (External Control)—prompted by the corporate scandals related to the extreme self-serving actions of some corporate executives and the lack of monitoring and control by some boards of directors.

   a. Many of the provisions of this act focus on defining the responsibilities of top executives and boards of directors to stockholders and the public at large.

   b. The act also defines the penalties for the failure to fulfill these responsibilities.

   c. Certification—it requires CEOs and CFOs of publicly traded companies to certify financial statements.

   d. Auditability—requires companies to develop and publish internal processes so that outsiders can confirm the existence of appropriate controls.

   e. Disclosure—companies must report financial results and material changes in corporate financial condition or operations "on a rapid and current basis."

   f. Accuracy—refers to the quality of the financial information reported to the public.

   g. Visibility—means that the internal information processes that make accuracy possible must be transparent.

   h. Criminal Accountability—criminal penalties for destroying, concealing, covering up, or falsifying records or documents may result in individual fines, imprisonment up to twenty years, or both.

   i. Whistleblower Protection—this act also protects employees of publicly traded companies who provide evidence of fraud on any rule or regulation of the SEC.

5. **Boards of Directors** (Internal Control)—are elected by stockholders and are expected to act in the owners' interests by monitoring and controlling the top-level executives. Many proposals have been offered as means of sharpening the accountability of boards of directors, these include:

   a. Independent Directors—the board should be composed of a substantial majority of independent (no present of former employment by the company or any significant financial or personal tie to the company or its management) directors.

   b. Self-Assessment—the board should have ways to evaluate and improve its performance in representing the shareholders.

   c. Executive Compensation—represents a window through which the effectiveness of the board may be viewed by shareholders and the public and thus the board should ensure a fair compensation program is in place. The board should ensure that the company describes clearly its overall compensation philosophy in the proxy statement to shareholders. It should also explain the rationale for the salary levels, incentive payments, and stock options granted to top executive officers.

   d. Evaluation of the CEO—a clear understanding between the board and the CEO regarding expected performance and how that performance will be measured is essential.

   e. Resource Allocation—every company needs to plan strategically to ensure future economic success.

   f. Fiduciary Responsibility and Control—the board has a primary duty to exercise its fiduciary responsibility and control in the best interests of the corporation and its shareholders.

MATCHING

Directions: Select the term that best identifies the statement listed below. Place the letter of the correct term in the space provided.

A. Stakeholder Control
B. Budgeting
C. Mechanistic Controls
D. Standards
E. Individual Self-Control
F. Machine Controls
G. Automation
H. Organizational Control
I. Financial Controls
J. Corrective Controls

K. Preventive Controls
L. Proxy Statement
M. Organic Controls
N. Principle of Selectivity
O. Group Control
P. Market Controls
Q. Corporate Governance
R. Corrective Control Model
S. Customer Monitoring
T. Green Marketing

_____ 1. Extensive rules and procedures, top-down authority, tightly written job descriptions, and other formal methods for preventing and correcting deviations from desired behaviors and results.

_____ 2. The pattern of relations and controls between the stockholders, the board of directors, and the top management of a company.

_____ 3. Mechanisms intended to reduce or eliminate unwanted behaviors and thereby achieve conformity with the organization's regulations and standards.

_____ 4. The process of categorizing proposed expenditures and linking them to goals.

_____ 5. Sale of products and services considered to be environmentally friendly, which makes the producing organizations environmentally responsible.

_____ 6. A document sent by publicly listed corporations to their shareholders providing material information on corporate matters subject to vote at the general shareholders' meeting.

_____ 7. The guiding mechanisms that operate consciously and unconsciously within each person.

_____ 8. Pressures from outside sources on organizations to change their behaviors.

_____ 9. The use of data to monitor sales, prices, costs, and profits, to guide decisions and to evaluate results.

_____ 10. The use of devices and processes that are self-regulating and operate independently of people.

_____ 11. The norms and values that group members share and maintain through rewards and punishments.

_____ 12. A wide range of methods, techniques, and procedures intended to prevent the misallocation of financial resources.

_____ 13. Flexible authority, loose job descriptions, individual self-controls, and other informal methods of preventing and correcting deviations from desired behaviors and results.

_____ 14. Consists of ongoing efforts to obtain feedback from customers concerning the quality of goods and services.

_____ 15. Criteria against which qualitative and quantitative characteristics are evaluated.

_____ 16. Mechanisms intended to reduce errors and thereby minimize the need for corrective actions.

_____ 17. A small number of characteristics always account for a large number of effects.

_____ 18. A process for detecting and eliminating or reducing deviations from an organization's established standards.

_____ 19. The use of instruments to prevent and correct deviations from desired results.

_____ 20. Comprises the formal rules and procedures for preventing or correcting deviations from plans and for achieving desired goals.

TRUE OR FALSE

<u>Directions</u>: Write True or False in the space provided.

❖1❖

_____ 1.   At FedEx, its controls help identify which customers generate the greatest profits and which actually end up costing the company.

_____ 2.   Planning and control are not related since planning is the first managerial function and controlling is the last.

_____ 3.   Rules, regulations, and standards function primarily as corrective controls.

_____ 4.   Organizations that use green marketing may increase consumer approval but will also increase costs.

_____ 5.   Group control comprises the formal rules and procedures for preventing or correcting deviations from plans and for achieving desired goals.

_____ 6.   Controls should be linked to the strategic goals of the organization.

❖2❖

_____ 7.   The preventive control model has six interconnected steps.

_____ 8.   In Nigeria, executives expect meetings to begin and end at certain times.

_____ 9.   If standards are known, overcontrolling becomes less likely and employees can use their time more effectively.

_____ 10. The principle of selectivity holds that a small number of characteristics always account for a large number of effects.

_____ 11. Once a characteristic can be controlled means that it always should be controlled.

❖3❖

_____ 12. Organic controls include top-down authority, tightly written job descriptions, and other formal methods for preventing and correcting deviations from desired behaviors and results.

_____ 13. Johnson & Johnson and Home Depot are classic examples of organizations that use mechanistic controls.

_____ 14. One goal of profit-sharing plans is to establish a more equitable reward system.

_____ 15. The current ratio is computed to assess an organization's ability to pay its long-term financial commitments.

_____ 16. There has been a steady shift in the last five years toward more human controls and less machine controls in production operations.

_____ 17. Automation usually involves linking machines with other machines to perform tasks.

❖4❖

___ 18. The board of directors are elected by the shareholders of a corporation to oversee the management of the corporation.

___ 19. A proxy statement refers to the public dissemination of material—particularly market-influencing information.

___ 20. Many provisions of the Sarbanes-Oxley Act focus on defining the responsibilities of top executives and boards of directors to stockholders and the public at large.

MULTIPLE CHOICE

<u>Directions</u>: Select the best answer in the space provided.

❖1❖

___ 1. Which of the following statements is <u>false</u> regarding control?
  a. Control helps maintain or redirect actual behaviors and results.
  b. Control provides some essential information that managers need.
  c. Control is seldom the focus of controversy and policy struggles within organizations.
  d. To most people the word *control* has a negative connotation.

___ 2. When a FedEx dispatcher sends messages to drivers to change their pick-up to satisfy customers needs, this is an example of a _____ control.
  a. post-action
  b. preventive
  c. corrective
  d. process

___ 3. _____ control refers to pressures from outside sources on organizations to change their behaviors.
  a. Community
  b. Stakeholder
  c. Corrective
  d. Preventive

___ 4. _____ control includes rules, standards, budgets, and audits.
  a. Organizational
  b. Individual
  c. Bureaucratic
  d. Organic

_____   5.   _____ comprises the guiding mechanisms that operate consciously and unconsciously within each person.
a. Group control
b. Organic self-control
c. Psychological control
d. Individual self-control

❖2❖

_____   6.   Which of the following is <u>not</u> a step in the corrective control model?
a. collect information
b. link to desired goals
c. define the system
d. make comparisons

_____   7.   The _____ holds that a small number of characteristics always account for a large number of effects.
a. principle of standards
b. comparative analysis
c. effects test
d. principle of selectivity

_____   8.   _____ is/are criteria for evaluating qualitative and quantitative characteristics and should be set for each characteristic measured.
a. Procedures
b. Policies
c. Standards
d. Pareto's law

_____   9.   The turnover of field sales personnel should be no more than _____ per 100 salespeople per month and no more than _____ per 100 salespeople annually.
a. 5; 30
b. 1; 10
c. 3; 15
d. 3; 30

_____   10.   When formal controls emphasize punishment, strong _____ controls often emerge to distort the information that is reported to management.
a. organizational
b. group
c. individual
d. organic

_____ 11. Which of the following statements is true regarding control systems?
   a. If information is collected by the individual or group whose performance is to be controlled, its validity must be checked.
   b. Information about actual results must be compared with performance standards.
   c. Computer-based management information systems often help in overcoming inadequacies in corrective controls.
   d. All of the above

❖3❖

_____ 12. _____ controls involve the extensive use of rules and procedures, top-down authority, tightly written job descriptions, and other formal methods for preventing and correcting deviations from desired behaviors and results.
   a. Organic
   b. Mechanistic
   c. Market
   d. Participative

_____ 13. _____ controls are consistent with a clan culture.
   a. Organic
   b. Market
   c. Bureaucratic
   d. Financial

_____ 14. To be effective, market controls generally require that _____.
   a. the costs of the resources used in producing outputs be measured monetarily
   b. the value of the goods and services produced be defined clearly and monetarily priced
   c. the prices of the goods and services produced be set competitively
   d. all of the above

_____ 15. Two of the control methods that can satisfy the market control requirements are _____ and _____.
   a. organizational control; financial control
   b. profit-sharing plans; customer monitoring
   c. stakeholder control; corrective control
   d. group control; bureaucratic control

_____ 16. _____ generally is considered to be the most important profitability ratio because it indicates how efficiently the organization is using its resources.
   a. Quick ratio
   b. Return on investment
   c. Debt ratio
   d. Current ratio

_____   17.   A _____ budget targets spending for major tangible assets and often requires a time horizon beyond one year.
a.   strategic
b.   financial
c.   capital
d.   research and development

❖4❖

_____   18.   Which of the following refers to a document statement the rules of internal governance for a corporation as adopted by its board of directors?
a.   annual report
b.   disclosure
c.   proxy Statement
d.   bylaws

_____   19.   _____ is the pattern of relations and controls between the stockholders, the board of directors, and the top management of a company.
a.   Disclosure
b.   Whistleblower protection
c.   Corporate governance
d.   Activity-based costing

_____   20.   One requirement of the Sarbanes-Oxley Act is _____, which indicates that if CFOs and CEOs falsify documents, they are liable for criminal and civil penalties.
a.   certification
b.   auditability
c.   disclosure
d.   visibility

ESSAY QUESTIONS

❖1❖

1.   Explain the two general types of organizational controls: preventive and corrective.

2.   Identify and discuss the four primary sources of control in most organizations.

3. What criteria should be included in an effective control system?

❖2❖

4. Discuss the six steps of the corrective control model.

❖3❖

5. Explain the difference between market and financial controls.

6. What are the benefits and limitations of activity-based costing?

❖4❖

7. Explain the Sarbanes-Oxley Act and define its major provisions.

CHAPTER 10
CONTROLLING IN ORGANIZATIONS

MATCHING SOLUTIONS

1. C - Mechanistic Controls
2. Q - Corporate Governance
3. J - Corrective Controls
4. B - Budgeting
5. T - Green Marketing
6. L - Proxy Statement
7. E - Individual Self-Control
8. A - Stakeholder Control
9. P - Market Controls
10. G - Automation
11. O - Group Control
12. I - Financial Controls
13. M - Organic Controls
14. S - Customer Monitoring
15. D - Standards
16. K - Preventive Controls
17. N - Principle of Selectivity
18. R - Corrective Control Model
19. F - Machine Controls
20. H - Organizational Control

TRUE/FALSE SOLUTIONS

Question	Answer	Page	Explanation
1.	True		
2.	False	266–267	<u>Planning</u> is the formal process of developing goals, strategies, tactics, and standards and allocating resources. <u>Controls</u> help ensure that decisions, actions, and results are consistent with those plans. Thus planning and controlling go hand in hand. Planning prescribes desired behaviors and results. Controls help maintain or redirect actual behaviors and results. Controls provide some essential information to managers. Thus, planning and control complement and support each other.

3.	False	267	Preventive controls are mechanisms intended to reduce errors and thereby minimize the need for corrective action. Rules and regulations, standards, recruitment and selection procedures, and training and development programs function primarily as preventive controls. Corrective controls are mechanisms intended to reduce or eliminate unwanted behaviors or results and thereby achieve conformity with the organization's regulations and standards.
4.	False	268	Green marketing is the name for marketing of products and services considered environmentally friendly that make their organizations "environmentally responsible." Organizations use green marketing not only to increase consumer approval, but also to cut costs.
5.	False	269	Organizational control comprises the formal rules and procedures for preventing or correcting deviations from plans and for achieving desired goals. Group control comprises the norms and values that group members share and maintain through rewards and punishments.
6.	True		
7.	False	272	The corrective control model is a process for detecting and eliminating or reducing deviations from an organization's established standards. The corrective control model has six interconnected steps: (1) define the system, (2) identify the key characteristics to be measured, (3) set standards, (4) collect information, (5) make comparisons, and (6) diagnose problems and make corrections.
8.	False	274	U.S. and Canadian executives expect meetings to begin and end at certain times, but Latins arrive later than the stated times and are not concerned about ending meetings at the specified time. In Nigeria, a starting time for a meeting is only an approximation, and tardiness is readily accepted.
9.	True		
10.	True		
11.	False	275	Diagnosis involves assessing the types, amounts, and causes of deviations and correct problems. However, the fact that a characteristic can be controlled doesn't necessarily mean that it should be controlled.

12.	False	277	<u>Mechanistic controls</u> involve the extensive use of rules and procedures, top-down authority, tightly written job descriptions, and other formal methods for preventing and correcting deviations from desired behaviors and results. <u>Organic controls</u> involve the use of flexible authority, relatively loose job descriptions, individual self-controls, and other informal methods for preventing and correcting deviations from desired behaviors and results.
13.	False	277	Organic controls are consistent with a clan culture. A <u>clan</u> is simply a group united by common interests (goals) and characteristics. In clan-type organizational cultures, such as The Associates, Johnson & Johnson, and Home Depot, members share pride in membership and a strong sense of identification with management.
14.	True		
15.	False	280	The <u>current ratio</u> indicates an organization's ability to pay bills on time. <u>Debt ratio</u> is computed to assess an organization's ability to meet its long-term financial commitments.
16.	False	285	The impact of automatic machine controls on management has been reported in a number of studies. One researcher found that the introduction of an advanced automated system in one large factory reduced the number of middle management jobs by 34 percent. There has been a steady shift toward machine controls in production operations.
17.	True		
18.	True		
19.	False	287	A <u>proxy statement</u> is a document sent by publicly listed corporations to their shareholders providing material information on corporate matters subject to vote at the general shareholders' meeting. <u>Disclosure</u> is the public dissemination of material, market-influencing information.
20.	True		

MULTIPLE CHOICE SOLUTIONS

Question	Answer	Page	Explanation
1.	c	266	<u>Control</u> involves the use of mechanisms to ensure that behaviors and performance conform to an organization's rules and procedures. Most employees and many shoppers resent control practices because of their deeply held values of freedom and individualism. Thus controls often are the focus of controversy and policy struggles within organizations.
2.	c	267	<u>Preventive controls</u> are mechanisms intended to reduce errors and thereby minimize the need for corrective action. <u>Corrective controls</u> are mechanisms intended to reduce or eliminate unwanted behaviors or results and thereby achieve conformity with the organization's regulations and standards. At FedEx, dispatchers send messages to drivers to change their pick-up routes to satisfy customer needs.
3.	b	268	<u>Stakeholder control</u> refers to pressures from outside sources on organizations to change their behaviors. Stakeholders may be unions, governmental agencies, customers, shareholders, and others who have direct interests in the well-being of an organization.
4.	a	269	<u>Organizational control</u> comprises the formal rules and procedures for preventing or correcting deviations from plans and for achieving desired goals. Examples include rules, standards, budgets, and audits.
5.	d	269	<u>Individual self-control</u> comprises the guiding mechanisms that operate consciously and unconsciously within each person. Standards of professionalism are becoming an increasingly important aspect for individual self-control.
6.	b	272	The <u>corrective control model</u> is a process for detecting and eliminating or reducing deviations from an organization's established standards. It has six interconnected steps: (1) define the system, (2) identify the key characteristics to be measured, (3) set standards, (4) collect information, (5) make comparisons, and (6) diagnose problems and make corrections.

7.	d	273	The <u>principle of selectivity</u> (also known as Pareto's law) holds that a small number of characteristics always account for a large number of effects.
8.	c	273	<u>Standards</u> are criteria for evaluating qualitative and quantitative characteristics and should be set for each characteristic measured. Increasingly, control systems are being based on performance standards.
9.	d	274	The turnover of field sales personnel should be no more than 3 per 100 salespeople per month and no more than 30 per 100 salespeople annually.
10.	b	274	When formal controls emphasize punishment, strong group controls often emerge to distort the information that is reported to management. Such reporting often obscures responsibility for failure to achieve goals or meet standards.
11.	d	274–275	Employees and managers have an incentive to distort or conceal information if negative results will be used to criticize or punish them. All of the statements listed are true.
12.	b	277	<u>Organic controls</u> involve the use of flexible authority, relatively loose job descriptions, individual self-controls, and other informal methods for preventing and correcting deviations from desired behaviors and results. <u>Mechanistic controls</u> involve the extensive use of rules and procedures, top-down authority, tightly written job descriptions, and other formal methods for preventing and correcting deviations from desired behaviors and results.
13.	a	277	Organic controls are consistent with a clan culture. A <u>clan</u> is a group united by common interests and characteristics. In clan cultures, members share pride in membership and a strong sense of identification with management.
14.	d	278	To be effective, marketing control mechanisms generally require that (1) the costs of the resources used in producing outputs be measured monetarily, (2) the value of the goods and services produced be defined clearly and priced monetarily, and (3) the prices of the goods and services produced be set competitively.

15.	b	278–279	Two of the control methods that can satisfy the market control requirements are profit-sharing plans and customer monitoring. Profit-sharing plans provide employees with supplemental income based on the profitability of an entire organization or a selected subunit. Customer monitoring consists of ongoing efforts to obtain feedback from customers concerning the quality of goods and services.
16.	b	280	Return on investment (ROI) generally is considered to be the most important profitability ratio because it indicates how efficiently the organization is using its resources. A ratio value greater than 1.0 indicates that the organization is using its resources effectively.
17.	c	282	A capital budget is targeted at spending for major tangible assets (e.g., new or renovated headquarters building, new factory, or major equipment), and often requires a time horizon beyond one year.
18.	d	286	Bylaws are documents and statements the rules of internal governance for a corporation as adopted by its board of directors.
19.	c	286	Corporate governance refers to a document statement the rules of internal governance for a corporation as adopted by its board of directors.
20.	a	287	The Sarbanes-Oxley Act requires CEOs and CFOs of publicly traded companies to certify financial statements. Those who knowingly falsify documents are liable for criminal and civil penalties. This certification is the CEOs and CFOs personal guarantee that valid financial/accounting processes have been established to ensure the proper flow of financial disclosure.

ESSAY SOLUTIONS

[Page 267]

1. There are two general types of organizational controls: preventive and corrective. Preventive controls are mechanisms intended to reduce errors and thereby minimize the need for corrective action. Rules and regulations, standards, recruitment and selection procedures, and training and development programs function primarily as preventive controls. They all direct and limit the behaviors of managers and employees alike. The assumption is that, if managers and employees comply with these requirements, the organization is likely to achieve its goals.

Corrective controls are mechanisms intended to reduce or eliminate unwanted behaviors or results and thereby achieve conformity with the organization's regulations and standards. Similarly, an air traffic controller exercises corrective control by instructing a pilot to change altitude and direction to avoid another plane.

[Pages 268–269]

2. Stakeholder control is expressed as pressures from outside sources on organizations to change their behaviors. Stakeholders may include unions, government agencies, customers, shareholders, and others who have direct interests in the well-being of an organization. Organizational control comprises the formal rules and procedures for preventing or correcting deviations from plans and for achieving desired goals. Examples include rules, standards, budgets, and audits. Group control comprises the norms and values that group members share and maintain through rewards and punishments. Individual self-control comprises the guiding mechanisms that operate consciously and unconsciously within each person. Standards of professionalism are becoming an increasingly important aspect for individual self-control.

[Pages 270–271]

3. Designing effective organizational controls and control systems is not simple, because many issues must be considered. Control systems are more likely to be effective if the following criteria are considered.

   a. *Linkage to Desired Goals.* Control or control systems should be linked to the desired goals of the organization. These goals often include improving customer service, protecting the organization's assets, and improving the quality of goods and/or services.

   b. *Objective.* An objective control is impartial and cannot be manipulated by employees for personal gain.

   c. *Complete.* A complete control or control system encompasses all the desired behaviors and goals. Thus, balancing quantitative (measurable) controls with more qualitative (subjective) controls is necessary.

   d. *Timely.* A timely control or control system provides information when it is most needed. Computer-based information systems have played a major role in increasing the timely flow of information.

   e. *Acceptable.* An acceptable control or control system is recognized as necessary and appropriate. If a control system is widely ignored, managers need to find out why. Perhaps the controls should be dropped or modified, should be backed up with rewards for compliance and punishments for noncompliance, or should be linked more closely to desired results.

[Pages 272–276]

4. The <u>corrective control model</u> is a process for detecting and eliminating or reducing deviations from an organization's established standards. This process relies heavily on information feedback and the needed reactions to it. The corrective control model has the following six interconnected steps.

   a. *Define the System.* A formal control system might be created and maintained for an employee, a department, or an entire organization. The control mechanisms could focus on specific inputs, transformation processes, or outputs. Input controls often limit the amount by which raw materials used in the transformation process can vary from the organization's standards.

   b. *Identify Key Characteristics.* The key types of information to be obtained about a person, team, department, or organization must be identified. Establishing a formal corrective control requires early determination of the characteristics that can be measured, the costs and benefits of obtaining information about each characteristic, and whether variations in each characteristic are likely to affect performance.

   c. *Set Standards.* Standards are criteria for evaluating qualitative and quantitative characteristics and should be set for each characteristic measured. Increasingly, control systems are being based on performance standards (performance goals).

   d. *Collect Information.* Information on each of the standards can be collected manually or automatically. If information is collected by the individual or group whose performance is to be controlled, its validity must be checked. Employees and managers have an incentive to distort or conceal information if negative results will be used to criticize or punish them.

   e. *Make Comparisons.* Comparisons are needed to determine whether what *is* happening is what *should be* happening. Information about actual results must be compared with performance standards. Making these comparisons allow managers and team members to concentrate on controlling deviations or exceptions.

   f. *Diagnose and Correct Problems.* Diagnosis involves assessing the types, amounts, and causes of deviations from standards. Action is needed to eliminate those deviations and correct problems. Computer-based management information systems often help in overcoming inadequacies in corrective controls.

[Pages 278–282]

5. <u>Market controls</u> involve the use of data to monitor sales, prices, costs, and profits, to guide decisions and evaluate results. To be effective, market controls generally require that the costs of the resources used in producing outputs be measured monetarily, the value of the goods and services produced be defined clearly and monetarily priced, and the prices of the goods and services produced be set competitively. Two of the control methods that can satisfy these requirements are profit-sharing plans and customer monitoring.

Financial controls include a wide range of methods, techniques, and procedures intended to prevent or correct the misallocation of resources. Three essential financial control methods are comparative financial analysis, budgeting, and activity-based costing. Evaluation of a firm's financial condition for two or more time periods is called comparative financial analysis. When data are available from similar firms, they are used in making comparisons. The most common method of comparison is ratio analysis. Ratio analysis involves selecting two significant figures, expressing their relationship as a proportion or fraction, and comparing its value for two periods of time or with the same ratio of similar organizations. The process of categorizing proposed expenditures and linking them to goods is known as budgeting. Budgets usually express the dollar cost of various tasks or resources. Activity-based costing is a system that focuses on activities as the fundamental cost centers. In contrast to most financial control mechanisms, activity-based costing focuses on the work activities associated with operating a business.

[Pages 282–285]

6. Activity-based costing (ABC) is a system that focuses on activities as the fundamental cost centers. Activities become the focal point for the organization. An activity is any event that drives costs, including energy consumed, miles driven, computer hours logged, quality inspections made, shipments made, and scrap/rework orders filled.

   Using an activity-based accounting control system yields at least four benefits. First, costs are pinpointed by activity instead of being charged to overhead. Second, cost allocations are based on the portion of activities that can be directly traced to a product or job itself, as opposed to the volume of production. Third, costs associated with an activity for a particular product can now be traced. Finally, the use of ABC shifts managers' thinking from accounting to managerial decision making.

   The benefits of activity-based accounting control systems are offset somewhat by two limitations. First, managers must still make some arbitrary cost allocations based on volume. Second, high measurement costs are associated with multiple activity centers and cost drivers.

[Pages 287–288]

7. Sarbanes-Oxley Act (External Control)—prompted by the corporate scandals related to the extreme self-serving actions of some corporate executives and the lack of monitoring and control by some boards of directors.

   a. Many of the provisions of this act focus on defining the responsibilities of top executives and boards of directors to stockholders and the public at large.

   b. The act also defines the penalties for the failure to fulfill these responsibilities.

   c. *Certification*—it requires CEOs and CFOs of publicly traded companies to certify financial statements.

   d. *Auditability*—requires companies to develop and publish internal processes so that outsiders can confirm the existence of appropriate controls.

e.   *Disclosure*—companies must report financial results and material changes in corporate financial condition or operations "on a rapid and current basis."

f.   *Accuracy*—refers to the quality of the financial information reported to the public.

g.   *Visibility*—means that the internal information processes that make accuracy possible must be transparent.

h.   *Criminal Accountability*—criminal penalties for destroying, concealing, covering up, or falsifying records or documents may result in individual fines, imprisonment up to twenty years, or both.

i.   *Whistleblower Protection*—this act also protects employees of publicly traded companies who provide evidence of fraud on any rule or regulation of the SEC.

Chapter 11
ORGANIZATIONAL DESIGN

LEARNING OBJECTIVES

After studying this chapter, you should be able to:

❖**1**❖   Describe the two fundamentals of organizing.

❖**2**❖   Explain the five aspects of an organization's vertical design.

❖**3**❖   Describe the four types of horizontal design.

❖**4**❖   Describe two methods of integration.

OUTLINE

❖**1**❖   Describe the two fundamentals of organizing.

   I.   **Fundamentals of Organizing**

      1. **Organization Design**—the decisions and actions that result in a structure.

      2. **Organization Chart**—is a diagram showing the reporting relationships of functions, departments, and individual positions within an organization

         a. It provides four major pieces of information about an organization's structure:

            1. The boxes represent different units (marketing, legal, human resources).

            2. The titles in each box show the work performed by that person.

            3. Reporting relationships are shown by the lines connecting superiors and subordinates.

            4. Levels of the organization are indicated by the number of vertical layers in the chart.

         b. One advantage is that such a chart shows employees how the pieces of the entire organization fit together.

         c. Another advantage is that the chart may indicate gaps or duplication of services.

         d. A major disadvantage of the organization chart is that it is just a piece of paper; it simply can't show everything about an organization's structure nor much about the way things really get done.

      e. Differentiation—means that the organization is composed of units that work on specialized tasks using different work methods and requiring employees with unique competencies.

         1. *Division of labor*—means that the work of the organization is divided into smaller tasks.

         2. *Specialization*—is the process of identifying particular tasks and assigning them to departments, teams, or divisions.

      f. Integration—means that the various units must be put back together so that work is coordinated.

❖**2**❖   Explain the five aspects of an organization's vertical design.

  II. **Vertical Design**

    1. **Hierarchy**—is a pyramid showing relationships among levels.

      a. The CEO occupies the top position and is the senior member of top management.

      b. The CEO and members of the top management team set the strategic direction of the organization.

    2. **Span of Control**—refers to the number of employees directly reporting to a person.

      a. Holding size constant, narrow spans of control lead to more hierarchical levels.

      b. Wider spans create a flatter organization with fewer hierarchical levels.

      c. Four key factors that can influence the span of control in any situation:

         1. The competence of both the manager and the employee.

         2. The similarity or dissimilarity of tasks being supervised.

         3. The incidence of new problems in the manager's department.

         4. The extent of clear operating standards and rules.

    3. **Authority**—is the right to make a decision.

      a. Authority is the glue that holds the vertical and horizontal parts together.

      b. Authority implies both responsibility and accountability. By exercising authority, managers accept the responsibility for acting and are willing to be held accountable for success or failure.

    4. **Responsibility**—is an employee's obligation to perform assigned tasks.

      a. The employee acquires this obligation upon accepting a job or a specific assignment.

      b. Managers should give employees sufficient authority to get a job done.

5. **Accountability**—is the manager's expectation that the employee will accept credit or blame for his work.

   a. No manager can check everything an employee does. Therefore managers normally establish guidelines and performance standards within which responsibilities are carried out.

   b. Accountability flows from the bottom to the top.

   c. Accountability is the point at which authority and responsibility meet and is essential for effective performance.

6. **Delegation**—is the process by which managers assign to subordinates the right to make decisions and act in certain situations.

   a. Delegation starts when the design of the organization is being established and work is divided. Delegation continues as new jobs and tasks are added during day-to-day operations.

   b. Delegation of authority occurs in conjunction with the assignment of responsibilities.

   c. Effective Delegation:

      1. Establish goals and standards.

      2. Ensure clarity.

      3. Involvement.

      4. Expect completed work.

      5. Provide training.

      6. Timely feedback.

   d. Barriers to Delegation—delegation can only be as effective as the ability of people to delegate.

      1. The greatest psychological barrier to delegation is fear.

      2. Failure to define authority and responsibility clearly often serves as an organizational behavior.

7. **Centralization and Decentralization**

   a. Centralization—is the concentration of decision making at the top of an organization or department.

   b. Decentralization—is the delegation of authority to lower level employees or departments.

      1. It is an approach that requires managers to decide what and when to delegate, to select and train personnel carefully, and to formulate adequate controls.

    c. <u>No Absolutes</u>—neither centralization or decentralization is absolute in an organization.

        1. Potential advantages.

            a. It frees top managers to develop organizational plans and strategies.

            b. It develops lower-level managers' conceptual skills.

            c. Because subordinates often are closer to the action than higher level managers, they may have a better grasp of all the facts.

            d. It fosters a healthy, achievement-oriented atmosphere among employees.

    d. <u>Key Factors</u>—several factors can affect management's decision to centralize or decentralize decision-making responsibilities.

        1. *Cost of Decisions*—is perhaps the most important factor in determining the extent of centralization.

            a. As a general rule, the more costly it is to the organization, the more likely top management will make the decision.

        2. *Uniformity of Policy*—managers who value consistency favor centralization of authority.

            a. Uniform policies enable managers to compare the relative efficiencies of various departments.

        3. *Competency Levels*—many organizations work hard to ensure an adequate supply of competent managers and employees—an absolute necessity for decentralization.

        4. *Control Mechanisms*—even the most avid proponents of decentralization insist on controls to determine whether actual events are meeting expectations.

        5. *Environmental Influences*—external factors such as unions, federal and state regulatory agencies, and tax policies affect the degree of centralization in a firm.

❖**3**❖   Describe the four types of horizontal design.

III. **Horizontal Design**

    1. **Functional Design**—means grouping managers and employees according to their areas of expertise and the resources they use to perform their jobs.

        a. Designing by function is economical because it results in a simple structure. It keeps administrative expenses low because everyone in a department shares training, experience, and resources.

      b. Potential Benefits

         1. Supporting skill specialization.

         2. Reducing duplication of resources and increasing coordination within the functional area.

         3. Enhancing career development and training within the functional area.

         4. Allowing supervisors and subordinates to share common expertise.

         5. Promoting high-quality technical decision making.

      c. Potential Pitfalls

         1. Inadequate communication between units.

         2. Conflicts over product priorities.

         3. Difficulties with interunit coordination.

         4. Focus on departmental rather than organizational issues and goals.

         5. Developing managers who are experts only in narrow fields.

2. **Product Design**—means that all functions that contribute to a product are organized under one manager.

      a. Product designs are evaluated on the basis of their profit contributions to the entire organization.

      b. Because each division represents a product or group of products, senior management can measure the financial performance of each division.

      c. Potential Benefits

         1. Permitting fast changes in a product line.

         2. Allowing greater product line visibility.

         3. Fostering a concern for customer demands.

         4. Clearly defining responsibilities for each product line.

         5. Developing managers who can think across functional lines.

      d. Potential Pitfalls

         1. Not allowing efficient utilization of skills and resources.

         2. Not fostering coordination of activities across product lines.

         3. Encouraging politics and conflicts in resource allocation across product lines.

         4. Limiting career mobility for personnel outside their own product line.

3. **Geographic Design**—organizes activities around location.

      a. It allows organizations to develop competitive advantage in a particular region according to that area's customers, competitors, and other factors.

      b. This permits managers to specialize in particular markets.

    c. Potential Benefits

        1. Having facilities and the equipment used for production and/or distribution all in one place, saving time and costs.

        2. Being able to develop expertise in solving problems unique to one location.

        3. Gaining an understanding of customers' problems and desires.

        4. Getting production closer to raw material and suppliers.

    d. Potential Pitfalls

        1. Duplication of functions, to varying degrees, at each regional or individual location.

        2. Conflict between each location's goals and organizational goals.

        3. Added levels of management and extensive use of rules and regulations to coordinate and ensure uniformity of quality among locations.

4. **Network Design**—subcontracts some or many of its operations to other firms and coordinates them to accomplish specific goals.

    a. Sometimes called a *virtual organization*, managers need to coordinate and link up people (from many organizations) to perform activities in many locations.

    b. The network design enhances fast communications so that people can act together.

    c. Potential Benefits

        1. The organization brings together the special knowledge and skills or others to create value rather than hiring employees to perform this task.

        2. It brings together people with different insights into teams that work exclusively on a given project.

        3. Organizations with network design can work with a wide variety of different suppliers customers, and other organizations.

    d. Potential Pitfalls

        1. Other organizations can sometimes fail to live up to the deadlines that were established.

        2. Since the network design does not provide managers with knowledge to complete the process on their own, they must constantly monitor the quality of work provided by those in other organizations.

        3. Employees in the outsourced organization may not commit to the same values and sense of time urgency to which employees in the networked organization are committed.

        4. Since the network design requires managers working with many organizations, the lines of authority, responsibility, and accountability are not always clear. Thus projects are delayed and cost overruns do occur.

❖**4**❖ Describe two methods of integration.

   IV. **Organizational Integration**

     1. **Mechanistic System**—is one in which management breaks activities into separate, highly specialized tasks, relies extensively on standardized rules, and centralizes decision making at the top.

       a. It may be most appropriate when an organization's environment is stable and predictable.

     2. **Organic System**—encourages managers and subordinates to work together in teams and to communicate openly with each other.

       a. Employees are encouraged to communicate with anyone who might help them solve a problem.

       b. Decision making tends to be decentralized.

       c. Authority, responsibility, and accountability flow to employees having the expertise required to solve problems as they arise. As a result, an organic organization is well suited to a changing environment.

     3. **Technological Interdependence**—is the degree of coordination required between individuals and units to transform information and raw materials into goods and services.

       a. <u>Pooled Interdependence</u>—involves little sharing of information or resources among individuals within a unit or among units in the performance of tasks.

       b. <u>Sequential Interdependence</u>—involves the orderly step-by-step flow of information, tasks, and resources from one individual or team to another within the same unit or from one unit to another.

       c. <u>Reciprocal Interdependence</u>—involves the need for every individual and unit to work with every other individual and unit; information and resources flow back and forth freely until the goal is achieved.

MATCHING

Directions: Select the term that best identifies the statement listed below. Place the letter of the correct term in the space provided.

A. Specialization
B. Centralization
C. Network Design
D. Differentiation
E. Responsibility
F. Product Design
G. Organization Chart
H. Division of Labor
I. Authority
J. Sequential Interdependence

K. Accountability
L. Delegation
M. Functional Design
N. Mechanistic System
O. Span of Control
P. Decentralization
Q. Geographic Design
R. Pooled Interdependence
S. Reciprocal Interdependence
T. Coordination

_____   1.   This is described as the "glue" that holds the vertical and horizontal parts of organizational design together.

_____   2.   The process of identifying particular tasks and assigning them to individuals or teams who have been trained to do them.

_____   3.   A high degree of delegated decision making throughout an organization or department.

_____   4.   The expectation that each employee will accept credit or blame for results of their work.

_____   5.   The formal and informal procedures that integrate the activities of separate individuals, teams, and departments in an organization.

_____   6.   This means that the organization is composed of units that work on specialized tasks using different work methods and requiring employees with unique competencies.

_____   7.   This refers to the grouping of managers and employees according to their areas of expertise and the resources they use to perform their jobs.

_____   8.   This means that all functions that contribute to a product are organized under one manager.

_____   9.   Involves the need for every individual and unit to work with every other individual and unit with information and resources flowing back and forth until the goal is achieved.

_____   10.   Is the process by which managers assign to subordinates the right make decisions and act in certain situations.

_____   11.   An employee's obligation to perform assigned tasks.

_____   12.   The grouping of all functions for a geographic area at one location under one manager.

_____   13.   The concentration of decision making at the top of an organization or department.

_____ 14. This is being utilized when an organization divides its work into smaller tasks.

_____ 15. Involves little sharing of information or resources among individuals within a unit or among units in the performance of tasks.

_____ 16. This subcontracts some or many of an organization's operations to other firms and coordinates them to accomplish specific goals.

_____ 17. The principle that states that the number of people reporting directly to any one manager must be limited.

_____ 18. A diagram showing the reporting relationships of functions, departments, and individual positions within an organization.

_____ 19. This is the step-by-step flow of information, tasks, and resources from one individual or team to another within the same unit or from one unit to another.

_____ 20. This breaks management activities into separate, highly specialized tasks, relies extensively on standardized rules, and centralizes decision making at the top.

TRUE OR FALSE

<u>Directions</u>: Write True or False in the space provided.

❖1❖

_____ 1. Organization design includes the elements of the organizing function and the complex tradeoffs that must be considered in achieving a "fit" among these functions.

_____ 2. Specialization refers to the uniform and consistent procedures that employees are to follow in performing their jobs.

_____ 3. Integration means that the organization is composed of units that work on specialized tasks using different work methods and requiring employees with unique competencies.

_____ 4. An organization chart is a diagram showing the political structure and informal reporting relationships of functions, departments, and individual positions within an organization.

❖2❖

_____ 5. Span of control refers to the number of employees directly reporting to a person.

_____ 6. Responsibility refers to the right to make a decision.

_____ 7. Authority is the manager's expectation that the employee will accept credit or blame for his work.

_____ 8. The greatest psychological barrier to delegation is fear.

_____ 9. Delegation starts when the design of the organization is being established and work is divided.

____ 10. Decentralization is the concentration of decision making at the top of an organization or department.

____ 11. Neither centralization or decentralization is absolute in an organization.

❖3❖

____ 12. A potential benefit of network design is the reduction of duplication of resources and an increase in the coordination within each area.

____ 13. Designing by geography is economical because it results in a simple structure.

____ 14. A functional design is where all functions that contribute to a product are organized under one manager.

____ 15. Geographical design allows organizations to develop competitive advantage in a particular region according to that area's customers, competitors, and other factors.

____ 16. Organizations with a geographical design are sometimes called virtual organizations, where managers need to coordinate and link up people to perform activities in many locations.

❖4❖

____ 17. A mechanistic system relies extensively on standardized rules and centralizes decision making at the top.

____ 18. Sequential interdependence involves little sharing of information or resources among individuals within a unit or among units in the performance of tasks.

____ 19. Technological interdependence is the degree of coordination required between individuals and units to transform information and raw materials into goods and services.

____ 20. Reciprocal interdependence involves the need for every individual and unit to work with every other individual and unit.

MULTIPLE CHOICE

Directions: Select the best answer in the space provided.

❖1❖

____ 1. In organizational charts, the term *units* refer to:
   a. groups.
   b. teams.
   c. divisions.
   d. all of the above.

_____ 2. _____ refers to the decisions and actions that result in a structure.
a. Organizational charting
b. Organizational design
c. Integration
d. Organizational differentiation

_____ 3. _____ means that the organization is composed of units that work on specialized tasks using different work methods and requiring employees with unique competencies.
a. Integration
b. Specialization
c. Delegation
d. Differentiation

_____ 4. The process of identifying particular tasks and assigning them to departments, teams, or divisions is known as:
a. differentiation.
b. integration.
c. delegation.
d. specialization.

❖**2**❖

_____ 5. Which of the following is a pyramid showing relationships among levels of an organization?
a. hierarchy
b. span of control
c. organization design
d. organization chart

_____ 6. _____ refers to the number of employees directly reporting to a person.
a. Span of control
b. Responsibility
c. Authority
d. Accountability

_____ 7. Which of the following is an employee's duty to perform the assigned task?
a. authority
b. accountability
c. responsibility
d. span of control

_____ 8. No manager can check everything an employee does. Therefore managers usually establish guidelines and performance standards which are carried out. As such, _____ flows from the bottom to the top.
a. responsibility
b. accountability
c. authority
d. delegation

_____   9.   Which of the following is the process of giving authority to a person (or group or team) to make decisions and act in certain situations?
a. span of control
b. decentralization
c. centralization
d. delegation

_____   10.   _____ is the delegation of authority to lower level employees or departments.
a. Span of control
b. Decentralization
c. Centralization
d. Delegation

_____   11.   _____ is the concentration of authority at the top of an organization or department.
a. Span of control
b. Decentralization
c. Centralization
d. Delegation

_____   12.   Which of the following is perhaps the most important factor in determining the extent of centralization?
a. complexity levels
b. cost of decisions
c. control mechanisms
d. uniformity of policies

❖3❖

_____   13.   _____ means grouping managers and employees according to their areas of expertise and the resources they use to perform their jobs.
a. Network design
b. Geographic design
c. Product design
d. Functional design

_____   14.   _____ means that all functions that contribute to a product are organized under one manager.
a. Network design
b. Geographic design
c. Product design
d. Functional design

_____   15.   _____ organizes activities around location.
a. Network design
b. Geographic design
c. Product design
d. Functional design

_____ 16. Which of the following subcontracts some or many of its operations to other firms and coordinates them to accomplish specific goals?
a. network design
b. geographic design
c. product design
d. functional design

❖4❖

_____ 17. A(n) _____ is one in which management breaks activities into separate, highly specialized tasks, relies extensively on standardized rules, and centralizes decision making at the top.
a. pooled interdependence system
b. sequential interdependence system
c. organic system
d. mechanistic system

_____ 18. _____ interdependence involves little sharing of information or resources among individuals within a unit or among units in the performance of tasks.
a. Pooled
b. Technological
c. Sequential
d. Reciprocal

_____ 19. _____ interdependence involves the need for every individual and unit to work with every other individual and unit.
a. Pooled
b. Technological
c. Sequential
d. Reciprocal

_____ 20. _____ interdependence involves the orderly step-by-step flow of information, tasks, and resources from one individual or team to another within the same unit or from one unit to another.
a. Pooled
b. Technological
c. Sequential
d. Reciprocal

ESSAY QUESTIONS

❖1❖

1. Define *organization design* and describe the two fundamentals of organizing.

2. Identify and discuss the information an organization chart provides about an organization's structure.

❖2❖

3. Define span of control and the factors that influence its appropriate size for an organization.

❖3❖

4. What are the four basic types of horizontal design?

❖**4**❖

5.   Compare and contrast mechanistic and organic systems.

CHAPTER 11
ORGANIZATIONAL DESIGN

MATCHING SOLUTIONS

1. I - Authority
2. A - Specialization
3. P - Decentralization
4. K - Accountability
5. T - Coordination
6. D - Differentiation
7. M - Functional Design
8. F - Product Design
9. S - Reciprocal Interdependence
10. L - Delegation
11. E - Responsibility
12. Q - Geographical Design
13. B - Centralization
14. H - Division of Labor
15. R - Pooled Interdependence
16. C - Network Design
17. O - Span of Control
18. G - Organization Chart
19. J - Sequential Interdependence
20. N - Mechanistic System

TRUE/FALSE SOLUTIONS

Question	Answer	Page	Explanation
1.	True		
2.	False	300	Specialization is the process of identifying particular tasks and assigning them to individuals or teams who have been trained to do them.
3.	False	300	Differentiation means that the organization is composed of units that work on specialized tasks using different work methods and requiring employees with unique competencies. Integration means that the various units must be put back together so that the work is coordinated.
4.	False	299	In general, an organization chart provides four major pieces of information about an organization's structure: tasks, subdivisions, levels of management, and lines of authority. The organizational chart shows the formal relationships. It doesn't show who has the most political influence or where the vital informal channels of communication operate.
5.	True		
6.	False	302	Authority is the right to make a decision. Responsibility is an employee's obligation to perform an assigned task.
7.	False	302	Accountability is the manager's expectation that the employee will accept credit or blame for his work. Authority is the right to make decisions.
8.	True		
9.	True		
10.	False	304	Decentralization is the delegation of authority to lower level employees or departments. Centralization is the concentration of authority at the top of an organization or department.
11.	True		
12.	False	306	Functional design group managers and employees according to their areas of expertise and the resources they use to perform their jobs. Reducing duplication or resources and increasing coordination within the functional area.

| 13. | False | 306 | Designing by function is economical because it results in a simple structure. Management creates one department for each primary function to be performed. This design keeps administrative expenses low because everyone in a department shares training, experiences, and resources. |

| 14. | False | 307 | <u>Product design</u> refers to situations where all functions that contribute to a product are organized under one manager. |

| 15. | True | | |

| 16. | False | 310 | <u>Network design</u> subcontracts some or many of its operations to other firms and coordinates them to accomplish specific goals. Sometimes called a <u>virtual organization</u>, managers need to coordinate and link up people to perform activities in many locations |

| 17. | True | | |

| 18. | False | 317 | <u>Sequential interdependence</u> involves the orderly step-by-step flow of information, tasks, and resources from one individual or team to another within the same unit or from unit to another. <u>Pooled interdependence</u> involves little sharing of information or resources among individuals within a unit or among units in the performance of tasks. |

| 19. | True | | |

| 20. | True | | |

MULTIPLE CHOICE SOLUTIONS

<u>Question</u>	<u>Answer</u>	<u>Page</u>	<u>Explanation</u>
1.	d	299	The <u>organization chart</u> is a diagram that illustrates the reporting lines between units and people within the organization. The term units is used to refer to teams, groups, departments, or divisions.
2.	b	298	<u>Organization design</u> refers to the decisions and actions that result in a structure. All organizations have a set of jobs. In fact, the existence of structure is most visible in the familiar organization chart, but it is somewhat like the tip of the iceberg.

3.	d	300	<u>Differentiation</u> means that the organization is composed of units that work on specialized tasks using different work methods and requiring employees with unique competencies.
4.	d	300	<u>Specialization</u> is the process of identifying particular tasks and assigning them to departments, teams, or divisions.
5.	a	301	The <u>hierarchy</u> is a pyramid showing relationships among levels. The CEO occupies the top position and is the senior member of top management. The CEO and members of the top management team set the strategic direction of the organization.
6.	a	301	<u>Span of control</u> refers to the number of employees directly reporting to a person. It can be either too wide, too narrow, or appropriate.
7.	c	302	<u>Responsibility</u> is an employee's duty to perform the assigned task. Employees take this obligation whenever they accept a job assignment.
8.	b	302	<u>Accountability</u> is the manager's expectation that the employee will accept credit or blame for his work. No manager can check everything an employee does. Therefore managers normally establish guidelines and performance standards within which responsibilities are carried out. As such, accountability flows from the bottom to the top.
9.	d	302–303	<u>Delegation</u> is the process of giving authority to a person (or group or team) to make decisions and act in certain situations.
10.	b	304	<u>Decentralization</u> is the delegation of authority to lower level employees or departments. It requires managers to decide what and when to delegate, to select and train personnel carefully, and to formulate adequate controls.
11.	c	304	<u>Centralization</u> is the concentration of authority at the top of an organization or department.
12.	b	305	A number of factors can affect management's decisions to centralize or decentralize authority in various areas of decision making. *Cost of decisions* is perhaps the most important factor in determining the extent of centralization. As a general rule, the more costly the outcome, the more likely top management is to centralize the authority to make the final decision.

13.	d	306	<u>Functional design</u> means grouping managers and employees according to their areas of expertise and the resources they use to perform their jobs.
14.	c	307	<u>Product design</u> means that all functions that contribute to a product are organized under one manager. Sometimes called divisional structures, they simply divide the organization into self-contained units that are responsible for developing, producing, and selling their own products and services in their own markets.
15.	b	309	<u>Geographical design</u> organizes activities around location. It allows organizations to develop competitive advantage in a particular region according to that area's customers, competitors, and other factors.
16.	a	310	A <u>network design</u> subcontracts some or many of its operations to other firms and coordinates them to accomplish specific goals. Sometimes called a virtual organization, managers need to coordinate and link up people to perform activities in many locations.
17.	d	314	A <u>mechanistic system</u> is one in which management breaks activities into separate, highly specialized tasks, relies extensively on standardized rules, and centralizes decision making at the top.
18.	a	316	<u>Pooled interdependence</u> involves little sharing of information or resources among individuals within a unit or among units in the performance of tasks.
19.	d	317	<u>Reciprocal interdependence</u> involves the need for every individual and unit to work with every other individual and unit; information and resources flow back and forth freely until the goal is achieved.
20.	c	317	<u>Sequential interdependence</u> involves the orderly step-by-step flow of information, tasks, and resources from one individual or team to another within the same unit or from one unit or another.

ESSAY SOLUTIONS

[Pages 298–300]

1. <u>Organization design</u> means quite simply the decisions and actions that result in a structure. There are two fundamental concepts around which all organizations are organized: *differentiation* and *integration*.

   a. *Differentiation* means that an organization is composed of units that work on specialized tasks using different work methods and requiring employees with unique competencies.

   b. *Integration* means that the various units must be put back together so that work is coordinated.

[Page 299]

2. An <u>organization chart</u> is a diagram that illustrates the reporting lines between units and people within the organization. It basically is the skeleton of the organization. It provides four major pieces of information about an organization's structure:

   a. The boxes represent different units (marketing, legal, human resources).

   b. The titles in each box show the work performed by that person.

   c. Reporting relationships are shown by the lines connecting superiors and subordinates.

   d. Levels of the organization are indicated by the number of vertical layers in the chart.

[Pages 301–302]

3. The <u>span of control</u> refers to the number of employees directly reporting to a person. The span of control can either be too wide, narrow, or appropriate. The following key factors can influence the span of control in any situation:

   a. The competence of both the manager and the employee.

   b. The similarity or dissimilarity of tasks being supervised.

   c. The incidence of new problems in the manager's department.

   d. The extent of clear operating standards and rules.

[Pages 305–310]

4. Management can use any of four basic types of horizontal design:

    a. *Functional design* means grouping managers and employees according to their areas of expertise and the resources they use to perform their jobs. Functions vary widely according to the type of organization. Functional units are usually found in organizations that produce a high volume of a narrow range of products. They are also particularly well suited for small organizations.

    b. *Product design* means that all functions that contribute to a product are organized under one manager. Product design divides the organization into self-contained units, each capable of designing, producing, and marketing its own goods and/or services. Organizations that have worldwide operations often use this form of departmentalization. Each product competes against competitors in its own market. They are evaluated on the basis of their profit contributions to the entire organization.

    c. *Geographical design* organizes activities around location. It allows organizations to develop competitive advantage in a particular region according to that area's customers, competitors, and other factors. This form of design allows managers to specialize in particular markets.

    d. *Network design* subcontracts some or many of its operations to other firms and coordinates them to accomplish specific goals. Sometimes called a virtual organization, managers need to coordinate and link up people to perform activities in many locations.

[Pages 314–315]

5. A <u>mechanistic system</u> is one in which management breaks activities into separate, highly specialized tasks, relies extensively on standardized rules, and centralizes decision-making at the top. This system is most appropriate when an organization's environment is stable and predictable.

    An <u>organic system</u> encourages managers and subordinates to work together in teams and to communicate openly with each other. In fact, employees are encouraged to communicate with anyone who might help them solve a problem. Decision making tends to be decentralized. Authority, responsibility, and accountability flow to employees having the expertise required to solve problems as they arise. Thus, an organic organization is well suited to a changing environment.

CHAPTER 12
ORGANIZATIONAL CHANGE AND LEARNING

LEARNING OBJECTIVES

After studying this chapter, you should be able to:

❖**1**❖   Describe four types of organizational change.

❖**2**❖   Explain the planning process for organizational change.

❖**3**❖   Identify four methods of organizational change.

❖**4**❖   Describe how innovation relates to organizational change.

❖**5**❖   Discuss how learning organizations foster change.

OUTLINE

❖**1**❖   Describe four types of organizational change.

    I.   Types of Organizational Change

        1. **Organizational Change**—refers to any transformation in the design or functioning of an organization.

            a. If an organization creates or adopts a substantially new method of production, implementing the innovation is likely to require major organizational change.

            b. Massive changes in the way an organization operates occur occasionally, but more often change occurs in small steps.

                1. The desire to improve performance continuously in order to stay ahead of competitors is a common reason for smaller organizational changes.

        2. **Radical Change**—occurs when organizations make major adjustments in the ways they do business.

        3. **Incremental Change**—is an ongoing process of evolution over time, during which many small changes occur routinely. After enough time has passed, the cumulative effect of these changes may be to transform the organization totally.

            a. <u>Tempered radicals</u> are people who strive to create radical change but do so by prodding an organization to make many small incremental changes.

            b. Tempered radicals understand that they can get more done by working as an insider in the system they want to change.

4. **Timing of Change**—degree of change and timing of change combine to form different types of change:

   a. Reactive Change—occurs when an organization is forced to change in response to some event in the external or internal environment. These changes can be incremental or radical.

   b. Anticipatory Change—occurs when managers make organizational changes in anticipation of upcoming events or early in the cycle of a new trend.

❖**2**❖ Explain the planning process for organizational change.

II. **Planning for Organizational Change**

1. Change is most likely to be orderly when it has been planned.

2. The process of planned organizational change comprises a series of steps as shown in Figure 12.3.

3. **Assess the Environment**—both the degree and rate of change in the environment have implications for organizations.

   a. The four environmental factors most responsible for stimulating organizational change are customers, technology, competitors, and the workforce.

      1. Other factors that may pressure organizations to change include globalization and the actions of important stakeholders, such as shareholders, government regulators, unions, and political action groups.

4. **Determine the Performance Gap**—a performance gap is the difference between what the organization wants to do and what it actually does.

5. **Diagnose Organizational Problems**—the aim of diagnosis is to identify the nature and extent of problems before taking action in order to develop an understanding of the reasons behind gaps in performance.

   a. All too often results-oriented managers begin the change process prematurely and impatiently push for solutions before the nature of the problem itself is clear.

6. **Articulate and Communicate a Vision for the Future**—successful change efforts are guided by a clear vision for the future.

   a. To communicate the leader's vision, messages should be sent consistently and repeatedly through varying organizational channels by credible sources.

7. **Develop and Implement an Action Plan**—an action plan articulates the goals for change and describes the specific measure to be used to monitor and evaluate progress toward those goals.

   a. Consider Alternatives—when developing an action plan, management should consider all feasible alternatives, along with their advantages and disadvantages.

      b. <u>Set Goals</u>—for changes to be effective, goals should be set before the change effort is started.

         1. If possible, goals should be: (1) stated in clear and measurable terms, (2) consistent with the organization's overall goals and policies, and (3) realistically attainable.

  8. **Anticipate Resistance and Take Action to Reduce It**—to deal successfully with resistance, managers must learn to anticipate it and then head it off, if at all possible.

      a. Some resistance to change may actually be useful. Employees can operate as a check-and-balance mechanism to ensure that management properly plans and implements change.

      b. In general, people—and sometimes even entire organizations—tend to resist change for many reasons.

         1. *Fear*—some people resist change because they fear that they will be unable to develop the competencies required to be effective in the new situation.

         2. *Vested Interests*—people who have a vested interest in maintaining things as they are often resist change.

         3. *Misunderstandings*—people resist change when they do not understand its implications.

         4. *Cynicism*—over time, employees in some organizations see change efforts come and go so often that cynicism sets in and employees refuse to support yet another change "program."

  9. **Monitor the Changes**—as the process of change unfolds, managers need to monitor employees' reactions as well as results.

❖**3**❖   Identify four methods of organizational change.

  III. **Implementing Change**

      1. **Technological Change**—involves incremental adjustments or radical innovations that affect workflows, production methods, materials, and information systems.

         a. <u>Information Technology</u> (IT)—comprises complex networks of computers, telecommunication systems, and remote-controlled devices.

      2. **Organization Redesign**—involves incremental adjustments or radical innovations focused on realigning departments, changing who makes decisions, and merging or reorganizing departments that sell the organization's products.

         a. Two basic approaches to organization redesign are changing the organization's structure and changing the organization's process.

            1. *Restructuring*—means reconfiguring the distribution of authority, responsibility, and control in an organization.

2. *Reengineering*—focuses on creating new ways to get work done. The goal is to design the most effective process for making and delivering a product.

3. **Job Redesign**—involves modifying specific employee job responsibilities and tasks. To different ways of changing job designs are:

a. Job Simplification—involves the scientific analysis of tasks performed by employees in order to discover procedures that produce the maximum output for the minimum input.

1. The job specification states the tasks to be performed, the work methods to be used, and the workflow to be obtained.

2. The downside of job simplification is that it leads to low employee commitment and high turnover.

b. Job Enrichment—involves changing job specifications to broaden and add challenge to the tasks required in order to increase productivity.

1. Job enrichment is based on the assumption that interesting and challenging work can be a source of employee satisfaction and involvement.

2. Job enrichment directly changes employees' behaviors in ways that gradually lead to more positive attitudes about the organization and a better self-image.

3. Job enrichment offers numerous opportunities for initiating other types of organizational change.

4. Job enrichment can humanize an organization.

4. **Organization Development** (OD)—is a planned, long-range behavioral science strategy for understanding, changing, and developing an organization's workforce in order to improve its effectiveness.

a. Although OD methods frequently include design, technological, and task changes, their primary focus is on changing people.

b. The three most commonly used forms of OD methods available are:

1. *Focus Group Discussion*—is a carefully planned discussion among several employees about a specific topic or issue of interest, which is led by a trained facilitator.

2. *Survey Feedback*—allows managers and employees to report their thoughts and feelings about the organization and to learn about how others think and feel about their own behaviors.

a. Accurate feedback from others about behaviors and job performance is one of the primary characteristics and values on which OD is based.

b. Feedback is obtained by means of a questionnaire, which is developed and distributed to all employees, who complete it and turn it in anonymously.

3. *Team Building*—is a process that develops the ability of team members to collaborate effectively so they can perform the tasks assigned them.

4. *Enterprise Resource Planning (ERP)*—this software is designed to be an enterprise-wide solution to all the information technology needs a company might have.

❖**4**❖   Describe how innovation relates to organizational change.

IV.   **Role of Innovation in Organizational Change**

1. **Innovation**—is the process of creating and implementing a new idea.

    a. Successful organizations understand that both innovation and change are required to satisfy their most important stakeholders.

2. **Types of Innovation**

    a. Technical Innovation—is one major type of innovation that involves the creation of new products and services.

    b. Process Innovation—involves creating a new means of producing, selling, and/or distributing an existing product or service.

    c. Administrative Innovation—occurs when creation of a new organization design better supports the creation, production, and delivery of products and services.

3. **Architecture for Innovation**

    a. Briefly, managers should:

        1. Develop a learning environment and a learning orientation among employees.

        2. Foster workforce resilience.

        3. Provide a support system for innovation.

❖**5**❖   Discuss how learning organizations foster change.

V.   **Learning Organizations**

1. **Learning Organization**—has both the drive and the capabilities to improve its performance continuously. It learns from past experiences, its learns from customers, it learns from various parts of its company, and it learns from other companies.

    a. When the environment is unstable, learning may require a lot of exploration and experimentation.

    b. When the environment is more stable, learning is more likely to occur through a systematic process of testing alternative approaches.

    c. The five interrelated building blocks of a learning organization are: shared leadership, culture of innovation, customer-focused strategy, organic organization design, and intensive use of information.

2. **Shared Leadership**—all employees in a learning organization share at least some leadership responsibilities.

    a. In a learning organization, everyone is encouraged to find ways to improve products and services and to experiment with new methods to serve the organization.

3. **Culture of Innovation**—shared leadership goes hand in hand with innovation. For learning organizations, successful innovation is a never-ending process that becomes part of the daily routine.

    a. <u>Community</u>—learning organizations develop a sense of community and trust.

        1. Everyone needs to work together, respecting each other and being able to communicate openly and honestly.

        2. Conflict and debate are accepted as responsible forms of communication.

        3. When people feel that they are part of a community, they are more willing to make the extra effort needed to find and fix problems.

    b. <u>Continuous Learning</u>—is encouraged by learning organizations.

        1. *Empowerment*—places responsibility on employees for problem finding and problem solving

        2. The flat, team-based structure found in learning organizations facilitates learning because employees are involved in a broad range of activities and work with others from whom they can learn.

        3. Formal training is another way to ensure continuous learning.

        4. For managers in particular, continuous learning is essential to develop the competencies needed by generalists who are knowledgeable in several areas, as opposed to specialists who understand only finance, production, marketing, or some other function.

4. **Customer-Focused Strategy**—learning organizations add value for customers by identifying needs and then developing ways to satisfy those needs.

5. **Organic Organization Design**—the design of learning organizations often reflects their emphasis on organic rather than mechanistic systems. They emphasize the use of teams, strategic alliances, and boundaryless networks.

    a. <u>Teams</u>—in learning organizations, employees with dissimilar expertise form multidisciplinary teams. To encourage the free flow of ideas, these teams maybe formed only as needed, on a project-by-project basis where bosses are practically nonexistent.

    b. <u>Strategic Alliances</u>—many learning organizations use strategic alliances with suppliers, customers, and even competitors as a method of learning.

c. Boundaryless Networks—refers to an extreme design option for learning organizations to become a network of cooperating units connected by complex interdependencies and separated by few boundaries.

   1. Network structures maximize the linkages between organizations and provide learning opportunities and generate innovation in products and services.

6. **Intensive Use of Information**—information is the lifeblood of learning organizations. To be effective they must undertake extensive scanning, be measurement oriented, and foster shared problems and solutions.

   a. Scanning the Environment—to ensure that they do not miss an important new trend or change, learning organizations aggressively scan both the external and internal environments for information.

      1. Large amounts of information are obtained from the external environment on how customers are reacting to current products and services, how customers compare them to those of competitors, and whether new competitors may be on the horizon.

   b. Measurement Oriented—performance measurements make assessing improvements impossible. Organizations learn to improve.

      1. To judge improvements, an organization needs to know where it was before and where it is now.

   c. Communication—by sharing information about the problems they face and the solutions they discover, employees minimize the number of times they reinvent the wheel and speed up the process of organizational learning.

MATCHING

Directions: Select the term that best identifies the statement listed below. Place the letter of the correct term in the space provided.

A. Performance Gap
B. Job Enrichment
C. Organizational Diagnosis
D. Organizational Change
E. Reengineering
F. Process Innovation
G. Organization Redesign
H. Administrative Innovation
I. Survey Feedback
J. Restructuring

K. Information Technology
L. Innovation
M. Organization Development
N. Technical Innovation
O. Focus Group Discussion
P. Technological Change
Q. Job Simplification
R. Incremental Change
S. Tempered Radicals
T. Reactive Change

____ 1. Involves creating a new means of producing, selling, and/or distributing an existing product or service.

_____ 2. Complex networks of computers, telecommunications systems, and remote-controlled devices.

_____ 3. Are people who strive to create radical change but do so by prodding an organization to make many small incremental changes.

_____ 4. The difference between what the organization wants to do and what it actually does.

_____ 5. Its aim is to identify the nature and extent of problems before taking action.

_____ 6. The process of creating and implementing a new idea.

_____ 7. Is an ongoing process of evolution over time, during which many small changes occur routinely.

_____ 8. Occurs when creation of a new organization design better supports the creation, production, and delivery of products and services.

_____ 9. Reconfiguring the levels of authority, responsibility, and control in an organization.

_____ 10. Is a carefully planned discussion among several employees about a specific topic or issue of interest, which is lead by a facilitator.

_____ 11. Changing job specifications to broaden and add challenge to the tasks required in order to increase productivity.

_____ 12. Occurs when an organization is forced to change in response to some event in the external or internal environment.

_____ 13. Refers to any transformation in the design or functioning of an organization.

_____ 14. A major type of innovation that involves the creation of new products and services.

_____ 15. An OD method that allows managers and employees to report their thoughts and feelings about the organization and to learn about how others think and feel about their own behaviors.

_____ 16. When an organization chooses to use this for creating change, it focuses its attention on workflows, production methods, materials, and information systems.

_____ 17. This emphasizes internal structural changes: realigning departments, changing who makes decisions, and merging or reorganizing departments that sell the organization's products.

_____ 18. Scientific analysis of tasks performed in order to develop ways to produce the maximum output for the minimum input.

_____ 19. Creating new ways to get work done, often involving redesigning the process related to logistics, distribution, and manufacturing.

_____ 20. A planned long-range behavioral science strategy for understanding, changing, and developing an organization's workforce in order to improve its effectiveness.

TRUE OR FALSE

Directions: Write True or False in the space provided.

❖1❖

___ 1. Massive changes in the way an organization operates occur occasionally, but more often change occurs in small steps.

___ 2. Incremental change occurs when an organization is forced to change in response to some event in the external or internal environment.

___ 3. Successful companies are equally adept at making both minor and major changes.

❖2❖

___ 4. The four environmental factors most responsible for stimulating organizational change are customers, employees, technology, and stakeholders.

___ 5. The organizational diagnosis is the difference between what the organization wants to do and what it actually does.

___ 6. The performance gap is the difference between what the organization wants to do and what it actually does.

___ 7. For a plan to be effective, those who will be affected must buy into it.

___ 8. To maximize goal effectiveness, goals should be set after the change effort has started.

___ 9. Some resistance to change may actually be useful.

___ 10. People often resist change when they don't understand its implications

❖3❖

___ 11. When an organization chooses technological change, it focuses primarily on means of reconfiguring the distribution of authority, responsibility, and control in an organization.

___ 12. Reengineering emphasizes internal structure changes.

___ 13. Job redesign focuses on creating new ways to get work done.

___ 14. The oldest task approach to change is job simplification.

___ 15. Job enrichment involves changing job specifications to broaden and add challenge the tasks required to increase productivity.

❖4❖

___ 16. Process innovation refers to the creation of new goods and services.

___ 17. Administrative innovation occurs when creation of a new organization design better supports the creation, production, and delivery of goods and services.

❖5❖

____   18. When an organization's environment is stable, learning may require a lot of exploration and experimentation.

____   19. The design of learning organizations often reflect their emphasis on mechanistic systems.

____   20. Information is the lifeblood of learning organizations.

MULTIPLE CHOICE

<u>Directions</u>: Select the best answer in the space provided.

❖1❖

____   1. _____ refers to any transformation in the design or functioning of an organization.
           a. Organizational change
           b. Organizational innovation
           c. Transgenerational structuring
           d. Innovative restructuring

____   2. Which of the following is a true statement about organizational change?
           a. Effective managers understand when change is needed and are able to guide their organizations through the change process.
           b. If a substantially new and better method of production becomes available, adopting that new method is likely to require major organizational change.
           c. Often, effective managers learn by watching what other organizations are doing.
           d. All of the above

____   3. _____ change occurs when an organization is forced to change in response to some event in the external or internal environment.
           a. Incremental
           b. Organizational
           c. Anticipatory
           d. Reactive

____   4. _____ change is an ongoing process of evolution over time, during which many small changes occur routinely.
           a. Incremental
           b. Organizational
           c. Anticipatory
           d. Reactive

❖2❖

_____ 5. The process of planned organizational change comprises the following steps except:
   a. reduce resistance.
   b. assess environment.
   c. structure evaluation.
   d. determine performance gap.

_____ 6. The environmental factor most responsible for stimulating organizational change is _____.
   a. customers
   b. technology
   c. competitors
   d. all of the above

_____ 7. The aim of a _____ is to identify the nature and extent of problems before taking action.
   a. learning organization
   b. organizational diagnosis
   c. organic organization
   d. performance gap

_____ 8. If possible, goals should be:
   a. realistically attainable.
   b. consistent.
   c. attainable.
   d. all of the above

_____ 9. Which of the following statements is <u>false</u>?
   a. To be able to reduce resistance to change, managers first of all must not be afraid of resistance.
   b. All resistance to change is unuseful and harmful to the organization and thus must be eradicated.
   c. A common obstacle to organizational change is the reluctance of managers and employees to change their attitudes and learn the new behaviors the organization requires.
   d. People who have vested interests in maintaining things as they are often resist change.

❖3❖

_____ 10. _____ focuses its attention on workflows, production methods, materials, and information systems.
   a. Organization redesign
   b. Job redesign
   c. Technological change
   d. Reengineering

____   11.   _____ emphasizes internal structural changes: realigning departments, changing who makes decisions, and merging or reorganizing departments that sell the organization's products.
   a.   Organization redesign
   b.   Job redesign
   c.   Technological change
   d.   Reengineering

____   12.   The downsides of job simplification include
   a.   low employee commitment.
   b.   high turnover.
   c.   low amount of challenge.
   d.   all of the above

____   13.   _____ is a planned, long-range behavioral science strategy for understanding, changing, and developing an organization's workforce in order to improve its effectiveness.
   a.   Organization development
   b.   Organization culture
   c.   Team building
   d.   Learning organization

____   14.   _____ is an OD method that allows managers and employees to report their thoughts and feelings about the organization and to learn about how others think and feel about their own behaviors.
   a.   Interpersonal relations
   b.   Delphi technique
   c.   Survey feedback
   d.   Team building

❖4❖

____   15.   Virtual teams and other information management systems are examples of _____ innovation.
   a.   technical
   b.   process
   c.   advanced
   d.   administrative

____   16.   Which of the following involves creating a new way of producing, selling, and/or distributing an existing good or service?
   a.   technical innovation
   b.   administrative innovation
   c.   advanced innovation
   d.   process innovation

❖5❖

___ 17. Which of the following is <u>not</u> one of the key features of an architecture for innovation?
   a. a support system for innovation
   b. a resilient workforce
   c. a state of unreadiness
   d. a learning orientation among employees

___ 18. Which of the following is <u>not</u> one of the five interrelated building blocks of a learning organization?
   a. culture
   b. mentoring
   c. use of information
   d. shared leadership

___ 19. Which of the following statements about learning organizations is <u>false</u>?
   a. Organizational memory loss is a problem facing many learning organizations.
   b. Bosses are essential and take responsibility for training, safety, scheduling vacations, and purchases.
   c. Learning organizations develop a sense of community and trust.
   d. In learning organizations, empowered employees are encouraged to identify and experiment with new methods and approaches.

___ 20. The design of learning organizations often reflects their emphasis on _____ rather than _____ systems.
   a. organic; mechanistic
   b. technology; people
   c. process; innovative
   d. mechanistic; organic

ESSAY QUESTIONS

❖1❖

1. Contrast incremental and reactive change.

❖2❖

2. Discuss the reasons why people and sometimes organizations resist change.

❖3❖

3. Explain the difference between reengineering and restructuring

❖4❖

4. Define *innovation* and discuss technical, process, and administrative innovation

❖5❖

5. Identify and briefly discuss the five interrelated building blocks of a learning organization.

CHAPTER 12
ORGANIZATIONAL CHANGE AND LEARNING

MATCHING SOLUTIONS

1. F - Process Innovation
2. K - Information Technology
3. S - Tempered Radicals
4. A - Performance Gap
5. C - Organizational Diagnosis
6. L - Innovation
7. R - Incremental Change
8. H - Administrative Innovation
9. J - Restructuring
10. O - Focus Group Discussion
11. B - Job Enrichment
12. T - Reactive Change
13. D - Organization Change
14. N - Technical Innovation
15. I - Survey Feedback
16. P - Technological Change
17. G - Organization Redesign
18. Q - Job Simplification
19. E - Reengineering
20. M - Organization Development

TRUE/FALSE SOLUTIONS

Question	Answer	Page	Explanation
1.	True		
2.	False	326	Reactive change occurs when an organization is forced to change in response to some event in the internal or external environment.
3.	True		
4.	False	330	The four environmental factors most responsible for stimulating organizational change are customers, technology, competitors, and the workforce.

| 5. | False | 330 | The aim of the <u>organizational diagnosis</u> is to identify the nature and the extent of problems before taking action. A <u>performance gap</u> is the difference between what the organization wants to do and what it actually does. |

6.   True

7.   True

| 8. | False | 332 | For change to be effective, goals should be set before the change is started. |

9.   True

10.   True

| 11. | False | 335 | <u>Technological change</u> focuses its attention on workflows, production methods, materials, and information systems. <u>Restructuring</u> typically means reconfiguring the distribution of authority, responsibility, and control in an organization. |

| 12. | False | 337 | <u>Reengineering</u> focuses on creating new ways to get work done. |

| 13. | False | 337 | <u>Job redesign</u> concentrates on changing specific employee job responsibilities and tasks. <u>Reengineering</u> focuses on creating new ways to get work done. |

14.   True

15.   True

| 16. | False | 341–342 | <u>Process innovation</u> involves creating a new way of producing, selling, and/or distributing an existing good or service. <u>Technical innovation</u> is the creation of new goods and services. |

17.   True

| 18. | False | 343 | When an organization's environment is unstable, learning may require a lot of exploration and experimentation. |

| 19. | False | 346 | The design of learning organizations often reflects their emphasis on organic rather than mechanistic systems. |

20.   True

MULTIPLE CHOICE SOLUTIONS

Question	Answer	Page	Explanation
1.	a	324	Organizational change refers to any transformation in the design or functioning of an organization.
2.	d	325	All of the statements listed are true. Successful companies are equally adept at making both minor and major changes.
3.	d	326	Reactive change occurs when an organization is forced to change in response to some event in the external or internal environment.
4.	a	325–326	Incremental change is an ongoing process of evolution over time, during which many small changes occur routinely.
5.	c	329	The process of planned organizational change comprises these seven steps: assess the environment, determine the performance gap, diagnose organizational problems, articulate and communicate a vision for the future, develop and implement an action plan, anticipate resistance and take action to reduce it, and monitor the changes.
6.	d	330	Learning organizations are keenly aware of the need to scan the environment for information that may signal the need for change. The four environmental factors most responsible for stimulating organizational change are customers, technology, competitors, and the workforce. Other factors that may pressure organizations to change include globalization and the actions of important stakeholders, such as shareholders, government regulators, unions, and political action groups.
7.	b	330	The aim of organizational diagnosis is to identify the nature and extent of problems before taking action.
8.	d	332	For change to be effective, goals should be set before the change effort is started. If possible, the goals should be (1) stated in clear and measurable terms, (2) consistent with the organization's overall goals and politics, and (3) realistically attainable.
9.	b	333	Some resistance to change may actually be useful. Employees can act as a check-and-balance mechanism to ensure that management properly plans and implements change.

10.	c	335	Technological change focuses its attention on workflows, production methods, materials, and information systems.
11.	a	336	Organization redesign emphasizes internal structural changes: realigning departments, changing who makes decisions, and merging or reorganizing departments that sell the organization's products.
12.	d	337	Job simplification involves the scientific analysis of tasks performed by employees in order to discover procedures that produce the maximum output for the minimum input. The downside of job simplification is that it leads to low employee commitment and high turnover. Most current competitive challenges require a committed and involved workforce that is able to make decisions and experiment with new ways of doing things. Many people seek jobs that allow greater discretion and offer more of a challenge.
13.	a	338	Organization development (OD) is a planned, long-range behavioral science strategy for understanding, changing, and developing an organization's workforce in order to improve its effectiveness. Although OD methods frequently include design, technological, and task changes, their primary focus is on changing people.
14.	c	338	Of the many OD methods available, one of the most commonly used is survey feedback. Survey feedback allows managers and employees to report their thoughts and feelings about the organization and to learn about how others think and feel about their own behaviors.
15.	d	341–342	Innovation is the process of creating and implementing a new idea. The creation of new products and services is one major type of innovation and is often referred to as technical innovation. Process innovation involves creating a new means of producing, selling, and/or distributing an existing product or service. Administrative innovation occurs when creation of a new organization design better supports the creation, production, and delivery of products and services. Examples of administrative innovation include virtual teams and other information management systems.

16.	d	342	<u>Process innovation</u> involves creating a new means of producing, selling, and/or distributing an existing product or service.
17.	c	343	Key features of an architecture of innovation include a learning environment and learning orientation among employees, workforce resilience, and a support system for innovation.
18.	b	344	The five interrelated building blocks of learning organizations are: shared leadership, culture of innovation, strategy, organic organization design, and intensive use of information.
19.	b	346	In learning organizations, "bosses" are practically eliminated as team members take responsibility for training, safety, scheduling vacations, and purchases. The other statements are true.
20.	a	346	The design of learning organizations often reflects their emphasis on organic rather than mechanistic systems. In particular, they emphasize the use of teams, strategic alliances, and boundaryless networks.

ESSAY SOLUTIONS

[Pages 325–326]

1. <u>Incremental change</u> is an ongoing process of evolution over time, during which many small changes occur routinely. <u>Reactive change</u> occurs when an organization is forced to change in response to some event in the external environment.

[Pages 333–334]

2. In general, people—and sometimes even entire organizations—tend to resist change for numerous reasons:

   a. *Fear.* Some people resist change because they fear that they will be unable to develop the competencies required to be effective in the new situation. A common obstacle to organizational change is the reluctance of managers and nonmanagers alike to change their attitudes and learn the new behaviors that their organizations require.

   b. *Vested Interests.* People who have a vested interest in maintaining things as they are often resist change. Successful change requires getting people to let go of vested interests and consider how a different future might actually be a better future.

    c.   *Misunderstandings*. People resist change when they do not understand its implications. Unless quickly addressed, misunderstandings and lack of trust build resistance. Getting employees to discuss their problems openly is crucial to overcoming resistance to change.

    d.   *Cynicism*. Over time, employees see change efforts come and go and eventually cynicism sets in and they refuse to support yet another change program. Organizations can reduce cynicism by involving employees throughout the change process.

[Pages 336–337]

    3. <u>Reengineering</u> focuses on creating new ways to get work done. It often involves the redesign of processes related to logistics, manufacturing, and distribution. The goal is to design the most effective process for delivering a service or product. Effective processes are those that cost the least while at the same time producing goods and providing services of excellent quality rapidly. Successful reengineering requires managers to examine the breadth of activities to be redesigned and the depth of the changes needed.

       <u>Restructuring</u> typically means reconfiguring the distribution of authority, responsibility, and control in the organization. Entire businesses or divisions might be combined or spun off.

[Pages 341–342]

    4. <u>Innovation</u> is the process of creating and implementing a new idea. Because new ideas can take various forms, many types of innovation are possible. The creation of new products and services is one major type of innovation and is often referred to as <u>technical innovation</u>. <u>Process innovation</u> involves creating a new means of producing, selling, and/or distributing an existing product or service. <u>Administrative innovation</u> occurs when creation of a new organization design better supports the creation, production, and delivery of products and services.

[Pages 343–347]

    5. A <u>learning organization</u> involves all employees in identifying and solving problems, thus enabling the organization to continuously experiment, improve, and increase its capacity to deliver new and improved goods or services to customers. The following are the five interrelated building blocks of learning organizations.

    a.   *Shared Leadership*—all employees in a learning organization share at least some leadership responsibility. Everyone is encouraged to find ways to improve products and services and to experiment with new methods to serve their organization.

    b.   *Culture of Innovation*—in learning organizations, empowered employees are encouraged to identify and experiment with new methods and approaches.

    c.   *Customer – Focused Strategy*—regardless of the strategy chosen, learning organizations need to address three key issues: customers focus, long-term perspective, and internal alignment.

    d.   *Organic Organization Design*—the design of learning organizations often reflects their emphasis on organic rather than mechanistic systems. They emphasize the use of teams, strategic alliances, and boundaryless networks.

    e.   *Intensive Use of Information Communication*—information is the lifeblood of learning organizations. To be effective they must undertake extensive scanning, be measurement oriented, and foster shared problems and solutions.

CHAPTER 13
MANAGING HUMAN RESOURCES

LEARNING OBJECTIVES

After studying this chapter, you should be able to:

❖1❖   Explain the strategic importance of managing human resources effectively.

❖2❖   Describe several important laws and government regulations that affect how organizations manage their human resources.

❖3❖   Explain the objective of human resources planning and describe how organizations respond to the unpredictability of future business needs.

❖4❖   Describe the hiring process.

❖5❖   Describe several types of training and development programs.

❖6❖   Describe several principles for improving the accuracy of managerial appraisals of employee performance.

❖7❖   Describe the basic elements of a monetary compensation package.

OUTLINE

❖1❖   Explain the strategic importance of managing human resources effectively.

    I. Strategic Importance

        1. **Human Resource Management** (HRM)—refers to the philosophies, policies, and practices that an organization uses to affect the behaviors of people who work for the organization.

            a. HRM includes activities related to staffing, training and development, performance review and evaluation, and compensation.

            b. Gaining and sustaining competitive advantage is done by meeting three conditions:

                1. Employees must be a source of value added.

                2. Employees must be "rare" or unique in some way.

                3. Competitors must not be able to copy or imitate easily the company's approach to human resource management.

     c. **Bottom-Line Consequences**—estimating the dollar value of investments in human resource activities is a topic of increasing interest to financial analysts and accountants.

       1. Investors' judgments about the value of company's human resources often are formed on the basis of reputation and other forms of public recognition for excellence.

     d. **Social Value**—In the U.S., society often judges organizations in terms of the fairness with which they treat their employees.

❖**2**❖ Describe several important laws and government regulations that affect how organizations manage their human resources.

   II.   **The Legal and Regulatory Environment**

     1. **Equal Employment Opportunity (EEO)**—states that job applicants and employees should be judged on characteristics that are related to the work that they are being hired to do and on their job performance after being hired, and they should be protected from discrimination based on their personal background characteristics, such as gender, race, ethnicity, religion, and so forth.

       a. <u>Title VII of the Civil Rights Act of 1964</u>—prohibits discrimination in all phases of employment on the basis of race, color, religion, sex, or national origin.

         1. Enforcement of U.S. EEO Laws—power to enforce Title VII rests with the *Equal Employment Opportunity Commission (EEOC)*. The EEOC has the authority to make rules, conduct investigations, make judgments about guilt, and impose sanctions.

         2. Failure to comply with EEO laws exposes a company to lawsuits.

       b. The challenge of meeting legal requirements concerning employment practices is greater for international firms because laws take many different forms in countries around the world.

     2. **Compensation and Benefits**—several laws influence compensation and benefit practices.

       a. <u>Fair Labor Standards Act (FLSA) of 1938</u>—is a federal law that specifies a national minimum wage rate and requires payment for overtime work by covered employees.

       b. <u>Equal Pay Act of 1963</u>—requires men and women to be paid equally when they are doing equal work (in terms of skill, effort, responsibility, and working conditions) in the same organization.

       c. <u>Comparable Worth</u>—is state legislation that requires employers to assess the worth of all jobs and ensure that jobs of comparable worth are paid similarly.

❖**3**❖ Explain the objective of human resources planning and describe how organizations respond to the unpredictability of future business needs.

III. **Human Resources Planning**

 1. **Human Resource Planning**—involves forecasting the organization's human resources needs and developing the steps to be taken to meet them.

  a. At the heart of planning are two tasks: determining an organization's future human resource needs and developing a strategy to meet those needs.

   1. More than 60 percent of all large firms utilize some type of expert forecasting to project HR needs.

  b. Contingent Workers—are employees who are hired by companies for specific tasks or short periods of time with the understanding that their employment may be ended at any time.

  c. Layoffs—when business is slow, many companies reduce their workforce by laying off employees.

   1. Layoffs are typically a short-term solution to difficult economic conditions or an expected decline in the company's business.

   2. The problem seems to be that managers use layoffs as a quick method of cost cutting. In the longer term, layoffs create problems because the overall trend is that the size of the labor force is growing very slowly.

  d. Competency Inventories—is a detailed file maintained for each employee that lists level of education, training, experience, length of service, current job title and salary, and performance history.

   1. There are many different competency models, but their purpose is the same: to keep track of the talent in the organization so that it can be nurtured and used effectively.

   2. Many organizations use computerized human resources information systems for storage and easy retrieval of such vital job-related information.

❖**4**❖ Describe the hiring process.

IV. **The Hiring Process**—includes activities related to the recruitment of applicants to fill open positions in an organization and the selection of the best applicants for a position.

 1. **Recruitment**—is the process of searching, both inside and outside the organization, for people to fill vacant positions. During recruitment, the organization develops a pool of job candidates from which to select qualified employees. After recruiting candidates, the organization selects those who are most likely to perform well on the job.

  a. Employers inform potential applicants about employment opportunities using a variety of methods.

1. They place ads, post notices on the company bulletin board, accept applications from people who simply walk in to their recruiting offices, and so on.

2. Instead of using just one recruiting method, most employers use multiple methods.

3. *Electronic and Other Media*—virtually every company has a Web site to which applicants as well us customers can go to learn about the company. Many of these sites have specific information about job postings, required competencies, career progression programs, mentoring, diversity initiatives, and benefits.

4. *Job Postings*—prominently display current job openings to all employees in an organization.

5. *Employee Referrals*—occur when current employees inform people they know about openings and encourage them to apply.

2. **Selection**—the process of employee selection involves deciding which of the recruits should actually be hired and for which positions. The most common forms of information for making selection decisions are:

   a. Résumés—a well-written résumé is clear, concise, and easy to read and understand.

   b. Reference Checks—because résumés can be falsified easily, managers should request references and conduct reference checks.

   c. Interviews—although commonly used, don't always predict on-the-job performance accurately. Research indicates that interviewers tend to decide about a person early in the interview and then spend the rest of the time seeking information to support that decision.

      1. Key to their success is developing a structured and systematic approach.

      2. *Situational Interviews (a.k.a. Behavioral)*—are those in which a manager or human resource professional role plays a situation you could face on the job. Observers watch how you behave and give you a score.

   d. Tests—many organizations use tests in addition to interviews to screen and select candidates.

      1. *Cognitive Ability Test*—measures general intelligence; verbal, numerical, and reasoning ability; and the like.

      2. *Personality Test*—assesses the unique blend of characteristics that define an individual.

      3. *Performance Test*—requires a candidate to perform simulations of actual job *tasks*.

❖**5**❖   Describe several types of training and development programs.

V.   Training and Development

1. **Training**—refers to activities that help employees overcome limitations and improve performance in their current jobs.

2. **Development**—refers to practices that help employees gain the competencies they will need in the future in order to advance their careers.

3. **Orientation Training**—almost all new hires need to "learn the ropes." Every organization has its own ways of doing things, which are important for employees to understand.

    a. A few hours of training during the first day or two helps ease them into their jobs.

4. **Basic Skills Training**—may be need by employees who are unable to read, write, do arithmetic, or solve problems well enough to perform even simple tasks.

5. **E-Learning**—when training is delivered using Web-based technologies. It allows employees to develop their skills at their own pace and at a time that is personally convenient.

6. **Team Training**—often seek to enhance the teamwork competency in response to such events as organizational downsizing and mergers with other firms.

    a. The jobs of many employees are likely to change in fundamental ways and hence training often is needed to help employees adjust.

7. **Career Development**—the intent of such development programs is to improve an employee's competencies in preparation for future jobs.

8. **One-on-One Mentoring and Coaching**—besides training employees in groups, some companies use more personal approaches.

    a. Mentoring—occurs when an established employee guides the development of a less experienced worker, or protégé.

    b. Coaching—an expert observes the employee in his or her job over a period of weeks or months and provides continuous feedback and guidance on how to improve.

❖**6**❖   Describe several principles for improving the accuracy of managers' appraisals of employee performance.

VI.   Performance Appraisal and Feedback

1. **Performance Appraisal**—refers to a formal, structured system for evaluating an employee's job performance.

2. **Uses of Performance Appraisal Results**—appraisal results influence who is promoted, demoted, transferred, and dismissed, and the size of raises that employees receive.

a. While it necessarily reflects the past, it isn't an end to be achieved. Rather, it's a means for moving into a more productive future.

b. Performance Feedback Sessions—is where a manager and subordinates meet to exchange information and discuss how to improve future performance.

3. **Performance Appraisal Accuracy**—there are several things that managers can do to be more accurate when conducting performance appraisals:

a. Performance Rating Scale—is used by managers to record their judgements of employee performance. The rating process is similar to assigning a grade. Performance ratings tend to be more accurate when the rating scales are precise.

b. Memory Aids—everyone involved in making appraisals should regularly record behaviors or outcomes—good or bad—that relate to an employee's performance.

c. Rater Training—rating accuracy can also be improved through training that focuses on improving the observation skills of raters.

d. Rewards—one cause of rating inaccuracy is a lack of rater motivation. Without rewards, raters may find it easier to give high ratings than to give accurate ratings.

e. Multiple Raters—360-Degree Appraisal System—measures performance by obtaining assessments of the employee from a variety of sources—supervisors, subordinates, colleagues inside the company, people outside the organization with whom the employee does business, and even a self-appraisal by the employee.

4. **Performance Appraisals for Teams**—teams frequently take full responsibility for constructing and conducting their own performance appraisals. Team members are well acquainted with each other's strengths and weaknesses, so it makes sense that they become the primary performance evaluators.

❖**7**❖   Describe the basic elements of a monetary compensation package.

VII. **Compensation**

1. **Nonmonetary compensation**—includes many forms of social and psychological rewards—recognition and respect from others and opportunities for self-development.

2. **Monetary compensation**—includes direct payments such as salary, wages, and bonuses, as well as benefits such as covering the costs of insurance plans. Two objectives of particular relevance to compensation are:

a. Attracting and retaining the talent required for a sustainable competitive advantage.

b. Maximizing productivity.

3. **Importance of Pay Fairness**—pay fairness refers to what people believe they deserve to be pain in relation to what others deserve to be paid.

4. **Base Pay**—the guaranteed pay offered for a job.

5. **Incentive Pay**—when monetary compensation is linked to the level of performance exhibited by employees.

    a. In addition to increasing importance, incentive pay can reduce turnover among good performers.

6. **Employee Benefits**—are generally defined as in-kind payments or services provided to employees for their membership in the organization.

MATCHING

<u>Directions</u>: Select the term that best identifies the statement listed below. Place the letter of the correct term in the space provided.

A. Comparable Worth
B. Orientation Training
C. Basic Skills Training
D. Contingent Workers
E. Team Training
F. Development
G. Equal Employment Opportunity
H. Fair Labor Standards Act
I. Human Resource Management
J. Title VII of the Civil Rights Act

K. Competency Inventory
L. Recruitment
M. Employee Referrals
N. Performance Appraisals
O. Situational Interview
P. Human Resource Planning
Q. Pay Fairness
R. Cognitive Ability Test
S. E-Learning
T. Mentoring

_____ 1. Is the process of searching, both inside and outside the organization, for people to fill vacant positions.

_____ 2. Refers to training delivered using Web-based technologies.

_____ 3. Training given to employees in their first day or two to help them "learn the ropes."

_____ 4. The philosophies, policies, programs, and practices that affect the people who work for an organization.

_____ 5. Is where a manager or human resource professional role plays a situation you could face on the job.

_____ 6. Requires employers to assess the worth of all jobs and ensure that jobs of similar worth are paid similarly.

_____ 7. Prohibited discrimination by employers, employment agencies, and unions on the basis of race, color, religion, sex, or national origin.

_____ 8. A written test that measures general intelligence, verbal ability, numerical ability, reasoning ability, and so on.

_____ 9. Is a detailed file maintained for each employee that lists level of education, training, experience, length of service, current job title and salary, and performance history.

_____ 10. Are employees who are hired by companies for specific tasks or short periods of time with the understanding that their employment may be ended at any time.

_____ 11. Occur when current employees inform people they know about openings and encourage them to apply.

_____ 12. Specifies a national minimum wage and requires payment for overtime work by covered employees.

_____ 13. When employers offer opportunities to help its employees attain the competencies to advance their careers.

_____ 14. The process of systematically evaluating each employee's job-related strengths, developmental needs, and progress toward meeting goals and determining ways to improve the employee's job performance.

_____ 15. Examples include training of employees who are unable to read, write, or do basic math.

_____ 16. Refers to what people believe they deserve to be paid in relation to what others deserve to be paid.

_____ 17. The principle of this legislation is that individuals not be discriminated against based on their personal background characteristics.

_____ 18. Forecasting the organization's human resources needs and developing the steps to be taken to meet them.

_____ 19. This type of training is often employed in response to company downsizing or mergers in order to help the employees work together to enhance their teamwork competency.

_____ 20. Occurs when an established employee guides the development of a less experienced worker, or protégé.

TRUE OR FALSE

Directions: Write True or False in the space provided.

❖1❖

_____ 1. Managing human resources is necessary in all organizations, from the smallest to the largest.

_____ 2. Human resource management is a system of philosophies, policies, and practices that affect the people who work for an organization.

❖**2**❖

_____　3.　Power to enforce Title VII of the Civil Rights Act rests primarily with the U.S. Attorney General's office.

_____　4.　The Equal Pay Act of 1963 specifies a national minimum wage and requires payment for overtime work covered by employees.

_____　5.　The Fair Labor Standards Act requires men and women to be paid equally when they are doing equal work.

_____　6.　The Equal Pay Act requires employers to assess the worth of all jobs and ensure all are paid similarly.

❖**3**❖

_____　7.　Less than 50% of large firms utilize some form of forecasting to project their human resource needs.

_____　8.　Estimates place the number of contingent workers at about 8 percent of the U.S. workforce.

❖**4**❖

_____　9.　The hiring process involves two primary activities: recruitment and selection.

_____　10.　Development includes activities related to the recruitment of applicants to fill open positions in an organization and the selection of the best applicants for a position.

_____　11.　Recruitment is the process of searching, both inside and outside the organization, for people to fill vacant positions.

_____　12.　Managers infrequently conduct reference checks because résumés cannot be falsified easily.

_____　13.　Most interviewers wait until the end of an interview to make a decision on the candidate.

❖**5**❖

_____　14.　Mentoring can increase an employees' competencies, achievement, and understanding of the organization.

_____　15.　The intent of development programs is to improve an employee's competencies in preparation for future jobs.

❖**6**❖

_____　16.　Performance appraisals are used to enhance organizational goal attainment by employees and not to make pay decisions.

_____　17.　During a performance feedback session, both manager and subordinate meet to exchange information and discuss how to improve performance.

_____　18.　Rater accuracy cannot be improved.

❖7❖

___ 19. Nonmonetary compensation includes many forms of social and psychological rewards.

___ 20. Comparable worth refers to what people believe they deserve to be paid in relation to what others deserve to be paid.

MULTIPLE CHOICE

<u>Directions</u>: Select the best answer in the space provided.

❖1❖

___ 1. _____ includes activities related to staffing, training and development, performance review and evaluation, and compensation.
   a. Human resource planning
   b. Human resource inventory
   c. Human resource management
   d. Replacement analysis

___ 2. Which of the following statements about gaining a sustainable competitive advantage is <u>false</u>?
   a. Employees must be a source of value added.
   b. Employees must be "rare" or unique in some way.
   c. Competitors must not be able to copy or imitate easily the company's approach to human resource management.
   d. All of the above

❖2❖

___ 3. Which of the following prohibited discrimination by employers, employment agencies, and unions on the basis of race, color, religion, sex, or national origin?
   a. Equal Pay Act
   b. Title VII of the Civil Rights Act
   c. Fair Labor Standards Act
   d. Comparable Worth Act

___ 4. The _____ of 1938 is a federal law that specifies a national minimum wage rate and requires payment for overtime work by covered employees.
   a. WHSA
   b. FLSA
   c. NLRA
   d. AWDA

_____ 5. The _____ requires that men and women be paid equally for doing equal work in the same organization.
   a. Landrum-Griffin Act
   b. Fair Labor Standards Act
   c. Equal Pay Act
   d. Griswold Employer Act

❖3❖

_____ 6. Which of the following was enacted to address the imbalances in pay in occupations dominated by women?
   a. Equal Pay Act
   b. Fair Labor Standards Act
   c. Title VII of the Civil Rights Act
   d. comparable worth legislation

_____ 7. A ____ is a detailed file maintained for each employee that lists such things as his/her level of education, experience, and training.
   a. competency inventory
   b. job description
   c. job analysis
   d. realistic preview

❖4❖

_____ 8. The _____ involves two primary activities: recruitment and selection.
   a. job analysis process
   b. competency inventory process
   c. hiring process
   d. performance appraisal process

_____ 9. Which of the following is contained in a résumé?
   a. career objectives
   b. personal data
   c. education
   d. all of the above

_____ 10. Which of the following selection devices often suffers from managers forming favorable/unfavorable impressions early and let their stereotypes affect their judgments about individual candidates?
   a. reference checks
   b. interviews
   c. résumés
   d. tests

_____ 11. Henry Alber, a vice president of a pharmaceutical company, requires all candidates who apply for sales positions to take a(n) _____ test and score high in extraversion.
   a. performance
   b. personality
   c. cognitive ability
   d. honesty

❖5❖

_____ 12. Which of the following is one of the most common sources of information for making selection decisions?
   a. interviews
   b. tests
   c. reference checks
   d. all of the above

_____ 13. The main purpose of _____ is to overcome the limitations, current or anticipated, that are causing an employee to perform at less than the desired level.
   a. training and development
   b. orientation
   c. a performance appraisal
   d. disciplinary procedures

_____ 14. Which of the following is a true statement about e-learning?
   a. Many companies are using electronic media to deliver training instead of relying on traditional classroom approaches.
   b. E-learning is delivered using Web-based technology.
   c. E-learning allows employees to develop their skills at their own pace and at a time that is personally convenient.
   d. All of the above.

❖6❖

_____ 15. _____ refers to a formal structured system for evaluating an employee's job performance.
   a. Performance appraisal
   b. Interviewing
   c. M.B.O.
   d. Human resource management

_____ 16. For which of the following means of improving performance appraisals, is it suggested that individuals record behavior—good or bad?
   a. memory aids
   b. rating scales
   c. rater training
   d. none of the above

_____ 17. Which of the following measures performance by obtaining assessments from a variety of sources including supervisors, subordinates, and the employee him/her self?
a. job analysis
b. rating scales
c. 360-degree appraisal
d. performance appraisal

❖**7**❖

_____ 18. _____ pay is intended to link at least a portion of pay to job performance to encourage superior performance.
a. Competency-based
b. Incentive
c. Job-based
d. Indirect

_____ 19. _____ includes many forms of social and psychological rewards—recognition and respect from others and opportunities for self-development.
a. Pay fairness
b. Incentive pay
c. Nonmonetary compensation
d. Base pay

_____ 20. Employees who receive _____ that is on par with the market average—or even above the market—are more likely to feel fairly paid than those who are paid below the going rate.
a. gainsharing
b. merit pay
c. incentive pay
d. base pay

ESSAY QUESTIONS

❖**1**❖

1. Define _human resource management_ and discuss what it includes.

❖2❖

2.   Explain the main provisions of the Equal Pay Act.

❖3❖

3.   Define *competency inventory*.

❖4❖

4.   Define the *hiring process* and its two primary activities.

❖5❖

5.   Discuss the concepts of training and development.

❖6❖

6.   Discuss performance appraisals.

❖7❖

7. Discuss pay fairness and the three components that employees consider to determine it.

CHAPTER 13
MANAGING HUMAN RESOURCES

MATCHING SOLUTIONS

1. L - Recruitment
2. S - E-Learning
3. B - Orientation Training
4. I - Human Resource Management
5. O - Situational Interview
6. A - Comparable Worth
7. J - Title VII of the Civil Rights Act
8. R - Cognitive Ability Test
9. K - Competency Inventory
10. D - Contingency Workers
11. M - Employee Referrals
12. H - Fair Labor Standards Act
13. F - Development
14. N - Performance Appraisals
15. C - Basic Skills Training
16. Q - Pay Fairness
17. G - Equal Employment Opportunity
18. P - Human Resource Planning
19. E - Team Training
20. T - Mentoring

TRUE/FALSE SOLUTIONS

Questions	Answer	Page	Explanation
1.	True		
2.	True		
3.	False	357	Power to enforce Title VII of the Civil Rights Acts rests with the Equal Employment Opportunity Commission (EEOC).
4.	False	359	The Fair Labor Standards Act of 1938 specifies a national minimum wage and requires payment for overtime work by covered workers.
5.	False	359–360	The Equal Pay Act of 1963 requires men and women to be paid equally when they are doing equal work in the same organization.
6.	False	360	Comparable worth legislation requires employers to assess the worth of all jobs and ensure that jobs of comparable worth are paid similarly.
7.	False	360	More than 60% of all large firms utilize some type of forecasting to project their future human resource needs.
8.	True		
9.	True		
10.	False	362	The hiring process include activities related to the recruitment of applicants to fill open positions in an organization and the selection of the best applicants for a position.
11.	True		
12.	False	366	Because résumés can be falsified easily, managers may request references and conduct reference checks. Many employers routinely check educational qualifications, including schools attended, majors, degrees awarded, and dates.
13.	False	366	Research indicates that interviewers tend to decide about a person early in the interview and then spend the rest of the time seeking information to support that decision.
14.	True		
15.	True		

16.	False	371	Performance appraisal refers to a formal, structured system for evaluating an employee's job performance. Its focus is on documenting how productive the employee is and which areas of performance could be improved. Appraisal results influence who is promoted, demoted, transferred, and dismissed, and the size of raises that employees receive.
17.	True		
18.	False	374	Rating accuracy can also be improved through training that focuses on improving the observation skills of raters.
19.	True		
20.	False	375	Pay fairness refers to what people believe they deserve to be paid in relation to what others deserve to be paid.

MULTIPLE CHOICE SOLUTIONS

Question	Answer	Page	Explanation
1.	c	354	Human resources management (HRM) is a system of the philosophies, policies, and practices that affect the people who work for an organization. It includes activities related to staffing, training and development, performance review and evaluation, and compensation.
2.	d	355	To gain sustainable competitive advantage through HRM, three conditions must be met: 1) employees must be a source of value added; 2) employees must be "rare" or unique in some way, and 3) competitors must not be able to copy or imitate easily the company's approach to HRM.
3.	b	357	Title VII of the Civil Rights Act of 1964 and its subsequent amendments, prohibits discrimination in all phases of employment on the basis of race, color, religion, sex, or national origin.
4.	b	359	The Fair Labor Standards Act (FSLA) of 1938 is a federal law that species a national minimum wage rate and requires payment for overtime work by covered employees.

5.	c	359	The Equal Pay Act requires that men and women be paid equally for doing equal work in the same organization.
6.	d	360	Comparable worth legislation requires employers to assess the worth of all jobs and ensure that jobs of comparable worth are paid similarly. If one occupation tends to be dominated by women and the other by men, chances are that the occupation dominated by women will be paid less.
7.	a	362	A competency inventory is a detailed file maintained for each employee that lists level of education, training, experience, length of service, current job title and salary, and performance history.
8.	c	362	The hiring process involves two primary activities: recruitment and selection.
9.	d	365–366	A well-written résumé is clear, concise, and easy to read and understand. It gives: (1) personal data (name, address, and telephone number), (2) career objectives, (3) education (including grade point average, degree, and major and minor fields of study), (4) work experience, highlighting special skills and responsibilities, (5) descriptions of relevant competencies, activities, and personal information, and (6) the names, addresses, and telephone numbers of references.
10.	b	366	Too often, managers form favorable impressions of candidates during an interview simply because they share superficial similarities with the manager. Also, managers may let their stereotypes affect their judgments about the candidates during the interview.
11.	b	366	A personality assesses the unique blend of characteristics that define an individual. Personality tests have no right or wrong answers. In jobs that involve a great deal of contact with other people, such as sales agents and many types of service jobs, a personality characteristic referred to as extraversion is a good predictor of future job performance. Extraverts tend to be talkative, good-natured, and gregarious—characteristics that facilitate smooth interactions with customers and clients.
12.	d	365	The most common sources of information for making selection decisions are résumés, reference checks, interviews, and tests.

13.	a	367	The main purpose of <u>training and development</u> is to overcome the limitations, current or anticipated, that are causing an employee to perform at less than the desired level. An organization may save money by recruiting trained individuals, but many organizations have found that training and development programs are preferable to hiring experienced employees.
14.	d	368	All of the statements listed about <u>e-learning</u> are true.
15.	a	371	<u>Performance appraisal</u> refers to the formal structured system for evaluating an employee's job performance. Its focus is on documenting how productive the employee is and which areas of performance could be improved. Appraisal results influence who is prompted, demoted, transferred, and dismissed, and the size of raises that employees receive.
16.	a	374	Everyone involved in making appraisals should regularly record behaviors or outcomes—good or bad—that relate to an employee's performance. Reviewing these memory aids at the time of the performance appraisal ensure that the rater uses all available and relevant information.
17.	c	374	A <u>360-degree appraisal</u> measures performance by obtaining assessments of the employee from a variety of sources—supervisors, subordinates, colleagues inside the company, people outside the organization with whom the employee does business, and even a self-appraisal by the employee.
18.	b	376	<u>Incentive pay</u> is intended to link at least a portion of pay to job performance to encourage superior performance. To be effective, incentives must be aligned with the behaviors that help achieve the organization's goals.
19.	c	375	<u>Nonmonetary</u> compensation includes many forms of social and psychological rewards—recognition and respect from others and opportunities for self-development.
20.	d	375	<u>Base pay</u> involves the guaranteed pay offered for a job. Employees who receive base pay that is on par with the market average—or even above the market—are more likely to feel fairly paid than those who are paid below the going rate.

ESSAY SOLUTIONS

[Page 354]

1. <u>Human resource management</u> (HRM) is a system of philosophies, policies, and practices that affect the people who work for an organization. It includes activities related to staffing, training and development, performance review and evaluation, and compensation.

[Pages 359–360]

2. The <u>Equal Pay Act</u> of 1963 requires men and women to be paid equally when they are doing equal work (in terms of skill, effort, responsibility, and working conditions) in the same organization.

[Page 362]

3. <u>Competency inventory</u> is a detailed file maintained for each employee that lists level of education, training, experience, length of service, current job title and salary, and performance history. Also included are assessments of the employee's competency levels in terms of the factors included in the competency model used throughout this book.

[Pages 362–367]

4. The hiring process involves two primary activities: recruitment and selection. These activities are stimulated by vacancies in the organization. Recruitment is the process of searching, both inside and outside the organization, for people to fill vacant positions. Effective recruitment not only attracts individuals to the organization, but it also increases the chances of retaining them once they are hired. Employee selection involves deciding which recruits should actually be hired and for which positions. The decision about who to select often takes into account both a person's ability to do the job and how well that person is likely to fit into the organization.

[Page 367]

5. In addition to their orientation programs, many organizations offer employees more extensive training and development experiences. The main purpose of <u>training</u> is to overcome the limitations, current or anticipated, that are causing an employee to perform at less than the desired level. <u>Development</u> refers to practices that help employees gain the competencies they will need in the future in order to advance in their careers.

[Page 371]

6. <u>Performance appraisal</u> refers to a formal, structured system for evaluating an employee's job performance. Its focus is on documenting how productive the employee is and which areas of performance could be improved.

[Pages 375–376]

7. <u>Pay fairness</u> refers to what people believe they should be paid in relation to what others deserve to be paid. When evaluating whether a company's pay is fair, employees consider three basic components of the pay system: base pay, incentive pay, and benefits. The guaranteed pay offered for a job is called the <u>base pay</u>. When monetary compensation is linked to the level of performance exhibited by employees it is referred to as <u>incentive pay</u>. <u>Employee benefits</u> are generally defined as in-kind payments or services provided to employees for their membership in the organization.

CHAPTER 14
WORK MOTIVATION

LEARNING OBJECTIVES

After studying this chapter, you should be able to:

❖1❖ Describe four approaches that can be used to explain employee motivation and satisfaction.

❖2❖ Explain how managers can use goals and rewards to improve performance.

❖3❖ Describe how jobs can be designed to be motivating and satisfying.

❖4❖ State how the organization context affects motivation and satisfaction.

❖5❖ Describe how individual differences in needs can affect employees' work.

❖6❖ Describe how understanding motivation can help managers improve employee performance and satisfaction.

OUTLINE

❖1❖ Describe four approaches that can be used to explain employee motivation and satisfaction.

I. **Understanding Motivation and Satisfaction**

1. **Motivation and Satisfaction**—<u>Motivation</u> is a psychological state that is said to exist whenever internal and/or external forces stimulate, direct, or maintain behaviors. <u>Satisfaction</u> is a psychological state that indicates how a person feels about his or her situation, based on an evaluation of the situation.

2. **Managerial Approach**—managers can directly motivate and satisfy employees through personal communication, by setting realistic goals, and by offering recognition, praise, and monetary rewards to employees who achieve those goals.

3. **Job Design Approach**—an approach to motivating employees that emphasizes the design of jobs.

4. **Organization Approach**—the broader organizational context is also important. The appropriate benefits, reward structure, and development opportunities may attract new employees to the organization. Whether such policies serve to increase employee effort and desire to stay with the company depends partly on whether employees perceive them to be fair and equitable.

5. **Individual Differences Approach**—are the needs, values, competencies, and other personal characteristics that people bring to their jobs.

   a. Instead of treating everyone alike, managers should get to know their employees personally and treat them as unique individuals.

❖**2**❖   Explain how managers can use goals and rewards to improve performance.

  II. **Managerial Approach**—three practical things managers can do to enhance motivation of their employees: (1) inspire employees through one-on-one communication, (2) to be sure that employees have specific and challenging goals that they accept and will strive to achieve, and (3) to provide employees with praise, recognition, or other rewards so they feel good about achieving those goals.

    1. **Goal-Setting Theory**—states that managers can direct the performance of their employees by assigning specific, difficult goals that employees accept and are willing to commit to.

      a. <u>Management by Objectives</u>—is a participate goal-setting technique whereby a manager and employee set objectives (goals) for the future.

        1. Both parties accept the objectives as appropriate, with the understanding that future performance evaluations and rewards will reflect the employee's progress in meeting the agreed-upon goals.

      b. <u>Feedback</u>—goal setting works best when employees receive timely feedback about the progress they are making toward achieving their goals.

      c. <u>Team Goal Setting</u>—just as goals can improve the performance of individual employees, team goals can improve group performance.

        1. Like individual goals, team goals work best if they are difficult, yet doable.

        2. To keep a team focused, it is best not to set too many team goals—usually no more than three to five.

        3. Be sure that employees understand why it's important for them to achieve the goals.

    2. **Reinforcement Theory**—states that behavior is a function of its consequences (rewards or punishments).

      a. It was developed most extensively by noted psychologist B. F. Skinner, who gained much public attention when he revealed that he raised his children strictly by reinforcement theory principles.

      b. <u>Behavior Modification</u>—reinforcement focuses on changing behaviors, thus a manager who follows the principles of reinforcement will almost certainly be able to modify employee behaviors to some extent.

        1. *Positive Reinforcement*—increases the likelihood that a behavior will be repeated by using rewards to create a pleasant consequence.

        2. *Punishment*—involves creating a negative consequence to discourage a behavior whenever it occurs.

3. *Extinction*—the absence of any reinforcement, either positive or negative, following the occurrence of a behavior

4. *Negative Reinforcement*—when people engage in behavior to avoid unpleasant consequences in the future.

3. **Self-Management**—with a bit of training, employees can learn to set their own goals, provide their own reinforcements, and even monitor their results over time.

   a. Taking an active self-management approach to job performance and career progress is one way to improve long-term outcomes.

4. **Expectancy Theory**—states that people tend to choose behaviors that they believe will help them achieve their personal goals and avoid behaviors that they believe will lead to undesirable personal consequences.

   a. Goalsharing—employees receive financial rewards when their business unit meets its goals.

   b. When making a decision to exert more effort at work, an employee would normally consider three things:

      1. *Expectancy*—*effort* is the amount of physical and/or mental energy exerted to perform a task or to learn something new. *Expectancy* refers to a person's estimate of how likely it is that a certain level of effort will lead to the intended behavior or performance result.

      2. *Instrumentality*—refers to a person's perception of how useful the intended behavior or performance will be for obtaining desired outcomes (or avoiding undesired outcomes).

      3. *Valence*—is the value (weight) that an employee attaches to a consequence.

❖**3**❖ Describe how jobs can be designed to be motivating and satisfying.

III. **Job Design Approach**

   1. **Job Characteristics Theory**—states that employees are more satisfied and motivated when their jobs are meaningful, when jobs create a feeling of responsibility, and when jobs are designed to ensure that some feedback is available.

      a. Critical Psychological States—according to the job characteristics theory, three attitudes or feelings are essential for motivation:

         1. *Experienced meaningfulness*—refers to whether employees perceive their work as valuable and worthwhile.

         2. *Experienced responsibility*—refers to whether employees feel personally responsible for the quantity and quality of their work.

         3. *Knowledge of results*—refers to the extent to which employees receive feedback about how well they are doing.

b. <u>Key Job Characteristics</u>—are objective aspects of the job design that can be changed to improve the critical psychological states.

1. *Skill Variety*—is the degree to which the job involves a variety of different work activities or requires the use of a number of skills and talents.

2. *Task Identity*—is present when a job requires completing an identifiable piece of work; that is, doing a job with a visible beginning and outcome.

3. *Task Significance*—is present when a job has a substantial impact on the goals or work of others in the company.

4. *Autonomy*—is present when the job provides substantial freedom, independence, and discretion to the individual in scheduling work and determining the procedures to be used in carrying out tasks.

5. *Feedback*—is present when work results give the employee direct and clear information about his or her performance.

c. <u>Growth Need Strength</u>—refers to a desire for personal challenges, a sense of accomplishment, and learning.

1. Employees with a strong growth need are likely to respond positively to enriched jobs.

2. Employees with a weak growth need may experience enriched jobs as frustrating and dissatisfying.

❖**4**❖   State how the organization context affects motivation and satisfaction.

IV. **Organization Approach**

1. **Herzberg's Two-Factor Theory**—an approach to motivation that states that two separate and distinct aspects of the work context are responsible for motivating and satisfying employees. These two aspects of the context he referred to as motivator factors and hygiene factors.

a. <u>Hygiene Factors</u>—the two-factor theory states that hygiene factors determine how satisfied employees feel.

1. They are the nontask characteristics of the work environment—the organizational context—that create dissatisfaction.

2. Hygiene factors need to be present, at least to some extent, to avoid dissatisfaction.

3. The presence of hygiene factors alone, however, will not motivate employees.

4. The absence of dissatisfaction is an essential, but not sufficient, condition for creating a motivated workforce.

    b. <u>Motivator Factors</u>—are apects of the organizational context that create positive feelings among employees.

        1. These factors determine whether a job is exciting and rewarding. However, their presence alone does not guarantee that employees will be productive.

        2. Motivators lead to superior performance *only* if no dissatisfiers are present.

2. **Equity Theory**—employees judge whether they've been treated fairly by comparing the ratio of their outcomes and inputs to the ratios of others doing similar work.

    a. <u>Inputs</u>—are what an employee gives to the job, (e.g., time, effort, education, and commitment to the organization) to obtain desired outcomes.

    b. <u>Outcomes</u>—are what people get out of doing the job (e.g., the feelings of meaningfulness and responsibility associated with jobs, promotions, and increased pay).

    c. Generally, six alternatives are available to employees who want to reduce their feelings of inequity:

        1. Increase their inputs to justify higher rewards when they feel that they are overrewarded in comparison with others.

        2. Decrease their inputs to compensate for lower rewards when they feel underrewarded.

        3. Change the compensation they receive through legal or other actions, such as leaving work early, forming a union, and so on.

        4. Modify their comparisons by choosing another person to compare themselves against.

        5. Distort reality by rationalizing that the inequities are justified.

        6. Leave the situation (quit the job) if inequities cannot be resolved.

❖**5**❖   Describe how individual differences in needs can affect employees' work.

V. **Individual Differences Approach**

1. **Types of Needs**—a <u>need</u> is a strong feeling of deficiency in some aspect of a person's life that creates an uncomfortable tension. That tension becomes a motivating force, causing the individual to take actions to satisfy the need, reduce the tension, and diminish the intensity of the motivating force.

2. **Hierarchy of Needs**—is an approach to motivation that suggests that people have a complex five-level set of needs, and this theory describes the order in which people seek to satisfy their desires.

    a. Psychologist Abraham Maslow believed that people have five types of needs, which he arranged in a <u>hierarchy of needs</u>: physiological (at the base), security, affiliation, esteem, and self-actualization (at the top).

1. He suggested that, as a person satisfies each level of needs, motivation shifts to satisfying the next higher level of needs.

b. <u>Physiological Needs</u>—are those for food, clothing, and shelter which people try to satisfy before all others.

c. <u>Security Needs</u>—include the desire for safety and stability, and the absence of pain, threat, and illness.

1. Many workers express their security needs as a desire for a stable job with adequate medical, unemployment, and retirement benefits.

d. <u>Affiliation Needs</u>—are the desire for friendship, love, and belonging.

1. Employees with high affiliation needs enjoy working closely with others, while employees with low affiliation needs may be content to work on tasks by themselves.

2. When an organization does not meet affiliation needs, an employee's dissatisfaction may be expressed in terms of frequent absenteeism, low productivity, stress-related behaviors, and even emotional breakdown.

3. A manager who recognizes that a subordinate is striving to satisfy affiliation needs should act supportively by encouraging others to work more closely with the employee and suggest that the employee participate in the organization's social activities.

e. <u>Esteem Needs</u>—are desires for self-respect, a sense of personal achievement, and recognition from others.

1. To satisfy these needs, people seek opportunities for achievement, promotion, prestige, and status—all of which symbolize their competence and worth.

2. When the need for esteem is dominant, managers can promote job satisfaction and high-quality performance by providing opportunities for exciting, challenging work and recognition for accomplishments.

f. <u>Self-Actualization Needs</u>—are the desire for personal growth, self-fulfillment, and the realization of the individual's full potential.

g. <u>Satisfaction–Progression Hypothesis</u>—proposes that a satisfied need is no longer a motivator and that once a need has been satisfied another emerges to take its place.

1. Research supports Maslow's view that until their basic needs are satisfied, people will not be concerned with higher level needs.

h. <u>Frustration–Regression Hypothesis</u>—later research suggests that when an individual is frustrated in meeting higher level needs, the next lower level needs reemerge and again direct behavior.

❖**6**❖   Describe how understanding motivation can help managers improve employee performance and satisfaction.

   VI.   **Guidelines for Managers**

       1.   **Enhancing Employee Motivation**—maximizing employee performance through motivation requires several actions.

          a.   Clearly communicate the organization's mission to employees and explain their contribution to the organization will help the organization realize its mission.

          b.   State the behaviors and performance achievements that are desired and explain how they will be rewarded.

               1.   By working with employees to set specific and measurable goals, managers can clarify their expectations for employees.

               2.   When setting goals, managers should be careful not to fall into the trap of focusing only on goals that are easily quantified.

          c.   Design jobs with high motivating potential.

               1.   To determine whether jobs need to be redesigned, managers should assess the degree to which employees experience their work as meaningful, feel personally responsible for their work outcomes, and receive adequate feedback.

          d.   Provide frequent and constructive feedback.

               1.   Giving appropriate feedback can be difficult, however, and inappropriate feedback may actually decrease motivation.

          e.   Provide rewards for desired behaviors and outcomes.

               1.   Effective managers ensure that the formal and informal rewards and punishments experienced by employees are aligned with the organization's desired behaviors and goal achievement.

          f.   Provide rewards that employees value.

               1.   To be motivators, rewards must be aligned with the things that employees value.

               2.   Some employees value monetary rewards above everything else, whereas others value scheduling flexibility, the opportunity to work on special projects, training and development opportunities, and so on.

          g.   Provide equitable rewards.

               1.   A well designed reward system will have little motivational value if employees misunderstand the system and rely on inferences and rumor when assessing whether the system is fair

h. Recognize that each person is unique.

1. Differences in employees' needs mean that rewards valued by one employee may not be valued by another employee

MATCHING

Directions: Select the term that best identifies the statement listed below. Place the letter of the correct term in the space provided.

A. Physiological Needs
B. Frustration–Regression Hypothesis
C. Key Job Characteristics
D. Punishment
E. Behavior Modification
F. Autonomy
G. Management by Objectives
H. Task Significance
I. Expectancy
J. Security Needs

K. Satisfaction–Progression Hypothesis
L. Reinforcement Theory
M. Esteem Needs
N. Experienced Meaningfulness
O. Task Identity
P. Goal-Setting Theory
Q. Goalsharing
R. Motivator Factors
S. Two-Factor Theory
T. Growth Need Strength

_____ 1. The extent to which the job provides substantial freedom, independence, and discretion to the individual in scheduling work and determining the procedures to be used in carrying out tasks.

_____ 2. This hypothesis states that when a need is satisfied, it ceases to be a motivator and another need emerges to take its place.

_____ 3. Is a desire for personal challenge, accomplishment, and learning.

_____ 4. Involves creating a negative consequence to discourage a behavior whenever it occurs.

_____ 5. The extent to which a job involves completing an identifiable piece of work, that is, doing a job with a visible beginning and outcome.

_____ 6. Job characteristics (challenge of the work, responsibility, recognition, achievement, and advancement and growth) that, when present, should create high levels of motivation.

_____ 7. The desires for safety and stability and the absence of pain, threat, and illness.

_____ 8. This hypothesis holds that when an individual is frustrated in meeting a higher level needs, the next lower level needs will reemerge and again direct behavior.

_____ 9. The extent to which a job has a substantial impact on the goals or work of others in the company.

_____ 10. Herzberg's approach to motivation, which states that distinct types of experiences produce job satisfaction (motivator factors) and job dissatisfaction (hygiene factors).

_____ 11. The extent to which employees perceive their work to be valuable and worthwhile.

_____ 12. The most basic human desires for food, clothing, and shelter, which occupy the first level in Maslow's hierarchy.

_____ 13. An approach to motivation that states that managers can direct the performance of their employees by assigning specific, difficult goals and providing feedback to employees about their progress in achieving those goals.

_____ 14. The belief that a given level of effort will lead to improved performance.

_____ 15. Hackman and Oldham's view that the three critical psychological states are affected by skill variety, task identity, task significance, autonomy, and feedback.

_____ 16. When the principles of reinforcement theory are used, it is commonly referred to as this.

_____ 17. This is in evidence when employees receive financial rewards when their unit meets its goals.

_____ 18. An approach to motivation that suggests that behavior is a function of its consequences (rewards or punishments).

_____ 19. A management technique whereby a manager and employee set objectives (goals) for the future.

_____ 20. The desire for personal growth, self-fulfillment, and the realization of the individual's full potential.

TRUE OR FALSE

Directions: Write True or False in the space provided.

❖1❖

_____ 1. Satisfaction is a psychological state that exists whenever internal and/or external forces stimulate, direct, or maintain behaviors.

_____ 2. According to the individual differences approach, instead of treating everyone alike, managers should get to know their employees personally and treat them as unique individuals.

❖2❖

_____ 3. When it comes it motivating employees, communication should come first.

_____ 4. Done correctly, goal setting has been shown to be effective for increasing the performance of people working in a wide range of jobs.

_____ 5. Reinforcement theory states that managers can direct the performance of their employees by assigning specific, difficult goals that employees can accept and are willing to commit to.

_____ 6. Numerous studies have documented that performance is improved when managers set goals that are specific and nearly impossible to achieve.

_____ 7. Reinforcement theory states that behavior is a function of individual differences.

_____   8. Behavior modification involves the almost certain ability to modify employee behavior through the use of reinforcement strategies.

_____   9. Negative reinforcement involves creating a negative consequence to discourage a behavior whenever it occurs.

_____   10. Examples of equity theory are choices such as whether to call in work or call in sick or whether to leave work at the official quitting time or stay late.

_____   11. With goalsharing, employees receive financial rewards when their business unit meets its goals.

❖3❖

_____   12. Experienced responsibility is a critical psychological state that refers to whether employees feel personally responsible for the quantity and quality of their work.

_____   13. Task significance is present when a job involves completing an identifiable piece of work, that is, doing a job with a clear beginning and outcome.

_____   14. According to research in the U.S., employees who work in jobs that include all five key job characteristics feel involved in their work and exert more effort compared to those working in poorly designed jobs.

❖4❖

_____   15. Hygiene factors are those aspects of the organizational context that create positive feelings among employees.

_____   16. The two-factor theory is based on the assumption that motivator and hygiene factors are similar for all employees.

_____   17. Within equity theory, feelings of meaningfulness and responsibility associated with jobs, promotions, and increased pay are called inputs.

❖5❖

_____   18. Maslow's hierarchy of needs describes the order in which people seek to satisfy their desires.

_____   19. The frustration–regression hypothesis states that a need is a motivator until it becomes satisfied.

❖6❖

_____   20. It is recommended that managers design jobs with high motivating potential.

MULTIPLE CHOICE

<u>Directions</u>: Select the best answer in the space provided.

❖1❖

_____ 1. _____ is any influence that triggers, directs, or maintains goal-directed behavior.
  a. Motivation
  b. Valance
  c. MBO
  d. Goal setting

_____ 2. The _____ approach to motivating employees focuses on the behaviors of managers—in particular their use of goals and rewards.
  a. job and organization
  b. managerial
  c. individual differences
  d. all of the above

❖2❖

_____ 3. The _____ theory states that managers can direct the performance of their employees by assigning specific, difficult goals that employees accept and are willing to commit to.
  a. acceptance
  b. goal-setting
  c. ERG
  d. performance

_____ 4. After Jim met with his superior, he felt good about his sales quota for the next year since he had participated in its development. This is an example of _____.
  a. reinforcement theory
  b. positive reinforcement
  c. behavior modification
  d. management by objectives

_____ 5. B.F. Skinner attempted to apply his theory by raising his children according the principles of rewarding desired behaviors and punishing undesirable ones. This is an example of _____.
  a. management by objectives
  b. extinction
  c. reinforcement theory
  d. goal-setting theory

_____   6.   _____ states that people tend to choose behaviors that they believe will help them achieve their personal goals and avoid behaviors that they believe will lead to undesirable personal consequences.
   a.   Reinforcement theory
   b.   Two-factor theory
   c.   Equity theory
   d.   Expectancy theory

_____   7.   With _____, employees receive financial rewards when their business unit meets its goals.
   a.   goalsharing
   b.   autonomy
   c.   task identity
   d.   experienced meaningfulness

❖3❖

_____   8.   _____ considers individual differences to be important in determining how an employee reacts to job content.
   a.   Job characteristics theory
   b.   McClelland's learned needs
   c.   B. F. Skinner's reinforcement theory
   d.   Equity theory

_____   9.   _____ in the job characteristics theory refers to the extent to which employees receive feedback about how well they are doing.
   a.   Critical feedback
   b.   Knowledge of results
   c.   Experienced meaningfulness
   d.   Experienced responsibility

_____   10.   _____ is present when the outcome gives the employee direct and clear information about his or her performance.
   a.   Feedback
   b.   Autonomy
   c.   Task identity
   d.   Task significance

❖4❖

_____   11.   Under the _____ theory, researchers discovered that the presence of a particular job characteristic, such as responsibility, might increase job satisfaction.
   a.   Herzberg's two-factor
   b.   Alderfer
   c.   Hackman-Oldham job enrichment
   d.   equity

_____ 12. Hygiene factors include all of the following <u>except</u>:
a. working conditions.
b. recognition.
c. formal status.
d. supervision.

_____ 13. _____ theory is concerned with individuals' beliefs about how fairly they are treated compared with their peers.
a. Expectancy
b. Learned needs
c. Alderfer's
d. Equity

_____ 14. Which of the following is incorrect regarding how employees react to inequity? They can
a. increase their inputs to justify higher rewards when they feel that they are overrewarded compared to others.
b. modify their comparisons by choosing another person to compare themselves against.
c. increase their inputs to compensate for lower rewards when they feel underrewarded.
d. leave the situation if the inequalities can't be resolved.

❖5❖

_____ 15. An employee who has the desire for personal growth and self-fulfillment is experiencing a(n) _____ need.
a. affiliation
b. self-esteem
c. self-actualization
d. internal

_____ 16. Noel Abber works at a restaurant and has exhibited a number of difficulties lately. Noel's productivity is low, he is frequently absent, and has been very stressed at work. Which of Maslow's hierarchy of needs is not satisfied?
a. security
b. esteem
c. self-actualization
d. affiliation

_____ 17. The _____ hypothesis proposes that a satisfied need is no longer a motivator and that once a need has been satisfied another emerges to take its place.
a. emergence–progression
b. valance–regression
c. satisfaction–progression
d. frustration–regression

_____ 18. The _____ hypothesis holds that, when an individual is frustrated in meeting higher level needs, the next lower needs reemerge and again direct behavior.
a. emergence–progression
b. valance–regression
c. satisfaction–progression
d. frustration–regression

❖6❖

_____ 19. Managers can increase employee motivation levels by _____.
a. clearly communicating the organization's mission to employees and explain how their contribution to the organization will help the organization realize its
b. stating the behaviors and performance achievements that are desired and explain how they will be rewarded
c. designing jobs with high motivating potential
d. all of the above

_____ 20. Managers can increase employee motivation levels by _____.
a. providing frequent and constructive frequent feedback
b. providing rewards that employees value
c. providing equitable rewards
d. all of the above

ESSAY QUESTIONS

❖1❖

1. Define *motivation* and its four general approaches.

❖2❖

2. Explain goal-setting theory.

3. Identify and discuss the components of expectancy theory.

❖3❖

4. What are the five key job characteristics that are included in the job characteristics theory?

❖4❖

5. Explain Herberg's two-factor theory.

❖5❖

6. Define both the satisfaction–progression and frustration–regression hypotheses.

❖6❖

7. Describe the design and implementation of an effective performance management system.

CHAPTER 14
WORK MOTIVATION

MATCHING SOLUTIONS

1. F - Autonomy
2. K - Satisfaction–Progression Hypothesis
3. T - Growth Need Strength
4. D - Punishment
5. O - Task Identity
6. R - Motivator Factors
7. J - Security Needs
8. B - Frustration–Regression Hypothesis
9. H - Task Significance
10. S - Two-Factor Theory
11. N - Experienced Meaningfulness
12. A - Physiological Needs
13. P - Goal-Setting Theory
14. I - Expectancy
15. C - Key Job Characteristics
16. E - Behavior Modification
17. Q - Goalsharing
18. L - Reinforcement Theory
19. G - Management by Objectives
20. M - Esteem Needs

TRUE/FALSE SOLUTIONS

Question	Answer	Page	Explanation
1.	False	384	Satisfaction is a psychological state that indicates how a person feels about his or her situation, based on an evaluation of the situation. Motivation is a psychological state that exists whenever internal and/or external forces stimulate, direct, or maintain behaviors.
2.	True		
3.	True		
4.	True		

5.	False	387	<u>Goal-setting theory</u> states that managers can direct the performance of their employees by assigning specific, difficult goals that employees accept and are willing to commit to.
6.	False	388	Numerous studies have documented that performance is improved when managers set goals that are specific and difficult. In addition, employees must accept the goals as reasonable—that is, they shouldn't be so difficult they are considered impossible to achieve.
7.	False	390	<u>Reinforcement theory</u> states that behavior is a function of its consequences. Positive consequences are referred to as rewards and negative consequences are known as punishments.
8.	True		
9.	False	393	<u>Negative reinforcement</u> is when employees engage in a behavior in anticipation of avoiding unpleasant consequences in the future. <u>Punishment</u> involves creating a negative consequence to discouraging a behavior whenever it occurs.
10.	False	394	<u>Expectancy theory</u> states that people tend to choose behaviors that they believe will help them achieve their personal goals and avoid behaviors that they believe will lead to undesirable personal consequences. Examples of choices that are related to work performance include whether to go to work or call in sick, whether to leave work at the official quitting time or stay late, and whether to exert a great deal of effort or to work at a more relaxed pace.
11.	True		
12.	True		
13.	False	400	<u>Task significance</u> is present when a job has a substantial impact on the goals or work of others in the company. <u>Task identity</u> is present when a job involves completing an identifiable piece of work, that is, doing a job with a clear beginning and outcome.
14.	True		
15.	False	402	<u>Hygiene factors</u> are the nontask characteristics of the work environment—the organizational context—that create dissatisfaction. <u>Motivator factors</u> are aspects of the organizational context that create positive feelings among employees.

16.	True		
17.	False	404	<u>Outcomes</u> are what people get out of doing their jobs (e.g., feelings of meaningfulness and responsibility associated with jobs, promotions and increased pay are called inputs).
18.	True		
19.	False	409	The <u>frustration–regression hypothesis</u> holds that, when an individual is frustrated in meeting higher level needs, the next lower level needs reemerge and again direct behavior. The satisfaction–progression hypothesis states that a need is a motivator until it becomes satisfied.
20.	True		

MULTIPLE CHOICE SOLUTIONS

<u>Question</u>	<u>Answer</u>	<u>Page</u>	<u>Explanation</u>
1.	a	384	<u>Motivation</u> is a psychological state that exists whenever internal and/or external forces stimulate, direct, or maintain behaviors.
2.	b	385	<u>Managerial approaches</u> to motivating employees focuses on the behaviors of managers—in particular their use of goals and rewards.
3.	b	387	<u>Goal-setting theory</u> states that managers can direct the performance of their employees by assigning specific, difficult goals that employees accept and are willing to commit to. Providing feedback to employees about their program toward achieving those goals is also important if the goals are to be an effective motivator.
4.	d	389	<u>Management by objectives</u> is a participative goal-setting technique used in many types of organizations in the United States. The manager and employee agree to a set of goals that both parties accept as appropriate, with the understanding that future performance evaluations and rewards will reflect the employee's progress toward the agreed-upon goals.

5.	c	390	Reinforcement is sometimes referred to as behavior modification where the desired outcome is the changing of an individual's behavior. B.F. Skinner gained much public attention—and generated considerable controversy—when he revealed that he raised his children strictly by reinforcement principles.
6.	d	394	Expectancy theory states that people tend to choose behaviors that they believe will help them achieve their personal goals and avoid behaviors that they believe will lead to undesirable personal consequences.
7.	a	394	With goalsharing, employees receive financial rewards when their business unit meets its goals.
8.	a	399	Unlike the two-factor theory, job characteristics theory considers individual differences to be important in determining how an employee reacts to job content. In particular, employees' growth needs influence how they react to their jobs.
9.	b	399	The job characteristics theory states that three critical psychological states are needed to create high levels of motivation in the workplace. Experienced meaningfulness refers to whether employees perceive their work as valuable and worthwhile. Experienced responsibility refers to whether employees feel personally responsible for the quantity and quality of their work. Knowledge of results refers to the extent to which employees receive feedback about how well they are doing. When all three of these psychological states are experienced, employee motivation is high.
10.	a	400	Feedback is present when the outcome gives the employee direct and clear information about his or her performance
11.	a	402	Herzberg's two-factor theory identifies aspects of the job and organizational contexts that contribute to satisfaction and motivation. Herzberg initially examined the relationship between job satisfaction and productivity for 200 accountants and engineers. In carrying out their research, Herzberg and his associates asked participants to describe job experiences that produced good and bad feelings about their jobs. The researchers discovered that the presence of a particular job characteristic, such as responsibility, might increase job satisfaction.

12.	b	402	Motivator factors are aspects of the job and organizational contexts that create positive feelings among employees. Motivator factors are job characteristics (challenge of the work itself, responsibility, recognition, achievement, advancement, and growth) that, when present, should create high levels of motivation. Motivators lead to superior performance only if no dissatisfiers are present. Hygiene factors are the nontask characteristics of the work environment that create dissatisfaction. They include aspects of the environment that are closely associated with the job (e.g., compensation and level of responsibility) and certain aspects of the broader organization (working conditions, company policies, supervision, co-workers, salary, formal status, and job security). They need to be present, at least to some extent, to avoid dissatisfaction.
13.	d	404	The equity theory is an approach to motivation that is concerned with individuals' beliefs about how fairly they are treated compared with peers, based on their relative levels of inputs and outcomes.
14.	c	406	They can decrease their inputs to compensate for lower rewards when they feel underrewarded.
15.	c	408	Self-actualization needs are the desire for personal growth, self-fulfillment, and the realization of the individual's full potential. Physiological needs are those for food, clothing, and shelter. Security needs include the desire for safety and stability, and the absence of pain, threats, and illness. Affiliation needs are the desire for friendship, love, and belonging. Esteem needs are the desire for self-respect, a sense of personal achievement, and recognition from others.
16.	d	408	Affiliation needs are the desire for friendship, love, and belonging. Employees with high affiliation needs enjoy working closely with others. Employees with low affiliation needs may be content to work on tasks by themselves. When an organization does not meet affiliation needs, an employee's dissatisfaction may be expressed in terms of frequent absenteeism, low productivity, stress-related behaviors, and even emotional breakdown.

17.	c	409	The <u>satisfaction–progression hypothesis</u> proposes that a satisfied need is no longer a motivator and that once a need has been satisfied another emerges to take its place. In general, lower level needs must be satisfied before higher needs become strong enough to motivate behavior. Thus people are always striving to satisfy some higher need.
18.	d	409	The <u>frustration-regression hypothesis</u> holds that, when an individual is frustrated in meeting higher level needs, the next lower needs reemerge and again direct behavior.
19.	d	410–411	All of the statements are true. By clearly communicating the organization's mission to employees and explaining how their contribution to the organization will help the organization realize its mission will help increase employee motivation levels. Stating the behaviors and performance achievements that are desired and explaining how they will be rewarded, designing jobs with high motivating potential will increase employee motivation levels.
20.	d	410–411	All of the statements are true. By providing frequent and constructive frequent feedback, rewards that employees value and equitable rewards, managers can increase employee motivation levels.

ESSAY SOLUTIONS

[Pages 384–386]

1. <u>Motivation</u> is a psychological state that exists whenever internal and/or external forces stimulate, direct, or maintain behaviors. The four approaches include: (1) the managerial approach, which focuses on the behavior of managers—in particular, their use of goals and rewards, (2) the job design approach, which emphasizes the design of jobs, (3) the organization approach which looks at motivation in a broader organizational context, and finally (4) the individual differences approach, which treats motivation and satisfaction as characteristics of individuals.

[Page 387]

2. <u>Goal-setting theory</u> states that managers can direct the performance of their employees by assigning specific, difficult goals that employees accept and are willing to commit to. Done correctly, goal setting has been shown to be effective for increasing the performance of people working in a wide range of jobs.

[Pages 394–397]

3.   <u>Expectancy theory</u> states that people tend to choose behaviors that they believe will help them achieve their goals (e.g., a promotion or job security) and avoid behaviors that they believe will lead to undesirable consequences (e.g., a demotion or criticism).

When making behavioral choices, employees normally consider questions of expectancy, instrumentality, and valence. <u>Expectancy</u> is the belief that a certain level of effort will lead to improved performance. Employees who believe that exerting more effort results in better performance generally show higher levels of performance than employees who do not believe that their efforts will pay off. <u>Instrumentality</u> is the perceived usefulness of performance as a means for obtaining desired outcomes (or avoiding undesired outcomes). To be willing to expend the effort needed to achieve the desired performance, employees must believe that the performance is instrumental to them. The <u>valence</u> of an outcome associated with performance is the weight that a particular employee attaches to the outcome. Valences are subjective; the same outcome may have a high valence for one person and a low valence for another.

[Pages 399–401]

4.   Job characteristics theory suggests that the three critical psychological states are affected by five key job characteristics. <u>Key job characteristics</u> are objective aspects of the job design that can be changed to improve the critical psychological states.

a.   *Skill Variety*—the degree to which the job involves many different work activities or requires several skills and talents.

b.   *Task Identity*—is present when a job involves completing an identifiable piece of work, that is, doing a job with a visible beginning and outcome.

c.   *Task Significance*—is present when a job has a substantial impact on the goals or work of others in the company.

d.   *Autonomy*—is present when the job provides substantial freedom, independence, and discretion to the individual in scheduling work and determining the procedures to be used in carrying out tasks.

e.   *Feedback*—is present when work results give the employee direct and clear information about his or her performance.

This theory argues that employees are motivated to the extent that their jobs have all five of these key job characteristics. When all are present at a significant level, employees feel involved in their work, and involved employees exert more effort.

[Pages 402–403]

5.   Herzberg's <u>two-factor theory</u> states that two separate and distinct aspects of the work context are responsible for motivating and satisfying employees. <u>Hygiene factors</u> are the nontask characteristics of the work environment that create dissatisfaction. <u>Motivator factors</u> are aspects of the organizational context that create positive feelings among employees.

[Page 409]

6. The <u>satisfaction–progression hypothesis</u> proposes that a satisfied need is no longer a motivator and that once a need has been satisfied another emerges to take its place. In general, lower level needs must be satisfied before higher needs become strong enough to motivate behavior. Thus, people are always striving to satisfy some higher need. The <u>frustration–regression hypothesis</u> holds that, when an individual is frustrated in meeting higher level needs, the next lower level needs reemerge and again direct behavior.

[Pages 410–411]

7. <u>Effective performance management systems</u> reflect the key principles of several theories of motivation. These principles include clearly communicating the organization's mission to employees and explaining how their contribution to the organization will help the organization realize its mission, stating the behaviors and performance achievements that are desired and explaining how they will be rewarded, designing jobs with high motivating potential, providing frequent and constructive feedback, providing rewards for desired behaviors and outcomes, providing rewards that employees value, providing equitable rewards, and recognizing that each person is unique.

CHAPTER 15
DYNAMICS OF LEADERSHIP

LEARNING OBJECTIVES

After studying this chapter, you should be able to:

❖**1**❖   Explain what leadership means.

❖**2**❖   Describe the personal characteristics that enable leaders to be effective.

❖**3**❖   Describe the types of behaviors required for leadership.

❖**4**❖   Identify the contingencies that may shape how leaders behave.

❖**5**❖   State the key characteristics and behaviors of transformational leadership.

❖**6**❖   Describe how organizations develop leaders.

OUTLINE

❖**1**❖   Explain what leadership means.

    I.   **The Meaning of Leadership**

        1. **Leadership**—is an influence relationship among leaders and followers who strive for real change and outcomes that reflect their shared purposes.

            a. <u>Influence</u> is perhaps the most essential aspect of leadership. Managers use many means to influence subordinates which include the authority of their *formal positions*, *coercion*, *expertise*, and *charisma*.

            b. <u>Shared Purposes</u>—leaders often strive to create a vision that reflects the concerns and aspirations of followers.

            c. <u>Change</u>—the need for change is constant in modern organizations yet for a variety of reasons, employees often resist change.

❖**2**❖   Describe the personal characteristics that enable leaders to be effective.

    II.   **Personal Characteristics of Effective Leaders**

        1. The personal characteristics of leaders are the relatively stable attributes that make each person unique, including their physical, social, and psychological traits.

2. **Emotional Intelligence**—is a group of abilities and traits that enable individuals to recognize and understand their own and others' feelings and emotions and to use these insights to guide their own thinking and actions. Emotional intelligence includes such traits as:

   a. Self-Awareness—is the ability to recognize and understand your moods, emotions, and drives, as well as their impact on others.

   b. Self-control—which is the ability to regulate and redirect one's own disruptive impulses and moods.

   c. Social Awareness—is the ability to understand the emotional makeup of other people, and the skill to treat people according to their emotional reactions.

   d. Social Skill—is the ability to build social networks, manage relationships, find common ground, and build rapport.

❖**3**❖ Describe the types of behaviors required for leadership.

III. **Leadership Behaviors**

1. **Behavioral Models**—leadership models that focus on differences in the actions of effective and ineffective leaders.

   a. Because behaviors can be learned, individuals can be trained to lead more effectively.

2. **Theory X and Theory Y**—are a way to contrast two sets of assumptions and beliefs held by leaders. What separates them are their assumptions about what motivates their subordinates and what are the best ways to carry out management responsibilities.

   a. Theory X—is a composite of propositions and underlying beliefs that take a command and control view of management based on a negative view of human nature.

      1. Theory X managers view management as a process that involves directing, controlling, and modifying their subordinates' behaviors to fit the needs of the organization.

      2. They view employees as basically lazy and self-centered and thus must be persuaded, rewarded, punished, and their activities tightly controlled.

   b. Theory Y—is a composite of propositions and beliefs that take a leadership and empowering view of management based on a positive view of human nature.

      1. According to this view, employees are not by nature passive or resistant to organizational needs.

      2. The motivation, the potential for development, the capacity for assuming responsibility, and the readiness to direct behavior toward organizational goals are all present in employees.

3. **Managerial Grid**—identifies five leadership styles that combine different proportions of concern for production and concern for people.

   a. <u>Impoverished</u>—is characterized by low concern for both people and production.

      1. The primary objective of managers who use this style is to stay out of trouble.

      2. They pass orders along to employees, go with the flow, and make sure that they can't be held accountable for mistakes.

      3. They exert the minimum effort required to get the work done and avoid being fired or demoted.

   b. <u>Country Club</u>—is identified as a high concern for people and a low concern for production.

      1. Managers who use this style try to create a secure and comfortable atmosphere and trust that their subordinates will respond positively.

      2. Attention to the need for satisfying relationships leads to a friendly, if not necessarily productive, atmosphere and work tempo.

   c. <u>Produce or Perish</u>—is characterized by a high concern for production and a low concern for people.

      1. Managers who use this style do not consider employees' personal needs to be relevant to achieving the organization's objectives.

      2. They use their legitimate and coercive influence tactics to pressure subordinates to meet production quotas.

      3. They believe that operational efficiency results from arranging the work so that employees merely have to follow orders.

   d. <u>Middle of the Road</u>—managers who use this style believe that the needs of people and organizations are in conflict and so it is difficult to satisfy both.

      1. Adequate performance is obtained by maintaining employee morale at a level sufficient to get the work done.

   e. <u>Team</u>—shows high levels of concern for both people and production.

      1. Leaders who use this style attempt to establish cohesion and foster feelings of commitment among workers.

      2. By introducing a "common stake" in the organization's purposes, the leader builds relationships of trust and respect.

❖**4**❖ Identify the contingencies that may shape how leaders behave.

IV. **Contingencies for Leadership Behavior**

1. **Contingency Models of Leadership**—is based on the idea that the situation determines the best style to use.

2. **Situational Leadership® Model**—states that the style of leadership used should be matched to the level of readiness of followers. It contains three basic components:

   a. Leadership Styles—according to the model, leaders can choose from among four leadership styles: *telling, selling, participating* and *delegating*. These four leadership styles involve combinations of two forms of behavior:

      1. *Task Behavior*—includes using one-way communication, spelling out duties, and telling followers what to do and where, when, and how to do it.

      2. *Relationship Behavior*—includes using two-way communication, listening, encouraging, and involving followers in decision making, and giving emotional support.

   b. Situational Contingency—according to this model, leaders should consider the situation before deciding which leadership style to use. The situational contingency in this model is the degree of follower *readiness*.

      1. *Readiness*—is a follower's ability to set high but attainable task-related goals and a willingness to accept responsibility for reaching them.

   c. Choosing a Leadership Style—the appropriate leadership style depends on the level of follower readiness.

      1. *Telling Style*—the leader provides clear instructions, gives specific directions, and supervises the work closely.

      2. *Selling Style*—the leader provides direction, encourages two-way communication, and helps build confidence and motivation on the part of the follower.

      3. *Participating style*—the leader encourages followers to share ideas and facilitates the work by being encouraging and helpful to subordinates.

      4. *Delegating style*—the leader turns over responsibility for making and implementing decisions to followers.

   d. Assessment—the Situational Leadership® Model helps leaders recognize that the same leadership style may be effective in some situations but not others. Furthermore, it highlights the importance of considering the followers' situation when choosing a leadership style.

      1. Like other contingency models, this one assumes that managers can accurately assess each situation and change their leadership styles to match different situations.

3. **Vroom–Jago Leadership Model**—prescribes a leader's choices among five leadership styles based on seven contingency variables, recognizing the time requirements and other costs associated with each style.

   a. Leadership Styles—the focus of this model is on how leaders involve a team of followers when making decisions. This model identifies five basic leadership styles:

      1. *Decide style*—the leader makes the decision and either announces or sells it to the team.

      2. *Consult Individually Style*—the leader presents the problem to team members individually, getting their ideas and suggestions without bringing them together as a group, and then makes the decision.

      3. *Consult Group Style*—the leader presents the problem to team members in a meeting, gets their suggestions, and then makes the decision.

      4. *Facilitate Style*—the leader presents the problem to the team in a meeting and acts as a facilitator, defining the problem to be solved and the constraints within which the decision must be made.

      5. *Delegate Style*—the leader permits the team to make the decision within prescribed limits.

   b. Situational Contingencies—the seven variables include:

      1. *Decision Significance*—How important is the technical quality of this decision?

      2. *Importance of Commitment*—How important is it for followers to be committed to the decision?

      3. *Leader Expertise*—Does the leader have the relevant information and competencies required to understand the problem fully and select the best solution?

      4. *Likelihood of Commitment*—If the leader makes the decision, will followers trust the leader's judgment?

      5. *Team Support*—Do the followers share the goals to be achieved by solving this problem?

      6. *Team Expertise*—Does the leader believe that followers have the abilities and information to make a high-quality decision?

      7. *Team Competence*—Are the followers capable of handling their own decision-making process?

     c. <u>Assessment</u>—if leaders can diagnose contingencies correctly, choosing the best leadership style for those situations becomes easier. These choices will enable them to make high-quality, timely decisions.

        1. Limitations:

            a. Most employees have a strong desire to participate in decisions affecting their jobs, regardless of the model's recommendation of a leadership style.

            b. Certain competencies of the leader play a key role in determining the relative effectiveness of the model.

❖**5**❖   State the key characteristics and behaviors of transformational leadership.

   V.   **Transformational Leadership**

      1. **Transformational Leaders**—inspire others with their vision, often promote this vision over opposition, and demonstrate confidence in themselves and their views. Although each transformational leader may be stronger in terms of some characteristics than others, all are likely to be present:

        a. <u>Visionary</u>—perhaps the most important characteristic that transformational leaders possess is their ability to create a vision that binds people to each other.

        b. <u>Charismatic and Ethical</u>—transformational leaders are charismatic, but not all charismatic leaders are transformational leaders.

            1. *Charismatic Leaders*—have the ability to influence others because of their inspirational qualities.

            2. Transformational leaders are charismatic and ethical.

        c. <u>Trustworthy</u>—transformational leaders strive to be ethical in their relations with others and are viewed as trustworthy.

        d. <u>Thoughtful</u>—transformational leaders are agents of thoughtful change and innovation. They challenge followers to build on their vision by offering innovative solutions and new ideas.

        e. <u>Considerate</u>—transformational leaders care about the needs of others and have a great capacity for empathy.

        f. <u>Confident</u>—transformational leaders project optimism and self-confidence.

❖**6**❖   Describe how organizations develop leaders.

VI.   **Leadership Development**

1. **On-the-Job Learning**—is important for all aspects of managerial work.

   a. Early in a person's career, working as an individual contributor on team projects provides many opportunities for learning effective leadership.

   b. Being a formal leader of a project allows an employee to use different types of power and observe how people react to the employee's attempt to influence them.

   c. On-the-job learning is most effective for people who take personal responsibility for their own development.

2. **Leadership Assessment and Training programs**—generally include evaluating the individual's style of leadership and providing educational experiences designed to improve the individual's effectiveness as a leader.

3. **Coaching and Mentoring**—leaders who prefer a more personal approach can hire a personal leadership coach or work with a mentor.

   a. Personal coaches can provide an intensive leadership development experience, but they can be quite expensive.

   b. Mentors are most often managers or senior colleagues in the organization who provide advice and guidance about a variety of career-related concerns.

      1. Mentors can help a manager understand how others respond to his or her behaviors and point out weaknesses or blind spots.

      2. Mentors also serve as role models that a manager can emulate, and provide valuable advice concerning the styles of leadership favored in the organization.

      3. Mentors often assist a manager in developing leadership capabilities by helping the manager find assignments that will foster on-the-job learning.

MATCHING

<u>Directions</u>: Select the term that best identifies the statement listed below. Place the letter of the correct term in the space provided.

A. Charismatic Leaders
B. Middle-of-the-Road Style
C. Team Style
D. Self-Awareness
E. Managerial Grid
F. Emotional Intelligence
G. Theory Y
H. Self-Control
I. Leadership
J. Readiness

K. Country Club Style
L. Produce or Perish Style
M. Task Behavior
N. Social Awareness
O. Social Skill
P. Delegating Style
Q. Transformational Leaders
R. Mentors
S. Team Expertise

_____ 1. Individuals that have an unshakable belief in their mission, are supremely confident that they and their followers can succeed, and have the ability to convey these certainties to their followers.

_____ 2. Is the ability to build social networks, manage relationships, find common ground, and build rapport.

_____ 3. Is a follower's ability to set high but attainable task-related goals and a willingness to accept responsibility for reaching them.

_____ 4. Consistent with Theory Y, leaders who use this style attempt to establish teamwork and foster feelings of commitment among workers.

_____ 5. Where the leader believes that followers have the abilities and information to make a high-quality decision.

_____ 6. Inspire others with their vision, and often promote this vision over opposition, and demonstrate confidence in themselves and their views.

_____ 7. Is a group of abilities and traits that enable individuals to recognize and understand their own and others' feelings and emotions and to use these insights to guide their own thinking and actions.

_____ 8. Influencing others to act toward the attainment of a goal.

_____ 9. Includes using one-way communication, spelling out duties, and telling followers what to do and where, when and how to do it.

_____ 10. Is the ability to regulate and redirect one's own disruptive impulses and moods.

_____ 11. Most often are managers or senior colleagues in the organization who provide advice and guidance about a variety of career-related concerns.

_____ 12. Recognition that others are ready to accomplish a particular task and are both competent and motivated to take full responsibility for it.

_____ 13. Is a composite of propositions and beliefs that take a leadership and empowering view of management based on a positive view of human nature.

_____ 14. Managers who use this style believe that the needs of people and organizations are in conflict and so it is difficult to satisfy both.

_____ 15. Is the ability to understand the emotional makeup of other people, and the skill to treat people according to their emotional reactions.

_____ 16. This style is characterized by a high concern for people and a low concern for production.

_____ 17. This is the ability to recognize and understand your moods, emotions, and drives, as well as their impact on others.

_____ 18. Are reflected by having a high concern for production and a low concern for people.

_____ 19. A model that identifies five leadership styles, each combining different proportions of concern for production and concern for people.

TRUE OR FALSE

Directions: Write True or False in the space provided.

❖1❖

_____ 1. Motivation is an influence relationship among leaders and followers who strive for real change and outcomes that reflect the shared purposes.

_____ 2. If subordinates believe their managers have more knowledge or technical skill than they do, they will accept the manager's view more easily.

_____ 3. Leaders who use their expertise and charisma to influence others are most effective in creating a sense of commitment.

❖2❖

_____ 4. Self-monitoring is the ability to recognize and understand your moods, emotions, and drives, as well as their impact on others.

_____ 5. Social awareness is the ability to build social networks, manage relationships, find common ground, and build rapport.

❖3❖

_____ 6. Because leadership behaviors can be learned, individuals can become effective leaders with the proper encouragement and support.

_____ 7. According to McGregor, Theory Y managers could be found everywhere in organizations and thus he argued for extensive use of management by direction.

_____ 8. Leaders who use the country club style do not consider employees' personal needs to be relevant to achieving the organization's objectives.

❖4❖

_____ 9. According to contingency models of leadership, the situation determines the best style to use.

_____ 10. Relationship behavior includes using one-way communication, spelling out duties, and telling followers what to do and where, when, and how to do it.

_____ 11. Readiness is a follower's ability to set high but attainable task-related goals and a willingness to accept responsibility for reaching them.

_____ 12. In using a telling style, the leader provides direction, encourages two-way communication, and helps build confidence and motivation on the part of the follower.

_____ 13. The facilitate style of leadership is typified by a leader that presents the problem to team members in a meeting, gets their suggestions, and then makes the decision.

_____ 14. Leader expertise is the degree to which the leader has relevant information and competencies to understand the problem fully and select the best solution.

❖5❖

_____ 15. Transformational leaders inspire others with their vision, often promote this vision over opposition, and demonstrate confidence in themselves and their views.

_____ 16. A charismatic leader is a person who has the ability to influence others because of his or her position of authority within the organization.

_____ 17. The Greek word kharisma means "able to motivate."

❖6❖

_____ 18. On-the-job learning is most effective for people who take personal responsibility for their own development.

_____ 19. Leadership assessment and training programs generally include evaluating the individual's style of leadership and providing educational experiences designed to improve the individual's effectiveness as a leader.

_____ 20. Mentors are most often supervisors or senior colleagues in the organization who provide advice and guidance about a variety of career-related concerns.

MULTIPLE CHOICE

Directions: Select the best answer in the space provided.

❖**1**❖

_____   1.   _____ is an influence relationship among leaders and followers who strive for real change and outcomes that reflect their shared purpose.
   a.   Leadership
   b.   Power
   c.   Empowerment
   d.   Reinforcement

_____   2.   Of the three aspects of leadership, _____ is perhaps the most essential.
   a.   formal position
   b.   a shared purpose
   c.   influence
   d.   coercion

_____   3.   Which of the following is not one of the three aspects of leadership?
   a.   change
   b.   shared purposes
   c.   influence
   d.   expert and referent powers

❖**2**❖

_____   4.   Which of the following is false regarding personal characteristics of a leader?
   a.   The personal characteristics are relatively stable attributes.
   b.   The personal characteristics include such things as their physical, social, and psychological traits.
   c.   The personal characteristics generally result in fairly predictable behavior over time and situations.
   d.   The personal characteristics can easily be changed. _

_____   5.   The ability to recognize and understand your moods, emotions, and drives, as well as their impact on others is known as _____.
   a.   self-control
   b.   genuineness
   c.   social awareness
   d.   self-awareness

_____   6.   _____ is the ability to build social networks, manage relationships, find common ground, and build rapport.
   a.   Social awareness
   b.   Social skill
   c.   Emotional intelligence
   d.   Transformational leadership

❖3❖

_____ 7. Carolyn Nuar is a manager who consults with her subordinates, seeks their opinions, and encourages them to take part in planning and decision making. Carolyn is exhibiting the _____ style of leadership.
a. Theory X
b. Theory Z
c. Theory Y
d. Theory T

_____ 8. Typical behaviors of a(n) _____ leader include displaying a high concern for people and a low concern for production.
a. country club style
b. produce or perish style
c. middle-of-the-road style
d. team style

_____ 9. The _____ style reflects high levels of concern for both people and production.
a. country club
b. team
c. produce or perish
d. middle of the road

_____ 10. Leaders who use the _____ style of the managerial grid attempt to establish cohesion and foster feelings of commitment among workers.
a. impoverished
b. team
c. produce or perish
d. country club

❖4❖

_____ 11. Which of the following models states that the style of leadership used should be based on the level of readiness of the followers?
a. managerial grid model
b. Situational Leadership® Model
c. House's path–goal model
d. leader-participation model

_____ 12. _____ occurs when a leader relies on two-way communication, listening, encouraging, and involving followers in decision making.
a. Relationship behavior
b. Path–goal behavior
c. Task behavior
d. Selling behavior

_____ 13. According to the Situational Leadership® Model, which of the following refers to the follower's ability rather than the leader's choice of leadership?
   a. task behavior
   b. relationship behavior
   c. readiness
   d. none of the above

_____ 14. The _____ style is appropriate for a leader whose followers are ready to accomplish a particular task and are both competent and motivated to take full responsibility for it.
   a. delegating
   b. selling
   c. participating
   d. telling

_____ 15. In using a ____ style, the leader encourages followers to share ideas and facilitates the work by being encouraging and helpful to subordinates.
   a. delegating
   b. participating
   c. selling
   d. telling

_____ 16. The _____ style of decision making in leadership is where the leader presents the problem to the team in a meeting, gets their suggestions, and then makes the decision. This decision may or may not reflect the team members' suggestions.
   a. facilitate
   b. delegate
   c. consult group
   d. consult individually

_____ 17. The _____ style of decision making is typified by a leader permitting the team to make the decision within prescribed limits.
   a. facilitate
   b. decide
   c. delegate
   d. consult team

❖5❖

_____ 18. John F. Kennedy and Franklin D. Roosevelt would be examples of _____ leaders.
   a. behavioral
   b. contingency
   c. transformational
   d. transfigurational

____ 19. The Greek word *kharisma* means _____.
       a. a vision
       b. divine gift
       c. active speaker
       d. empowerment

❖**6**❖

____ 20. Which of the following is a true statement about mentoring?
       a. Mentors are most often supervisors or senior colleagues in the organization who provide advice and guidance about a variety of career-related concerns.
       b. Talking with mentors about how to develop into a more effective leader is important to career advancement.
       c. Mentors serve as role models that a manager can emulate and provide valuable advice concerning the styles of leadership favored in the organization.
       d. All of the above

ESSAY QUESTIONS

❖**1**❖

1. Define *leadership* and discuss the three aspects of it.

❖**2**❖

2. Explain *emotional intelligence*.

❖**3**❖

3. Describe behavioral models of leadership.

❖4❖

4.   Define the *Situational Leadership® Model* and the differences between *task* and *relationship behaviors*.

❖5❖

5.   What are transformational leaders?

❖6❖

6.   Discuss how organizations develop effective leaders.

CHAPTER 15
DYNAMICS OF LEADERSHIP

MATCHING SOLUTIONS

1.   A - Charismatic Leaders
2.   O - Directive Behavior
3.   J - Readiness
4.   C - Referent Power
5.   S - Expert Power
6.   Q - Transformational Leaders
7.   F - Emotional Intelligence
8.   I   - Leadership
9.   M - Task Behavior
10. H - Self-Control
11. R - Mentors
12. P - Delegating Style
13. G - Theory Y
14. B - Middle-of-the-Road Style
15. N - Social Awareness

16. K - Country Club Style
17. D - Self-Awareness
18. L - Produce or Perish Style
19. E - Managerial Grid

TRUE/FALSE SOLUTIONS

Questions	Answer	Page	Explanation
1.	False	418	Leadership is an influence relationship among leaders and followers who strive for real change and outcomes that reflect their shared purposes.
2.	True		
3.	True		
4.	False	421	Self-Awareness is the ability to recognize and understand your moods, emotions, and drives, as well as their impact on others.
5.	False	422	Social skill is the ability to build social networks, manage relationships, find common ground, and build rapport. Social awareness is the ability to understand the emotional makeup of other people, and the skill to treat people according to their emotional reactions.
6.	True		
7.	False	424	McGregor believed that Theory X managers could be found everywhere in organizations, and that was a problem. According to him, management by direction and control was largely ineffective because it ignored the social, egoistic, and self-fulfillment needs of most employees.
8.	False	426	The country club style is identified as a high concern for people and a low concern for production. Managers who use this style try to create a secure and comfortable atmosphere and trust that their subordinates will respond positively. A high concern for production and a low concern for people are reflected in the produce or perish style. Leaders who use this style do not consider employees' personal needs to be relevant to achieving the organization's objectives.
9.	True		

10.	False	427	Task behavior includes using one-way communication, spelling out duties, and telling followers what to do and where, when, and how to do it. Relationship behavior includes using two-way communication, listening, encouraging, and involving followers in decision making.
11.	True		
12.	False	429	In using a selling style, the leader provides direction, encourages two-way communication, and helps build confidence and motivation on the part of the follower. In using a telling style, the leader provides clear instructions, gives specific directions, and supervises the work closely.
13.	False	430	Consult group style is typified by a leader that presents the problem to team members in a meeting, gets their suggestions, and then makes the decision. Facilitate style is typlifies by a leader that presents the problem to the team in a meeting and acts as a facilitator, defining the problem to be solved and the constraints within which the decision must be made.
14.	True		
15.	True		
16.	False	436	A charismatic leader is a person who has the ability to influence others because of his or her inspirational qualities.
17.	False	436	The Greek word *kharisma* means "divine gift."
18.	True		
19.	True		
20.	True		

MULTIPLE CHOICE SOLUTIONS

Questions	Answer	Page	Explanation
1.	a	418	Leadership is an influence relationship among leaders and followers who strive for real change and outcomes that reflect their shared purpose.
2.	c	418	Influencing others is perhaps the most essential aspect of leadership.

3.	d	418	Leadership is described as having three major aspects—<u>influence</u>, <u>shared purposes</u>, and <u>change</u>.
4.	d	420	A person can change some of her or his personal characteristics, but it is not easy to do so.
5.	d	421	The ability to recognize and understand your moods, emotions, and drives, as well as their impact on others is known as <u>self-awareness</u>.
6.	b	422	<u>Social skill</u> is the ability to build social networks, manage relationships, find common ground, and build rapport.
7.	c	423–424	<u>Theory Y</u> is a leadership style whereby leaders consult with their subordinates, seek their opinions, and encourage them to take part in planning and decision making. <u>Theory X</u> is a leadership style whereby leaders tell subordinates what is expected of them, instruct them in how to perform their jobs, insist that they meet certain standards, and make sure that everyone knows who is boss.
8.	a	426	The <u>country club style</u> is characterized by a high concern for people and a low concern for production.
9.	b	426	The <u>team style</u> reflects high levels of concern for both people and production.
10.	b	425–426	The <u>managerial grid</u>, developed by Robert Blake and Jane Mouton, identifies five leadership styles that combine different proportions of concern for production and concern for people. The <u>impoverished style</u> is characterized by a low concern for both people and production. The <u>country club style</u> is identified as a high concern for people and a low concern for production. A high concern for production and a low concern for people are reflected in the <u>produce or perish style</u>. Leaders who use a <u>middle-of-the-road style</u> seek a balance between workers' needs and the organization's productivity goals. The <u>team style</u> shows high levels of concern for both people and production. Leaders who use this style attempt to establish cohesion and foster feelings of commitment among workers.
11.	b	427	The <u>Situational Leadership® Model</u> states that the style of leadership used should be based on the level of readiness of the followers.

12.	a	427	<u>Relationship behavior</u> occurs when a leader relies on two-way communication, listening, encouraging, and involving followers in decision making.
13.	c	427	The contingency in the Situational Leadership® Model is the degree of follower readiness. <u>Readiness</u> is a follower's ability to set high but attainable task-related goals and a willingness to accept responsibility for reaching them.
14.	a	429	The <u>delegating style</u> is appropriate for a leader whose followers are ready to accomplish a particular task and are both competent and motivated to take full responsibility for it. A leader with a <u>telling style</u> provides clear instructions and specific direction. The <u>selling style</u> encourages two-way communication and helps build confidence and motivation on the part of the employee, although the leader still has responsibility for and controls decision making. In the <u>supportive style</u>, the leader and followers share decision making.
15.	b	429	In using a <u>participating style</u>, the leader encourages followers to share ideas and facilitates the work by being encouraging and helpful to subordinates.
16.	d	430	<u>Consult group style</u> is where the leader presents the problem to team members in a meeting, gets their suggestions, and then makes the decision. The decision may or may not reflect the team members' suggestions.
17.	c	431	The <u>delegate style</u> is typified by a leader that permits the team to make the decision within prescribed limits.
18.	c	434	<u>Transformational leadership</u> is leading by motivating. Transformational leaders provide extraordinary motivation by appealing to followers' ideals and moral values and inspiring them to think about problems in new ways. Joan of Arc, Abraham Lincoln, Franklin D. Roosevelt, John F. Kennedy, and Martin Luther King, Jr., among others, have transformed entire societies through their words and by their actions.
19.	b	436	The Greek word *kharisma* means "divine gift."
20.	d	440	All of the statements are true. <u>Mentors</u> often assist a manager in developing leadership capabilities by helping the manager find assignments that will foster on-the-job learning.

ESSAY SOLUTIONS

[Pages 418–420]

1. <u>Leadership</u> is an influence relationship among leaders and followers who strive for real change and outcomes that reflect their shared purposes. There are three major aspects of leadership: *influence*, *shared purposes*, and *change*. Influencing others is perhaps the most essential aspect of leadership and involves such things as using the authority of one's formal position in the firm, rewards, coercion, expertise, and charisma. Effective leaders also understand that they need to do more then simply convince others to follow them. They strive to create a vision that reflects the concerns and aspirations of followers. When a leader and followers have shared purposes, each can count on the other to act in ways that move everyone toward the common goal. Finally, the need for change seems constant in today's modern organizations. But, for a variety of reasons, employees often resist change.

[Page 421]

2. <u>Emotional intelligence</u> is a group of abilities that enable individuals to recognize and understand their own and others' feelings and emotions and to use these insights to guide their own thinking and actions. Like cognitive abilities, emotional intelligence may be affected by some aspects of our physiology. However, it is not fixed at birth and in fact develops over a period of many years as a person encounters various experiences and matures.

[Page 423]

3. <u>Behavioral models of leadership</u> focus on differences in the actions of effective and ineffective leaders. They seek to identify and understand what leaders actually do. Behavioral models of leadership assume that most people can learn to be effective leaders. Because leadership behaviors can be learned, individuals can become effective leaders with the proper encouragement and support.

[Pages 427–430]

4. The <u>Situational Leadership® Model</u> states the style of leadership used should be matched to the level of readiness of the followers. According to this model, leaders can choose from among four leadership styles (telling, selling, participating, and delegating) that involve various combinations of task and relationship behaviors. <u>Task behavior</u> includes using one-way communication, spelling out duties, and telling followers what to do and where, when, and how to do it. <u>Relationship behavior</u> includes using two-way communication, listening, encouraging, and involving followers in decision making, and giving emotional support.

[Pages 434–435]

5. <u>Transformational leaders</u> inspire others with their vision, often promote this vision over opposition, and demonstrate confidence in themselves and their views. They take an active and personal approach to influencing others. Transformational leaders alter feelings, desires, and expectations of others. They change perceptions of the possible and desirable. These leaders develop new approaches to long-standing problems and new options to open issues. They reflect excitement and enthusiasm and generate the same in others. They embrace risks to purse new opportunities. They are empathetic and intuitive in their ability to relate with others and, in general, are high in emotional intelligence.

[Pages 438–440]

6. Organizations use three approaches to develop effective leaders: placing employees in positions that promote learning on the job, providing employees with formal leadership assessments and training, and offering mentoring and coaching.

CHAPTER 16
ORGANIZATIONAL COMMUNICATION

LEARNING OBJECTIVES

After studying this chapter, you should be able to:

❖**1**❖   Explain the main elements of the communication process.

❖**2**❖   Identify hurdles to communication and describe ways to eliminate them.

❖**3**❖   State the guidelines for fostering effective communication.

❖**4**❖   Discuss two ethical issues in communications.

OUTLINE

❖**1**❖   Explain the main elements of the communication process.

    I.   The Communication Process

        1. **Communication**—is the transfer and exchange of information and understanding from one person to another through meaningful symbols.

           a. In organizations, managers use the communication process to carry out their four basic functions (planning, organizing, leading, and controlling).

               1. Because they must have access to relevant information in order to make sound decisions, effective managers build networks of contacts who facilitate information gathering, interpretation, and dissemination.

               2. Poor communication allows rumors to replace facts, fosters animosities between departments and work teams, and impedes successful organizational change.

               3. Most managers spend a large part of their working day communicating with superiors, peers, customers, and others; answering and writing e-mails, letters, and reports; and talking to others on the phone.

               4. The communication process involves six basic elements: sender (encoder), receiver (decoder), message, channels, feedback, and perception.

2. **Sender**—is the source of information and the initiator of the communication process.

   a. The sender tries to choose the type of message and the channel that will be most effective. The sender then encodes the message.

   b. Encoding—is the process of translating thoughts or feelings into a medium—written, visual, or spoken—that conveys the meaning intended.

   c. To increase encoding accuracy:

      1. *Relevancy*—make the message meaningful and significant.

      2. *Simplicity*—put the message in the simplest possible terms.

      3. *Organization*—arrange the message as a series of points to facilitate understanding

      4. *Repetition*—restate key points of the message at least twice.

      5. *Focus*—focus on the key points of the message at least twice.

3. **Receiver**—is the person who receives and decodes (or interprets) the sender's message.

   a. Decoding—is translating messages into a form that has meaning to the receiver.

   b. Both encoding and decoding are influenced by personal factors, such as education, personality, socioeconomic status, family, work history, culture, and gender.

   c. Listening—involves paying attention to the message, not merely hearing it.

4. **Message**—contains the verbal (spoken and written) symbols and nonverbal cues representing the information the sender wants to convey to the receiver.

   a. A message has two sides, and the message sent and the message received are not necessarily the same.

      1. Encoding and decoding of the message may vary because of differences between the sender's and the receiver's backgrounds and viewpoints.

      2. The sender may be sending more than one message.

   b. Nonverbal Messages—involve the use of facial expressions, body movement, gestures, and physical contact (often called body language) to convey meaning.

      1. When people communicate in person, as much as 60 percent of the content of the message is transmitted through facial expressions and body movement.

      2. *Body Language*—the body and its movement—particularly of the face and eyes, which are expressive—tell a lot about a person.

3. *Space*—how close you are to another person, where you sit or stand, and how you arrange your office can have a real impact on communication.

    a. The term <u>proxemics</u> refers to the study of ways people use physical space to convey messages.

    b. <u>Feng Shui</u>—is a system for arranging everything around you in such a way that your environment works for you and with you.

4. *Personal Appearance*—if you are dressed appropriately, customers and others may see you as a more competent person than someone who dresses inappropriately.

c. <u>Verbal Messages</u>—employees communicate verbally (speaking and writing) more often than in any other way.

1. Effective verbal communication requires the sender to encode the message in words (and nonverbal cues) that will convey it accurately to the receiver, present the message in a well-organized manner, and try to eliminate distractions.

d. <u>Written Messages</u>—are most appropriate when information has to be collected from or distributed to many people at scattered locations and when keeping a record of what was sent is necessary.

1. The following are some guidelines for preparing effective written messages.

    a. The message should be drafted with the receiver clearly in mind.

    b. The contents of the message should be well thought out ahead of time.

    c. The message should be as brief as possible, without extraneous words or ideas.

    d. Important messages should be prepared in draft form first and then polished.

    e. The message should be carefully organized.

5. **Channel**—is the path a message follows from the sender to the receiver.

a. <u>Information Richness</u>—is the information carrying capacity of the channel.

1. Written communications are low in richness.

2. Channels low in richness are considered lean because they are effective mainly for sending specific data and facts.

3. Face-to-face communication is the richest channel because it conveys several cues simultaneously, including spoken and nonverbal information.

4. The telephone is somewhat less rich than face-to-face communication, but not as lean as written surveys.

b. <u>Downward Channels</u>—all the means of sending messages from management to employees.

    1. Managers frequently use downward communication effectively as a channel, but it may be the most misused channel because it provides little opportunity for employees to respond.

    2. The fundamental problem with downward communication is that it is too often one way. It is a lean channel that does not encourage feedback from those on the receiving end.

c. <u>Upward Channels</u>—all the means used by employees to send messages to management.

    1. Such channels may be the only formal means that employees have for communicating with higher-level managers in the organization.

    2. Upward communication provides feedback on how well employees understand the messages they have received.

    3. If effective, upward communication can provide an emotional release and, at the same time, give employees a chance to participate, convey the feeling they are being listened to, and have a sense of personal worth.

d. <u>Horizontal Channels</u>—all the means used to send and receive messages across departmental lines, with suppliers, or with customers.

    1. Essential to the success of a network organization is maintaining effective communication among customers, suppliers, and employees in various divisions or functions.

    2. Messages communicated horizontally usually are related to coordinating activities, sharing information, and solving problems.

    3. Horizontal channels are extremely important in today's team-based organizations, where employees most often communicate among themselves to solve their clients' production or process problems.

e. <u>Informal Channels</u>—all the nonformal means for sender and receiver to communicate downward, upward, and horizontally.

    1. *Grapevine*—is an organization's informal communication system, along which information can travel in any direction.

    2. The term *grapevine* comes from a Civil War practice of hanging telegraph lines loosely from tree to tree, like a grapevine.

    3. In organizations, the path that messages follow along the grapevine is based on social interaction, not organization charts.

    4. *Employee Network Groups*—are informal groups who organize regularly scheduled social activities that promote informal communication among employees who share a common interest or concern.

f. <u>External Networking</u>—developing close, informal relationships with talented and interesting people outside the organization.

    1. People use these networks to help each other, trading favors and calling on each other's resources for career counseling or other types of information and support.

g. **Feedback**—is the receiver's response to the sender's message.

    1. It is the best way to show that a message has been received and to indicate whether it has been understood.

    2. Feedback should have the following characteristics:

        a. It should be helpful.

        b. It should be descriptive rather than evaluative.

        c. It should be specific rather than general.

        d. It should be well timed.

        e. It should not overwhelm.

6. **Perception**—is the meaning ascribed to a message by either sender or receiver.

a. Perceptions are influenced by what people see, by the ways they organize these elements in memory, and by the meanings they attach to them.

    1. How people interpret what they perceive is affected by their past.

b. <u>Selective Perception</u>—is the process of screening out information that a person wants or needs to avoid.

    1. Employees often filter out information about other areas of the organization and focus on information that is directly related to their own jobs.

c. <u>Stereotyping</u>—is the process of making assumptions about individuals solely on the basis of their belonging to a certain gender, race, age, or other group.

    1. Stereotyping distorts reality by suggesting that all people in a category have similar characteristics, which simply is not true.

❖**2**❖   Identify hurdles to communication and describe ways to eliminate them.

II. Hurdles to Effective Communication

1. **Organizational Hurdles**—the degree of specialization present in the organization may also affect clear communication.

a. <u>Authority and Status Levels</u>—when one person holds a higher formal position than another, that person has a higher level of authority.

    1. When one person is held in higher esteem than another, regardless of their positions in the organizations, that person has a higher status level.

2. *Status*—is a person's social rank in a group, which often is determined by a person's characteristics (e.g. age, educational level, family), in addition to the person's formal position.

3. When status and authority levels differ, communication problems are likely to occur.

b. Specialization—as knowledge becomes more specialized, professionals in many fields develop their own jargon, or shorthand, to simplify communication among themselves. That often makes communication with people outside the field difficult.

1. In an attempt to make themselves powerful, some people intentionally use the language of specialization to obscure what is going on.

c. Different Goals—open communication between people with differing goals speeds problem solving and improves the quality of solutions.

2. **Individual Hurdles**—the Center for Creative Leadership at Greensboro, North Carolina, estimates 50 percent of all managers and 30 percent of top managers have some difficulty in communicating with others.

a. Semantics—is the study of the way words are used and the meanings they convey.

1. When two people attribute different meanings to the same words but do not realize it, a barrier exists.

2. *Backtranslation*—involves having messages translated back to the original language to ensure the accuracy of the original translation.

3. Backtranslation is not foolproof because the meanings of words often depend on the context in which they are used—especially in high context cultures (e.g., Arabic, Japanese, and Chinese).

b. Emotions—are subjective reactions or feelings.

1. When people communicate, they convey emotions as well as facts and opinions.

2. The sender's feelings influence encoding of the message and may or may not be apparent to the receiver. The receiver's feelings affect decoding of the message and the nature of the response.

3. The antecedents of some emotions—anger, happiness, disgust, fear, sadness, and surprise—seem to be similar in most cultures, as are the facial expressions that accompany the emotions.

3. **Eliminating Hurdles**—barriers to effective communication can be overcome in the following ways:

a. Regulate the Flow of Information—if you receive too much information, you will suffer from information overload. You should set up a system that identifies priority messages for immediate attention.

      b. <u>Encourage Feedback</u>—you should follow up to determine whether important messages have been understood. Feedback lets you know whether the other person understands the message accurately.

      c. <u>Simplify the Language</u>—sentences should be concise, and jargon that others will not understand or that may be misleading should be avoided.

            1. In general, understanding is improved by simplifying the language used—consistent, of course, with the nature of the intended audience.

      d. <u>Listen Actively</u>—you need to become a good listener as well as a good message sender.

            1. Characteristics of effective listeners include: appreciative, empathic, comprehensive, discerning, and evaluative.

      e. <u>Restrain Negative Emotions</u>—when emotionally upset, both manager and subordinate are likely to misinterpret a message.

            1. The simplest answer in such a situation is to call a halt until the people involved can restrain their emotions—that is, until they can be more descriptive than evaluative.

      f. <u>Use Nonverbal Cues</u>—you should use nonverbal cues to emphasize points and express feelings.

            1. Make sure that your actions reinforce your words so that they do not send mixed messages.

      g. <u>Use the Grapevine</u>—use the grapevine to send information rapidly, test reactions before announcing a final decision, and obtain valuable feedback.

            1. The grapevine also frequently carries destructive rumors, reducing employee morale and organizational effectiveness. By being "plugged into" the grapevine, you can partially counteract this negative effect by being sure that relevant, accurate, meaningful, and timely information gets to others.

❖**3**❖   State the guidelines for fostering effective communication.

   III. **Fostering Effective Communication**

      1. The American Management Association's eight guidelines that can be used to improve communication skills are:

      a. <u>Clarify your ideas before communicating</u>.

            1. Analyze the topic or problem to clarify it in your mind before sending a message.

            2. Communication is often ineffective because the message is inadequately planned.

   b. Examine the true purpose of the communication.

       1. Before you send a message, ask yourself what you really want to accomplish with it.

       2. Decide whether you want to obtain information, convey a decision, or persuade someone to take action.

   c. Consider the setting in which the communication will take place.

       1. You convey meanings and intent by more than words alone.

       2. Trying to communicate with a person in another location is more difficult than doing so face-to-face.

   d. Consult with others, when appropriate, in planning communications.

       1. Encourage the participation of those who will be affected by the message.

       2. They often provide a viewpoint that you might not have considered.

   e. Be mindful of the nonverbal messages you send.

       1. Tone of voice, facial expression, eye contact, personal appearance, and physical surroundings all influence the communication process.

       2. The receiver considers both the words and the nonverbal cues that make up your message.

   f. Take the opportunity to convey something helpful to the receiver.

       1. Effective communicators really try to see the message from the listener's point of view.

   g. Follow up the communication.

       1. Follow up and ask for feedback to determine if the receiver understands the message.

❖4❖   Discuss two ethical issues in communications.

IV.   **Ethical Issues in Communications**

   1. **Computer ethics**—is concerned with the nature and social impact of information technologies and the formulation of policies for their appropriate use.

   2. **Privacy issues**—information that used to be inaccessible or very difficult to obtain is now instantly available for use by almost anyone.

   a. Protection of privacy through the legal system, organizational and managerial policies and practices, self-regulation through professional and trade associations, and consumer groups hasn't caught up with technological developments.

MATCHING

Directions: Select the term that best identifies the statement listed below. Place the letter of the correct term in the space provided.

A. Emotion
B. Nonverbal Messages
C. Upward Channels
D. Status
E. Listening
F. Communication
G. Information Richness
H. Stereotyping
I. Semantics
J. Decoding

K. Encoding
L. Feng shui
M. Proxemics
N. Grapevine
O. Employee Network Groups
P. Channel
Q. Selective Perception
R. Receiver
S. Horizontal Channels
T. Backtranslation

_____ 1. To avoid blunders or misinterpretation, companies routinely have their messages interpreted back to the original language to ensure the accuracy of the original interpretation.

_____ 2. The use of facial expressions, movements, body position, and physical contact to convey meaning.

_____ 3. This is a system for arranging everything around you in such a way that your environment works for you and with you.

_____ 4. Translating encoded messages into a form that has meaning to the receiver.

_____ 5. The path that a message follows from sender to receiver.

_____ 6. A person's social rank in a group.

_____ 7. An organization's informal communication system.

_____ 8. Paying attention to a message, not merely hearing it.

_____ 9. A subjective reaction or feeling.

_____ 10. All the means used to send and receive messages across departmental lines, with suppliers, or with customers.

_____ 11. The transfer of information and understanding from one person to another through meaningful symbols.

_____ 12. The study of ways people use physical space to convey a message about themselves.

_____ 13. Making assumptions about individuals solely on the basis of their belonging to a particular gender, race, age, or other group.

_____ 14. The person who receives and decodes the sender's message.

_____ 15. All the means used by employees to send messages to management.

_____ 16. Translating thoughts or feelings into a medium—written, visual, or spoken—that conveys the meaning intended.

_____ 17. These organize regularly scheduled social activities to promote informal communication among employees who share a common interest or concern.

_____ 18. The information carrying capacity of a channel of communication.

_____ 19. The process of screening out information that a person wants or needs to avoid.

_____ 20. The study of the way words are used and the meanings they convey.

TRUE OR FALSE

❖1❖

_____ 1. Poor communication seems to be the single most important reason for poor strategy implementation.

_____ 2. Encoding translates messages into a form that has meaning to the receiver.

_____ 3. Studies have shown that most people can recall immediately only about 75 percent of what someone tells them.

_____ 4. A message sent and a message received are always the same thing.

_____ 5. When people communicate in person, as much as 60 percent of the content of the message is transmitted through facial expressions and body movement.

_____ 6. Eye contact and posture play no role in the communication process.

_____ 7. All channels of communication carry the same richness, and written communication is high in richness.

_____ 8. Upward channels may be the only formal means that employees have for communicating with higher level managers in the organization.

_____ 9. Upon receiving rewarding feedback, the sender continues to produce the same kind of message.

_____ 10. Selective perception is the process of making assumptions about individuals solely on the basis of their belonging to a certain gender, race, age, or other group.

❖2❖

_____ 11. Flat organizations have relatively few authority levels and tend to be more egalitarian in terms of status.

_____ 12. Status is a person's social rank in a group, which is often determined by a person's characteristics, in addition to their formal position.

_____ 13. For feedback to be effective, it should be evaluative rather than descriptive.

_____ 14. The grapevine carries destructive rumors, has few positive attributes, and can be easily eliminated by management.

❖3❖

_____ 15. Communication is often ineffective because the message is inadequately planned.

_____ 16. Trying to communicate with a person in another location is more difficult than doing so face-to-face.

_____ 17. Effective communicators really try to see the message from the listener's point of view.

❖4❖

_____ 18. With the advances in technology allowing more employees to work from home, there has been less of an need for a formal code of ethics in organizations today.

_____ 19. Regarding credit information, consumers are today afforded tremendous protection of their privacy through the legal system, consumer groups and self-regulation.

_____ 20. With the increased threat of terrorism since September 11, 2001, the efforts of the U.S. government have focused on gaining access to more private information than on privacy protection.

MULTIPLE CHOICE

Directions: Select the best answer in the space provided.

❖1❖

_____ 1. _____ is the transfer and exchange of information and understanding from one person to another through meaningful symbols.
   a. Language
   b. Technology
   c. Communication
   d. Encoding

_____ 2. Which of the following statements about communication is false?
   a. Without effective communication, managers can accomplish little, which is why communication is one of the six key managerial competencies.
   b. Managers spend very little time communicating because subordinates are the ones responsible for writing memos, reports, and dealing with customers.
   c. Effective communication is necessary during times of expansion and growth.
   d. Poor communication seems to be the single most important reason for poor strategy implementation.

_____ 3. Which of the following is not an element of the communication process?
   a. proxemics
   b. perception
   c. channels
   d. encoder

____   4.   The _____ is the source of information and the initiator of the communication process.
   a.   sender
   b.   receiver
   c.   decoder
   d.   none of the above

____   5.   Which of the following is a guideline for effective listening?
   a.   Remove distractions
   b.   Try to see the other person's point of view.
   c.   Stop talking!
   d.   All of the above

____   6.   The _____ contains the verbal symbols and nonverbal cues representing the information that the sender wants to convey to the receiver.
   a.   channel
   b.   grapevine
   c.   message
   d.   richness

____   7.   _____ is a system for arranging everything around you in such a way that your environment works for you and with you.
   a.   Proxemics
   b.   Internal networking
   c.   Feng shui
   d.   Backtranslation

____   8.   Effective verbal communication requires the sender to _____.
   a.   encode the message in words (and nonverbal cues) that will convey it accurately to the receiver
   b.   convey the message in a well-organized manner
   c.   try to eliminate distractions
   d.   all of the above

____   9.   Which of the following is a false statement regarding information richness?
   a.   Written communications are high in richness.
   b.   Face-to-face interaction is the richest communication channel.
   c.   Channels low in richness are considered to be lean because they are effective mainly for sending specific data and facts.
   d.   Not all channels can carry the same richness of information.

____   10.   Feedback should have the following characteristics except:
   a.   it should be well timed.
   b.   it should be evaluative rather than descriptive.
   c.   it should be specific rather than general.
   d.   it should be helpful.

_____ 11. Which of the following is a true statement regarding perception?
a. The ability to perceive varies from person to person.
b. The attitudes that people bring to a situation color their perceptions of it.
c. How people interpret what they perceive is affected by their past.
d. All of the above.

❖**2**❖

_____ 12. Which of the following are considered organizational barriers to communication?
a. authority and status levels
b. different goals
c. status relationships among members
d. all of the above

_____ 13. Zolan Heckman, a sales representative, phoned in a special order to the company's shipping department. He asked that the item be shipped "as soon as possible" expecting that the order would receive top priority. Seven days later, the customer called saying the item had not yet arrived. When Zolan checked with the shipping department he was told that "as soon as possible" in their department meant to send the order with the next large shipment, not immediately. This is an example of a _____ problem.
a. semantic
b. selective perception
c. feedback
d. management

_____ 14. Exxon's original Japanese brand was Esso, which means stalled car when pronounced phonetically in Japanese. This is an example of Exxon's failure to do
_____.
a. market research
b. decoding
c. backtranslation
d. proxemics

_____ 15. All of the following are ways to overcome barriers to communication except:
a. encourage feedback.
b. restrain negative emotions.
c. eliminate nonverbal cues.
d. simplify the language used in the message.

_____ 16. Which of the following are characteristics of active listeners?
a. empathic
b. discerning
c. evaluative
d. All of the above.

_____ 17. As a manager you can use the _____ to send internal information rapidly, test reactions, and obtain valuable feedback.
   a. Internet
   b. bulletin board
   c. grapevine
   d. network groups

❖3❖

_____ 18. Which of the following is one of the American Management Association's eight guidelines for improving communication skills?
   a. Focus on the essential, or key points, of the message.
   b. Try to see the other person's point of view.
   c. Clarify your ideas before communicating.
   d. None of the above

❖4❖

_____ 19. _____ is concerned with the nature and social impact of information technologies and the formulation of policies for their appropriate use.
   a. Semantics
   b. Proxemics
   c. Computer ethics
   d. Teleconferencing

_____ 20. Which of the following statements is <u>false</u> regarding computer ethics?
   a. Computers make mistakes that no human being would make.
   b. Computers have huge capacities to store, copy, erase, retrieve, transmit, and manipulate information quickly and economically.
   c. Computers may collect and store data for only its designed purpose and can keep data for long periods of time.
   d. Computers have the effect of radically distancing originators, users, and subjects of programs and data from each other.

ESSAY QUESTIONS

❖1❖

1. Identify and discuss the six basic elements of the communication process.

2.   Define and discuss *selective perception* and *stereotyping*.

❖2❖

3.   How do emotions impact communication?

4.   State the methods for overcoming hurdles to effective communication.

❖3❖

5.   List the American Management Association's seven guidelines for improving effective communication.

❖4❖

6.   Define *computer ethics* and the ethical issues that arise surrounding the increased use of computers and their unique technological characteristics?

CHAPTER 16
ORGANIZATIONAL COMMUNICATION

MATCHING SOLUTIONS

1. T - Backtranslation
2. B - Nonverbal Messages
3. L - Feng shui
4. J - Decoding
5. P - Channel
6. D - Status
7. N - Grapevine
8. E - Listening
9. A - Emotion
10. S - Horizontal Channels
11. F - Communication
12. M - Proxemics
13. H - Stereotyping
14. R - Receiver
15. C - Upward Channels
16. K - Encoding
17. O - Employee Network Groups
18. G - Information Richness
19. Q - Selective Perception
20. I - Semantics

TRUE/FALSE SOLUTIONS

Question	Answer	Page	Explanation
1.	True		
2.	False	449–451	Encoding translates thoughts or feelings into a medium—written, visual, or spoken—that conveys the meaning intended. Decoding translates messages into a form that has meaning to the receiver.
3.	False	452	Listening involves paying attention to the message, not merely hearing it. Of the 75 percent or more of their time that managers spend in communicating, about half is spent listening to others. Becoming a better listener is an important way for people to improve their communication skills. Studies have shown that most people can recall immediately only

			about 50 percent of what someone tells them. Two months later, they can recall only about 25 percent.
4.	False	452	The <u>message</u> contains the verbal (spoken and written) symbols and nonverbal cues representing the information the sender wants to convey to the receiver. Like a coin, a message has two sides, and the message sent and the message received are not necessarily the same. Encoding and decoding of the message may vary because of differences between the sender's and the receiver's backgrounds and viewpoints.
5.	True		
6.	False	452–456	The ability to interpret facial expressions is an important part of communication. Eye contact is a direct and powerful way of communicating nonverbally. In the United States, social rules suggest that in most situations, brief eye contact is appropriate. Posture also communicates meaning by signaling a person's degree of self-confidence or interest in what is being discussed.
7.	False	457	The <u>channel</u> is the path a message follows from the sender to the receiver. <u>Information richness</u> is the information carrying capacity of the channel. Not all channels can carry the same richness of information. Written communications are low in richness. Channels low in richness are considered to be lean because they are effective mainly for sending specific data and facts.
8.	True		
9.	True		
10.	False	462–463	<u>Selective perception</u> is the process of screening out information that a person wants to avoid. <u>Stereotyping</u> is the process of making assumptions about individuals solely on the basis of their belonging to a certain gender, race, age, or other group. Stereotyping distorts reality by suggesting that all people in a category have similar characteristics, which simply is not true.
11.	True		
12.	True		

13.	False	462	If the receiver responds to the message in a descriptive manner, the feedback is likely to be effective. If the receiver is highly critical (or judgmental), the feedback is likely to be ineffective.
14.	False	468	As a manager, you could not get rid of the grapevine in an organization even if you tried, so you should use it to send information rapidly, test reactions before announcing a final decision, and obtain valuable feedback. Also, the grapevine frequently carries destructive rumors, reducing employee morale and organizational effectiveness. By being "plugged into" the grapevine, you can partially counteract this negative effect by being sure that relevant, accurate, meaningful, and timely information gets to others.
15.	True		
16.	True		
17.	True		
18.	False	469	The price for increased employee independence has led some organizations to monitor employee's work. Also, it is tempting for employees to engage in personal activities, such as checking stock quotes, or looking for another job, while on the job. Advances in communication are likely to increase the pressures on both management and employees to develop a code of ethics.
19.	False	471	The three large credit rating companies maintain credit information on more than 170 million people in the United States. Information that used to be inaccessible or very difficult to obtain is now instantly available for use by almost anyone. Protection of privacy through the legal system, organizational and managerial policies and practices, self-regulation through professional and trade associations, and consumer groups hasn't caught up with technological developments.
20.	True		

MULTIPLE CHOICE SOLUTIONS

<u>Question</u>	<u>Answer</u>	<u>Page</u>	<u>Explanation</u>
1.	c	449	<u>Communication</u> is the transfer and exchange of information and understanding from one person to another through meaningful symbols. It is a way of exchanging and sharing ideas, attitudes, values, opinions, and facts.
2.	b	449	In organizations, managers use the communication process to carry out their four basic functions (planning, organizing, leading, and controlling). Most managers spend a large part of their working day communicating with superiors, peers, customers, and others; writing memos, letters, and reports; and talking to others on the phone.
3.	a	449	The communication process involves six elements: sender (encoder), receiver (decoder), message, channels, feedback, and perception. <u>Proxemics</u> is the study of ways that people use physical space to convey a message about themselves.
4.	a	449	The <u>sender</u> is the source of information and the initiator of the communication process. The sender tries to choose the type of message and the channel that will be most effective. The sender then encodes the message.
5.	d	452	The guidelines for effective listening include: (1) Remember that listening is not just about receiving information—how you listen also sends a message back to the message sender. (2) Stop talking! You cannot listen if you are talking. (3) Show a talker that you want to listen. Paraphrase what's been said to show that you understand. (4) Remove distractions. (5) Avoid prejudging what the person thinks or feels. Listen first, then make judgments later. (6) Try to see the other person's point of view. (7) Listen for total meaning. This includes both the content of the words and the feeling or attitude underlying the words. (8) Attend to both verbal and nonverbal cues. (9) Go easy on argument and criticism, which put people on the defensive and may make them "clam up" or become angry. (10) Before each person leaves, confirm what has been said.

6.	c	452	The <u>message</u> contains the verbal (spoken and written) symbols and nonverbal cues representing the information that the sender wants to convey to the receiver.
7.	b	455	<u>Feng shui</u> is a system for arranging everything around you in such a way that your environment works for you and with you.
8.	d	456	Employees communicate verbally (speaking and writing) more often than in any other way. Effective verbal communication requires the sender to (1) encode the message in words (and nonverbal cues) that will convey it accurately to the receiver, (2) convey the message in a well-organized manner, and (3) try to eliminate distractions.
9.	a	457	<u>Information richness</u> is the information carrying capacity of the channel. Not all channels carry the same richness of information. Written communications are low in richness. The other statements are true.
10.	b	461–462	<u>Feedback</u> is the receiver's response to the sender's message. It is the best way to show that a message has been received and to indicate whether it has been understood. Procter & Gamble, 3M, IBM, and other companies have guidelines for providing effective feedback. According to these guidelines, feedback should have the following characteristics: (1) it should be helpful, (2) it should be descriptive rather than evaluative, (3) it should be specific rather than general, (4) it should be well timed, and (5) it should not overwhelm.
11.	d	462	<u>Perception</u> is the meaning ascribed to a message by either sender or receiver. Perceptions are influenced by what people see, by the ways they organize these elements in memory, and by the meanings they attach to them. All the statements listed are true.
12.	d	463	One of the first steps in communicating more effectively is to identify barriers to the process. Organizational barriers include: authority and status levels, specialization of task functions by members, different goals, and status relationships among members. Individual barriers to communication are: conflicting assumptions, semantics, and emotions.

13.	a	465–466	The study of the way words are used and the meanings they convey is called <u>semantics</u>. Misinterpretation of word meanings can play a large role in communication failure. When two people attribute different meanings to the same words but do not realize it, a barrier exists.
14.	c	466	To avoid blunders, companies should routinely have messages translated back to the original language to ensure the accuracy of the original translation—a process called <u>backtranslation</u>. If the original message and the backtranslated version agree, the translated version probably will not have unexpected meanings.
15.	c	467–468	People can overcome barriers to effective communication. Ways to overcome barriers to communication include: regulate the flow of information, encourage feedback, simplify the language used in the message, listen actively, restrain negative emotions, use nonverbal cues, and use the grapevine and informal networks.
16.	d	467–468	<u>Listening</u> is an active process in which listeners and speakers share equal responsibility for successful communication. The following are some characteristics of active listeners: appreciative, empathic, comprehensive, discerning, and evaluative.
17.	c	468	The <u>grapevine</u> is an organization's informal communication system. As a manager, you could not get rid of the grapevine in an organization even if you tried, so you should use it to send information rapidly, test reactions before announcing a final decision, and obtain valuable feedback.
18.	c	468–469	The American Management Association's seven guidelines to improve communication skills are: (1) Clarify your ideas before communicating. (2) Examine the true purpose of the communication. (3) Consider the setting in which the communication will take place. (4) Consult with others, when appropriate, in planning communications. (5) Be mindful of the nonverbal messages you send. (6) Take the opportunity to convey something helpful to the receiver. (7) Follow up the communication.
19.	c	469	<u>Computer ethics</u> is concerned with the nature and social impact of information technologies and the formulation of policies for their appropriate use.

20.   c   469   Computers may collect and store data for one purpose that can easily be used for another purpose and be kept for long periods of time.

ESSAY SOLUTIONS

[Pages 449–463]

1. <u>Communication</u> is the transfer and exchange of information and understanding from one person to another through meaningful symbols. The basic elements include:

   a. *Sender (Encoder)* is the source of information and the initiator of the communication process. The sender tries to choose the type of message and the channel that will be most effective. The sender then encodes the message. <u>Encoding</u> translates thoughts or feelings into a medium—written, visual, or spoken—that conveys the meaning intended.

   b. *Receiver (Decoder)* is the person who receives and decodes (or interprets) the sender's message. <u>Decoding</u> translates messages into a form that has meaning to the receiver. One of the main requirements of the receiver is the ability to listen.

   c. *Message* contains the verbal (spoken and written) symbols and nonverbal cues representing the information that the sender wants to convey to the receiver. Like a coin, a message has two sides, and the message sent and the message received are not necessarily the same. Managers and employees generally use three types of messages: nonverbal, verbal, and written.

   d. *Channel* is the path a message follows from the sender to the receiver. <u>Information richness</u> is the information carrying capacity of the channel. Not all channels can carry the same richness of information. In addition to selecting a level of information richness (such as written communication versus face-to-face communication), individuals must choose among several types of channels for communicating with others. They include downward, upward, and horizontal formal channels and informal channels, such as the grapevine and networking or caucus groups.

   e. *Feedback* is the receiver's response to the sender's message. It is the best way to show that a message has been received and to indicate whether it has been understood. Feedback should be helpful, descriptive, specific, well timed, and should not overwhelm.

   f. *Perception* is the meaning ascribed to a message by either sender or receiver. Perceptions are influenced by what people see, by the ways they organize these elements in memory, and by the meanings they attach to them. The ability to perceive varies from person to person. How people interpret what they perceive is affected by their past. Some problems in communication can be traced to two problems of perceptions: selective perception and stereotyping.

[Pages 462–463]

2. <u>Selective perception</u> is the process of screening out information that a person wants or needs to avoid. For example, many people "tune out" TV commercials. Most everyone has been accused at one time or another of listening only to what they want to hear.

   <u>Stereotyping</u> is the process of making assumptions about individuals solely on the basis of their belonging to a certain gender, race, age, or other group. Stereotyping distorts reality by suggesting that all people in a category have similar characteristics, which simply is not true. During the 1990s, organizations became increasingly sensitive to the potential negative consequences of stereotyping based on a person's gender, race, ethnicity, age, or sexual orientation. Many organizations have developed training programs and other initiatives designed to reduce the negative personal and organizational consequences of stereotyping.

[Page 466]

3. An <u>emotion</u> is a subjective reaction or feeling. Remembering experiences, an individual recalls not only events but also the feelings that accompanied them. Thus when people communicate they convey emotions as well as facts and opinions. The sender's feelings influence encoding of the message and may or may not be apparent to the receiver. The receiver's feelings affect decoding of the message and the nature of the response. Misunderstandings owing to differences in what arouses people's emotions often accompany cross-cultural communications.

[Pages 467–468]

4. People can overcome hurdles to effective communication. They must first be aware that barriers exist and can cause serious organizational problems. Then they must be willing to invest the effort and time to overcome the barriers. Several methods of overcoming barriers to communication include:

   a. *Regulate the Flow of Information.* If you receive too much information, you will suffer from information overload. A system should be set up that identifies priority messages for immediate attention.

   b. *Encourage Feedback.* You should follow up to determine whether important messages have been understood. Feedback lets you know whether the other person understands the message accurately.

   c. *Simplify the Language of the Message.* Because language can be a barrier, you should choose words that others will understand. Your sentences should be concise, and you should avoid jargon that others will not understand or that may be misleading.

   d. *Listen Actively.* You need to become a good listener as well as a good message sender. Listening is an active process in which listeners and speakers share equal responsibility for successful communication.

e.   *Restrain Negative Emotions.* When emotionally upset, you are more likely than at other times to phrase the message poorly. When emotionally upset, both manager and subordinate are likely to misinterpret a message.

f.   *Use Nonverbal Cues.* You should use nonverbal cues to emphasize points and express feelings. Your actions should reinforce your words so that they do not send mixed messages.

g.   *Use the Grapevine.* As a manager, you could not get rid of the grapevine in an organization even if you tried, so you should use it to send information rapidly, test reactions before announcing a final decision, and obtain valuable feedback.

[Pages 468–469]

5.   The American Management Association's seven guidelines for improving communication skills are as follows:

a.   Clarify your ideas before communicating.

b.   Examine the true purpose of the communication.

c.   Consider the setting in which the communication will take place.

d.   Consult with others, when appropriate, in planning communications.

e.   Be mindful of the nonverbal messages you send.

f.   Take the opportunity to convey something helpful to the receiver.

g.   Follow up the communication.

[Page 469]

6.   Computer ethics is concerned with the nature and social impact of information technologies and the formulation of policies for their appropriate use. Ethical issues surrounding computers arise from their unique technological characteristics, including:

a.   Computers make mistakes that no human being would make.

b.   Computers communicate over long distances at high speed and low cost.

c.   Computers have huge capacities to store, copy, erase, retrieve, transmit, and manipulate information quickly and economically.

d.   Computers have the effect of radically distancing originators, users, and subjects of programs and data from each other.

e.   Computers may collect and store data for one purpose that can easily be used for another purpose and be kept for long periods of time.

CHAPTER 17
MANAGING WORK TEAMS

LEARNING OBJECTIVES

After studying this chapter, you should be able to:

❖**1**❖   Explain the importance of work teams.

❖**2**❖   Identify four types of work teams.

❖**3**❖   State the meaning and determinants of team effectiveness.

❖**4**❖   Describe the internal team processes that can affect team performance.

❖**5**❖   Explain how to diagnose and remove barriers to poor team performance.

OUTLINE

❖**1**❖   Explain the importance of work teams.

    I.   **Work Teams and Other Groups**

        1. **Group**—is two or more individuals who come into personal and meaningful contact on a continuing basis.

        2. **Work Team**—consists of a small number of identifiable, interdependent employees who are held accountable for performing tasks that contribute to achieving an organization's goals.

           a. <u>Informal Group</u>—consists of a small number of individuals who frequently participate together in activities and share feelings for the purpose of meeting their mutual needs.

        3. **Why Organizations Use Work Teams**—the main reasons that managers give for organizing work around teams are generally similar for a variety of organizations.

           a. <u>Innovation</u>—creative thinking, the bedrock of new product ideas, is increased by bringing together people having a variety of experience and expertise to address a common problem or task.

           b. <u>Speed</u>—teams can also reduce the time required for product development.

           c. <u>Cost</u>—reducing costs and responding more quickly are key reasons for work teams.

           d. <u>Quality</u>—excellent quality is a primary goal of work teams.

❖**2**❖   Identify four types of work teams.

II.   **Types of Work Teams**

1. **Problem-Solving Work Team**—consists of employees from different areas of an organization who consider how something can be done better.

   a. Such a team may meet one or two hours a week on a continuing basis to discuss ways to improve quality, safety, productivity, or morale.

   b. Quality Circle (also called a TQM team)—is a group of employees who meet regularly to identify, analyze, and propose solutions to various types of workplace problems.

      1. Meetings usually lasting an hour or so are held once every week or two during or after regular working hours.

      2. Quality circles are expected to look for and propose solutions to quality-related problems continuously.

      3. Quality circles normally do not have the authority to implement their proposed solutions, which are presented to management for further consideration and action.

   c. Task Forces—are teams that are formed to accomplish specific, highly important goals for an organization.

2. **Functional Work Team**—includes members from a single department who have the common goal of considering issues and solving problems within their area of responsibility and expertise.

   a. Functional work teams formed for the purpose of completing their daily work are quite stable, enduring for as long as the organization maintains its same basic structure.

   b. A functional work team brought together as a task force to look at a specific issue or problem would disband as soon as it had completed its specific assignment.

3. **Multidisciplinary Work Team**—may consist of employees from various functional areas and sometimes several organizational levels who collectively work on specific tasks.

   a. In some respects, multidisciplinary teams are like task forces, but they differ from task forces in one important way: They are primary vehicles for accomplishing the core work of the organization.

   b. They are often used to speed design, production, and services processes or to enhance creativity and innovation.

   c. Product Development Team—a common type of multidisciplinary work team that exists for the period of time required to bring a product to market, which could vary from a couple of months to several years.

      1. In the telecommunications and electronic industries, multidisciplinary R & D teams bring together experts with a variety of knowledge and backgrounds to generate ideas for new products and services.

      2. To ensure that the products appeal to customers, the work teams may include representatives from marketing and the eventual end users.

4. **Self-Managing Work Team**—normally consists of employees who work together daily to make an entire product or deliver an entire service.

    a. The members all may be from a single functional area, but more often self-managing work teams are multidisciplinary.

    b. When it is truly empowered, a self-managing team does more than simply take over administrative duties.

    c. It also has a strong commitment to the organization's mission, the autonomy needed to control its own activities, belief in itself, and a chance to see directly the impact of its efforts.

❖**3**❖   State the meaning and determinants of team effectiveness.

  III. **A Framework For Team Effectiveness**

1. Although teams offer great potential, that potential isn't always realized.

2. Even when teams do fulfill their potential, team members and their organizations may experience unanticipated negative side effects, such as lingering political fights and turnover.

3. **Effectiveness Criteria**—measure the outcomes achieved by individual members and the team as a whole.

    a. A particular work team may be effective in some respects and ineffective in others.

    b. Whether the work team is viewed as effective overall depends on the relative importance of the various effectiveness criteria applied.

4. **Effectiveness Determinants**—the second step in achieving team effectiveness involves knowing about the various factors that determine how well the team is doing with respect to the effectiveness criteria.

    a. Effectiveness is determined by three main sets of influences: the external context in which the team operates, team design, and internal team processes.

❖**4**❖   Describe the internal team processes that can affect team performance.

  IV. **Internal Team Processes**

1. **Internal Team Processes**—include the development of the work team over time, personal feelings, and behavioral norms.

    a. In effective work teams, these processes support cooperation among team members and coordination of their work.

2. **Developmental Stages**—team functioning generally improves after a team has been together awhile. In general, the speed of team development seems to reflect the team's deadlines. As deadlines approach, team members feel more pressure to perform and often respond by resolving or setting aside personal differences in order to complete a task. No particular period of time is needed for a team to progress from one stage to the next. The stages include:

   a. <u>Forming Stage</u>—is the earliest stage of team development, at which the work team focuses on orientation to its goals and procedures.

      1. Most members may be anxious about what the team and they, as individual members, are supposed to do.

      2. In newly formed teams, task relationships often are guarded, cautious, and noncommittal.

      3. Understanding leadership roles and getting acquainted with other team members facilitate development.

   b. <u>Storming Stage</u>—is the stage of team development that begins when competitive or strained behaviors emerge and may involve resistance and impatience with the lack of progress.

      1. A few dominant members may begin to force an agenda without regard for the needs of other team members.

      2. Team members may challenge the leader, or they may isolate themselves from team discussion.

      3. If conflict spreads, frustration, anger, and defensive behavior may appear.

      4. If conflict is suppressed and not permitted to occur, resentment and bitterness may result, which in turn can lead to apathy or abandonment.

      5. Although conflict resolution often is the goal of work teams during the storming stage, conflict management is generally what is achieved.

   c. <u>Norming Stage</u>—is the stage of team development at which team members become increasingly positive about the team as a whole, the other members as individuals, and what the team is doing. The rules of behavior that are widely shared and enforced by the members of the work team develop.

      1. At the beginning of the norming stage, the dominant view might be: We are in this together, like it or not. Let us make the most of it.

      2. Problems are resolved through cooperation, open communication, and the acceptance of mutual influence.

      3. If the work team gets to the end of this stage, most members may like their involvement a great deal.

      4. If the work team focuses too much on "we-ness," harmony, and conformity, team members may avoid task-related conflicts that need to be resolved to achieve optimal performance.

d. <u>Performing Stage</u>—is the stage of team development by which members usually have come to trust and accept each other. Members are willing to risk presenting "wild" ideas without fear of being put down, and give accurate feedback to each other helps focus the team on its tasks and goals.

1. Leadership within the team is flexible and may shift among members in terms of who is most capable of solving a particular problem.

2. In terms of relationship behaviors, the team accepts the reality of differences and disagreements and works on them cooperatively and enthusiastically.

3. The team tries to reach consensus on important issues and to avoid internal politics.

4. The following characteristics lead to high levels of team performance:

   a. Members direct their energies toward the twin goals of getting things done (task behaviors) and building constructive interpersonal ties and processes (relationship behaviors).

   b. Members use procedures for making decisions, including how to share leadership.

   c. Members trust each other and are open among themselves.

   d. Members receive help from and give help to one another.

   e. Members are to be themselves while feeling a sense of belonging with others.

   f. Members accept and deal with conflicts.

   g. Members diagnose and improve their own functioning.

e. <u>Adjourning Stage</u>—is the stage of team development that involves terminating task behaviors and disengaging from relationships.

1. This stage is not always planned; however, a planned team conclusion often involves recognition for participation and achievement and an opportunity for members to say personal good-byes.

2. Adjournment of a work team charged with a particular task should be set for a specific time and have a recognizable ending point.

3. Ongoing work teams will have membership turnover, which will cause the team to recycle through earlier stages. Staggered terms of appointment can minimize the amount of recycling required.

3. **Feelings**—reflect the emotional climate of a group.

a. The four feelings most likely to influence work team effectiveness and productivity are the feelings of trust, openness, freedom, and interdependence.

   1. The more these feelings are present, the more likely the work team will be effective and the members will experience satisfaction.

b. <u>Cohesiveness</u>—the strength of members' desires to remain in the group and their commitment to it.

   1. It is a reflection of the members' feelings toward one another and the team as a whole.

   2. Team members may feel strongly committed to the team, even if they don't feel strongly committed to the organization.

   3. Cohesiveness cannot be dictated by managers or other work team members. It is a reflection of the members' feelings toward one another and the team as a whole.

   4. A cohesive team can work effectively for or against organizational goals.

4. **Behavioral Norms**—are the informal rules of behavior that are widely shared and enforced by members of a work team.

   a. Their main function is to regulate and standardize the behaviors viewed as important by team members.

      1. Norms may specify how much members should do, how customers should be treated, the importance that should be assigned to quality, what members should wear, what kinds of jokes are acceptable, how members should feel about the organization, how they should deal with their managers, and so on.

   b. A performance norm exists when three criteria have been met.

      1. There is a standard of appropriate behavior for team members.

      2. Members must generally agree on the standard.

      3. The members must be aware that the team supports the particular standard through a system of rewards and punishments—rewards for compliance and punishments for violations.

   c. <u>Free Rider</u>—is a team member who isn't contributing fully to team performance but still shares in team rewards.

   d. <u>Groupthink</u>—is an agreement-at-any-cost mentality that results in ineffective work team decision making and may lead to poor solutions.

      1. When decision-making work teams are so cohesive that conflict is stifled, groupthink can develop.

      2. The fundamental problem underlying groupthink is pressure on members to concede and accept what other members think.

      3. The likelihood of groupthink increases when: peer pressure to conform is great, a highly directive leader presses for a particular interpretation of the problem and course of action, the need to process a complex and unstructured issue under crisis conditions exists, and the group is isolated.

     e. <u>Productive Controversy</u>—occurs when team members value different points of view and seek to draw them out to facilitate creative problem solving.

       1. To ensure constructive controversy, work team members must establish ground rules to keep them focused on issues rather than people and defer decisions until various issues and ideas are explored.

❖**5**❖   Explain how to diagnose and remove barriers to poor team performance.

V. Diagnosing the Causes of Poor Team Performance

  1. **External System**—comprises outside organizational conditions and influences that exist before and after the work team is formed.

  2. **Team Design**—the design choices involved in creating a work team are numerous.

     a. <u>Team Size</u>—as the number of team members increases, changes occur in the team's internal decision-making processes.

       1. A good rule of thumb to remember is that understaffed teams tend to outperform overstaffed teams.

       2. Increasing team size causes the following effects: (1) demands on leader time and attention are greater; (2) the team's tolerance of direction from the leader is greater, and the team's decision making becomes more centralized; (3) the team atmosphere is less friendly, the actions are less personal, more cliques form within the team, and, in general, team members are less satisfied; (4) the team's rules and procedures become more formalized; and (5) the likelihood of some members being free riders increases.

     b. <u>Team Proximity</u>—refers to the location of a team's members.

       1. Two aspects of team location are (1) proximity to other work being done and (2) team members' proximity to each other.

       2. The ideal proximity among teams depends on the work being done.

     c. <u>Virtual Work Team</u>—is a work team that meets and does its tasks without everyone being physically present in the same place or even at the same time.

       1. Virtual work teams can be functional, problem-solving, multidisciplinary, or self-managing.

  3. **Culture**—the societal culture in which the work team operates is one major aspect of the external system.

     a. In an international work team, the natural tendency of team members is to behave according to the norms of their countries. When different cultures are present, misunderstandings are the likely result if team members are not familiar with the cultures represented on the team.

     b. Regardless of national cultures, work teams can function well if they are supported by the organization's culture.

    c. Organizational values that support participation by lower level employees increases the likelihood that work team members will embrace organizational goals and authority relations, rather than attempt to undermine them.

4. **Team Member Selection**—the characteristics needed in an employee who works in relative isolation are different from those needed in an employee who must work in a team environment.

    a. In work teams, the personality traits of <u>agreeableness</u> (persons who seek to find areas of common understanding with the members of the team) and <u>conscientiousness</u> (people who tend to stay focused on the task and seem to be good at organizing and coordinating activities) seem to be especially important.

    b. Of our six managerial competencies, communication and teamwork are essential for working in all types of teams.

    c. Personality traits are difficult to change, and both technical skills and managerial competencies develop slowly over time.   For these reasons, team-based organizations often use intensive and sophisticated selection procedures when hiring new employees.

5. **Team Training**—regardless of how many hours of team training organizations require, their goals are usually the same—to train members to perform a variety of managerial and leadership activities and to enhance team cohesiveness.

    a. <u>Management and Leadership Training</u>—responsibilities managers share include:

        1. Managing meetings.

        2. Supporting disagreement.

        3. Committing to a team decision.

        4. Using group-based technologies.

    b. <u>Building Team Cohesiveness</u>—to develop team cohesiveness, many organizations use experientially based adventure training.

6. **Reward Systems**—inform employees about how to direct their energies and reinforce them for making valuable contributions to the organization.

    a. Most experts agree that different team structures call for different reward systems.

    b. Thus, rather than prescribing a specific approach to rewarding work teams, understanding the basic choices involved in tailoring a reward system to an organization's situation is more useful.

MATCHING

<u>Directions</u>: Select the term that best identifies the statement listed below. Place the letter of the correct term in the space provided.

A. Virtual Work Team
B. Group
C. Cohesiveness
D. Task Force
E. Forming Stage
F. Problem-Solving Work Team
G. Work Team
H. Internal Team Processes
I. Feelings
J. Adjourning Stage

K. Team Proximity
L. Quality Circle
M. Storming Stage
N. Functional Work Team
O. Effectiveness Criteria
P. Performing Stage
Q. Multidisciplinary Work Team
R. External System
S. Behavioral Norms
T. Groupthink

_____ 1. The earliest stage of team development, at which the work team focuses on orientation to its goals and procedures.

_____ 2. Measurements of the outcomes achieved by individual members and the team as a whole.

_____ 3. Two or more individuals who come into personal and meaningful contact on a continuing basis.

_____ 4. The location of a team's members relative to the organization and relative to each other.

_____ 5. The activities that enable a team to coordinate and integrate the efforts of team members, including the development of the team over time, personal feelings, and behavioral norms.

_____ 6. The stage of team development that begins when competitive or strained behaviors emerge and may involve resistance and impatience with the lack of progress.

_____ 7. An agreement-at-any-cost mentality that results in an ineffective team decision-making process and may lead to poor solutions.

_____ 8. A work team that meets without everyone being physically present in the same place or even at the same time.

_____ 9. The stage of team development that involves terminating task behaviors and disengaging from relationships.

_____ 10. Members from a single department or unit, who jointly consider common issues and solve problems common to their area of responsibility and expertise.

_____ 11. The strength of members' desires to remain in the group or team and their commitment to it.

_____ 12. A group of employees who voluntarily meet regularly to identify, analyze, and propose solutions to problems in the workplace.

_____ 13. Employees from various functions and sometimes several organizational levels who collectively have specific tasks.

_____ 14. The emotions that reflect how team members feel about each other, including anger, happiness, trust, and distrust.

_____ 15. A team that is formed to accomplish a specific highly important goal for an organization.

_____ 16. Organizational conditions and influences outside the team that exist before and after a team is formed, including societal and organizational culture, organization design, and the human resource management system.

_____ 17. A small number of identifiable, interdependent employees who are held accountable for performing tasks that contribute to the achievement of organizational goals.

_____ 18. The stage of team development by which members usually have come to trust and accept each other.

_____ 19. Employees from different areas of a department who consider how something can be done better.

_____ 20. The informal rules of behavior that are widely shared and enforced by the members of a group.

TRUE OR FALSE

Directions: Write True or False in the space provided.

❖1❖

_____ 1. Work teams are primarily only found in the manufacturing operations.

_____ 2. The primary reasons for work teams in organizations include speed, innovation, cost reduction, and quality improvement.

❖2❖

_____ 3. Quality circles are often called TQM teams.

_____ 4. A functional work team may consist of employees from various functional areas and sometimes several organizational levels who collectively have specific goal-oriented tasks.

_____ 5. A self-managing work team normally consists of employees who work together daily to make an entire product or deliver an entire service.

❖3❖

_____ 6. Based on the productivity and outcomes of work teams, the popularity of team-based organizational structures is decreasing.

_____ 7. Effectiveness criteria measure the outcomes achieved by individual members and the team as a whole.

❖4❖

_____ 8. External processes include the development of the work team over time, personal feelings, and behavioral norms.

_____ 9. No particular period of time is needed for a team to progress from one stage to another in the developmental stage model.

_____ 10. In the norming stage of work team development, team members may challenge the leader, or they may isolate themselves from team discussion.

_____ 11. The performing stage involves terminating task behaviors and disengaging from relationships.

_____ 12. Throughout the stages of a work team's development, team members experience a variety of feelings, which reflect the emotional climate of a group.

_____ 13. A cohesive team always works effectively toward positive performance and accomplishment of organizational goals.

_____ 14. Groupthink refers to the rules of behavior that are widely shared and enforced by members of a work team.

_____ 15. The likelihood of groupthink increases when the group has a high degree of interaction with others in the organization.

❖5❖

_____ 16. A virtual work team meets and does its tasks without everyone being physically present in the same place or even at the same time.

_____ 17. Even within the United States, norms vary greatly between teams.

_____ 18. The most important personality trait for individuals in work teams sought during selection is extroversion.

_____ 19. The goals of team training organizations are usually the same—to train team members to perform a variety of managerial and leadership activities to enhance team cohesiveness.

_____ 20. Experiential training is the most optimal method of developing teamwork.

MULTIPLE CHOICE

<u>Directions</u>: Select the best answer in the space provided.

❖1❖

_____ 1. Six strangers waiting in Detroit, Michigan, to board a TWA flight to Los Angeles would be considered a(n) _____.
   a. work team
   b. group
   c. informal group
   d. none of the above

_____   2.   Which of the following is a true statement about informal groups?
         a.   They may support, oppose, or have no interest in organizational goals, rules, or higher authority.
         b.   Informal groups have little to do with completing tasks required by the employer.
         c.   A social group is one of the most common types of informal groups, within or outside the organization.
         d.   All of the above

❖2❖

_____   3.   At ConAgra, a diversified international food company, a _____ team's goals might include minimizing costs and ensuring that beef supplies are available to stores when needed.
         a.   high-performance
         b.   self-managing
         c.   functional
         d.   product development

_____   4.   Task forces and quality circles are examples of _____ work teams.
         a.   problem-solving
         b.   multidisciplinary
         c.   self-managing
         d.   functional

_____   5.   A _____ team is another common type of multidisciplinary work team.
         a.   product development
         b.   self-managing
         c.   functional
         d.   proximity

_____   6.   _____ work teams are composed of employees who work together daily to make an entire product or deliver an entire service.
         a.   Product development
         b.   Functional
         c.   Proximity
         d.   Self-managed

❖3❖

_____   7.   _____ measure the outcomes achieved by individual members and the team as a whole.
         a.   Effectiveness determinants
         b.   Effectiveness criteria
         c.   Internal team processes
         d.   Behavioral norms

❖**4**❖

_____ 8.   _____ team processes include the development of the work team over time, personal feelings, and behavioral norms.
   a. Internal
   b. Behavioral
   c. External
   d. Psychological

_____ 9.   The local chapter of NADD (Neighbors Against Drunk Drivers) membership is uncertain about what they as individuals and as a group are supposed to do. This group is in the _____ stage of work team development.
   a. storming
   b. norming
   c. forming
   d. adjourning

_____ 10.   At the beginning of the _____ stage of work team development, the dominant view might be: We are in this together, like it or not. Let's make the most of it.
   a. norming
   b. storming
   c. performing
   d. adjourning

_____ 11.   Which of the following characteristics lead to high levels of team performance?
   a. Members use procedures for making decisions, including how to share leadership.
   b. Members to accept and deal with conflicts.
   c. Members trust each other and are open among themselves.
   d. All of the above

_____ 12.   _____ is the strength of members' desires to remain in the group and their commitment to it.
   a. Cohesiveness
   b. Forming
   c. Interdependence
   d. Opennes

_____ 13.   At Emerson University, the professors in the Finance Department expect that all faculty in the department will dress professionally (no jeans) even though the university policy allows professors to wear any attire they desire. This is an example of _____.
   a. cohesiveness
   b. behavioral norms
   c. groupthink
   d. rules

_____ 14. When a member of a work team refuses to contribute to the team's project, and anticipates to reap the benefits of the project, this is known as _____.
  a. groupthink
  b. free riding
  c. gainsharing
  d. productive controversy

_____ 15. The underlying problem with _____ is pressure on members to concede and accept what other members think.
  a. feelings
  b. groupthink
  c. cohesiveness
  d. informal groups

_____ 16. A(n) _____ work team is simply a work team that meets and does its tasks without everyone being physically present in the same place or even at the same time.
  a. matrix
  b. independent
  c. virtual
  d. robotic

_____ 17. Virtual work team members that are geographically dispersed are more likely to function effectively if they follow all of the guidelines except:
  a. Whenever possible use a variety of communication technologies.
  b. Encourage team members to copy every e-mail message to the entire team for the purpose of promoting team interaction.
  c. Train team members to match their choice of technology to the task.
  d. Be sure that someone is responsible for facilitating the communication process.

❖5❖

_____ 18. To develop team _____, many organizations use experientially based adventure training.
  a. effectiveness
  b. performance
  c. rewards
  d. cohesiveness

_____ 19. Which of the following statements regarding reward systems is false?
  a. When employees work in a single team most of the time and it is essentially the employee's entire job, establishing team performance measures and using them to determine rates of pay is relatively easy.
  b. Most experts agree that different team structures call for different reward systems.
  c. In most organizations, individuals are assigned full time to a single team with their rewards based primarily on their group's performance.
  d. None of the above

____   20.   Which of the following is a <u>false</u> statement concerning team reward systems?
a. Both monetary and nonmonetary rewards should be used, taking into account differences in what individuals value most.
b. Employees should understand the reward system.
c. The reward system, to ensure fairness, should be the same for all teams in an organization.
d. The system should be designed to reward team efforts.

ESSAY QUESTIONS

❖1❖

1.   Explain why organizations use work teams.

❖2❖

2.   Explain the four most common types of work teams: functional, problem-solving, multidisciplinary, and self-managing.

❖3❖

3.   Define *effectiveness criteria*.

❖4❖

4.   Identify and discuss the stages of work team development.

5. Define *productive controversy* and discuss how it relates to norms.

❖**5**❖

6. Define *virtual work team* and the best practices to manage such teams.

CHAPTER 17
MANAGING WORK TEAMS

MATCHING SOLUTIONS

1. E - Forming Stage
2. O - Effectiveness Criteria
3. B - Group
4. K - Team Proximity
5. H - Internal Team Processes
6. M - Storming Stage
7. T - Groupthink
8. A - Virtual Work Team
9. J   - Adjourning Stage
10. N - Functional Work Team
11. C - Cohesiveness
12. L - Quality Circle
13. Q - Multidisciplinary Work Team
14. I - Feelings
15. D - Task Force
16. R - External System
17. G - Work Team
18. P - Performing Stage
19. F - Problem-Solving Work Team
20. S - Behavioral Norms

TRUE/FALSE SOLUTIONS

Question	Answer	Page	Explanation
1.	False	481	Work teams were found mostly in manufacturing operations a few years ago, but they have now spread throughout the service sector.
2.	True		
3.	True		
4.	False	485–486	A <u>functional work team</u> includes members from a single department who have the common goal of considering issues and solving problems common to their area of responsibility and expertise. A <u>multidisciplinary work team</u> consists of employees from various functional areas and sometimes several organizational levels who collectively have specific goal-oriented tasks.
5.	True		
6.	False	488	The increasing popularity of team-based organizational structures reflects the belief that teams can achieve outcomes that could not be achieved by the same number of individuals working alone.
7.	True		
8.	False	489	<u>Internal team processes</u> include the development of the work team over time, personal feelings, and behavioral norms. In effective work teams, these processes support cooperation among team members and coordination of their work.
9.	True		
10.	False	491–494	The <u>storming stage</u> begins when competitive or strained behaviors emerge. Initially, the storming process may involve resistance and impatience with the lack of progress. Team members may challenge the leader, or they may isolate themselves from team discussion. In the <u>norming stage</u>, team members become increasingly positive about the team as a whole, the other members as individuals, and what the team is doing. At the beginning of the norming stage, the dominant view might be: We are in this together, like it or not. Let's make the most of it. Thus the team members may begin to develop a sense of belonging and commitment.

11.	False	494	The <u>adjourning stage</u> involves terminating task behaviors and disengaging from relationships. <u>The performing stage</u> is where members usually come to trust and accept each other.
12.	True		
13.	False	494	<u>Cohesiveness</u> is the strength of members' desires to remain in the group and their commitment to it. Cohesiveness cannot be dictated by managers or other work team members. It is a reflection of the members' feelings toward one another and the team as a whole. A cohesive team can work effectively for or against organizational goals. For example, a cohesive team with negative feelings toward the organization may promote performance standards that limit productivity and pressure individual members to conform to them.
14.	False	495–496	<u>Behavioral norms</u> are the rules of behavior that are widely shared and enforced by members of a work team. <u>Groupthink</u> is an agreement-at-any-cost mentality that results in ineffective work team decision making.
15.	False	496	The likelihood of <u>groupthink</u> increases when: the group is isolated, needs to process a complex and unstructured issue under crisis conditions; has a highly directive leader pressing for a particular interpretation of the problem, and there is a high degree of peer pressure to conform.
16.	True		
17.	True		
18.	False	501	The characteristics needed in an employee who works in relative isolation are different from those needed in an employee who must work in a team environment. In work teams, the personality traits of <u>agreeableness</u> and conscientiousness seem to be especially important.
19.	True		
20.	False	504	Experiential training is an effective way to develop cohesiveness, but used alone it isn't likely to result in optimal teamwork. Teams can also benefit from more formal training.

MULTIPLE CHOICE SOLUTIONS

<u>Question</u>	<u>Answer</u>	<u>Page</u>	<u>Explanation</u>
1.	d	480	A <u>group</u> is two or more individuals who come into personal and meaningful contact on a continuing basis. Six strangers waiting to board a plane are not a group. The contact is not highly meaningful and most likely just a one-time event. A <u>work team</u> consists of a small number of identifiable, interdependent employees who are held accountable for performing tasks that contribute to achieving an organization's goals.
2.	d	482	An <u>informal group</u> consists of a small number of individuals who frequently participate together in activities and share feelings for the purpose of meeting their mutual needs. All of the statements listed are true.
3.	c	485	A <u>functional work team</u> includes members from a single department who have the common goal of considering issues and solving problems common to their area of responsibility and expertise. For example, at ConAgra, a diversified international food company, a functional team could be the purchasing manager and the purchasing agents in the department. Their goals might include minimizing costs and ensuring that beef supplies are available to stores when needed.
4.	a	484	A <u>problem-solving work team</u> usually consists of employees from different areas of an organization who consider how something can be done better. Such a team may meet one or two hours a week on a continuing basis to discuss ways to improve quality, safety, productivity, or morale. Task forces such as those used by Sears' CEO are perhaps the most common type of problem-solving work team. Quality circles are another form of problem-solving work teams.
5.	a	485–486	A <u>multidisciplinary work team</u> consists of employees from various functional areas and sometimes several organizational levels who collectively work on specific tasks. A product development team is a common type of multidisciplinary work team.

6.   d   486   <u>Self-managing work teams</u> normally consist of employees who work together daily to make an entire product or deliver an entire service.

7.   b   488   <u>Effectiveness criteria</u> measure the outcomes achieved by individual members and the team as a whole.

8.   a   489   <u>Internal team processes</u> include the development of work team norms over time, personal feelings, and behaviors.

9.   c   492–493   During the <u>forming stage,</u> a work team focuses on orientation to its goals and procedures. Most members may be anxious about what the team and they, as individual members, are supposed to do. In newly formed teams, task relationships are often guarded, cautious, and noncommittal. Understanding leadership roles and getting acquainted with other team members facilitate development.

10.   a   493–494   In the <u>norming stage</u>, team members become increasingly positive about the team as a whole, the other members as individuals, and what the team is doing. At the beginning of this stage, the dominant view might be: We are in this together, like it or not. Let's make the most of it. The <u>storming stage</u> begins when competitive or strained behaviors emerge. Team members may challenge the leader, or they may isolate themselves from team discussion. In the <u>performing stage</u> members usually have come to trust and accept each other. To accomplish tasks, diversity of viewpoints is supported and encouraged. The <u>adjourning stage</u> involves terminating task behaviors and disengaging from relationships.

11.   d   493–494   The following characteristics lead to high levels of team performance: (1) Members direct their energies toward the twin goals of getting things done and building constructive interpersonal ties and processes. (2) Members use procedures for making decisions, including how to share leadership. (3) Members trust each other and are open among themselves. (4) Members receive help from and give help to one another. (5) Members are free to be themselves while feeling a sense of belonging with others. (6) Members accept and deal with conflicts. (7) Members diagnose and improve their own functioning. The degree to which one or more of these characteristics is absent determines the extent to which teams are likely to be ineffective.

12.	a	494	<u>Cohesiveness</u> is the strength of members' desires to remain in the group and then commit to it.
13.	b	495	<u>Behavioral norms</u> are the informal rules of behavior that are widely shared and enforced by the members of a work team. They set standards for members' behaviors under specific circumstances. Norms may specify how much members should do, how customers should be treated, the importance that should be assigned to quality, what members should wear, what kind of jokes are acceptable, how members should feel about the organization, how they should deal with their managers and so on.
14.	b	495	When a team member isn't contributing fully to team performance but still shares in team rewards, that person is referred to as a <u>free rider</u>.
15.	b	496	<u>Groupthink</u> is an agreement-at-any-cost mentality that results in ineffective work team decision making and may lead to poor solutions. The fundamental problem underlying groupthink is pressure on members to concede and accept what other members think.
16.	c	498	A <u>virtual work team</u> is simply a work team that meets and does its tasks without everyone being physically present in the same place or even at the same time. Virtual work teams can be functional, problem-solving, multidisciplinary, or self-managing.
17.	b	498	Virtual teams that are geographically dispersed are more likely to function effectively if they follow some simple guidelines: (1) Whenever possible, use a variety of communication technologies. (2) Pay attention to the quality of the communication transmissions. (3) Encourage the team members to discuss cultural differences. (4) Be sure that someone is responsible for facilitating the communication process. (5) Encourage team members to interact one on one, without feeling obligated to copy every e-mail message to the entire team. (6) Train team members to match their choice of technology to the task.
18.	d	503	To develop team cohesiveness, many organizations use experientially based, adventure training. Such training often is held in a camplike environment and includes navigating river rapids, scaling cliffs, or completing a ropes course.

includes navigating river rapids, scaling cliffs, or completing a ropes course.

19.   c   504   When employees work in a single team most of the time and its is essentially the employee's entire job, establishing team performance measures and using them to determine rates of pay is relatively easy. In most organizations, however, people aren't assigned full time to a single team. Their primary responsibilities may derive from a job that they perform essentially as an individual, with work team participation added to their regular duties.

20.   c   505   Most experts agree that different team structures call for different reward systems. Thus, rather than prescribe a specific approach to rewarding work teams, it is more useful to understand the basic choices involved in tailoring a reward system to an organization's situation.

ESSAY SOLUTIONS

[Pages 483–484]

1. The main reasons that managers give for organizing work around teams are generally similar for a variety of organizations. They include servicing customers better through innovation, speed, cost reduction, and quality improvement. Innovation is increased by bringing together people having a variety of experience and expertise to address a common problem or task. Speed can be enhanced by teams who reduce the time required for product development. Costs are reduced often by better servicing customers in a more timely manner. Finally, excellent quality is the primary goal of work teams.

[Pages 484–487]

2. A <u>problem-solving work team</u> usually consists of employees from different areas of an organization whose purpose is to consider how something can be done better. Such a team may meet one or two hours a week on a continuing basis to discuss ways to improve quality, safety, productivity, or morale.

    A <u>functional work team</u> includes members from a single department who have the common goal of considering issues and solving problems common to their area of responsibility and expertise. Functional work teams formed for the purpose of completing their daily work are quite stable, enduring for as long as the organization maintains its same basic structure.

    A <u>multidisciplinary work team</u> may consist of employees from various functional areas and sometimes several organizational levels who collectively have specific tasks. The use of such teams is spreading rapidly and crosses all types of organizational boundaries.

A <u>self-managing work team</u> normally consists of employees who work together daily to make an entire product or deliver an entire service. These teams often perform various managerial tasks, including scheduling their members' work and vacations, rotating job tasks and assignments among members, ordering materials, deciding on team leadership, and setting production goals. In other words, to a large extent, they decide both what they need to do and how to do it.

[Pages 488–489]

3. <u>Effectiveness criteria</u> measure the outcomes achieved by individual members and the team as a whole. Whether the team is viewed as effective overall depends on the relative importance of the various effectiveness criteria applied.

[Pages 491–494]

4. During the <u>forming stage</u>, a work team focuses on orientation to its goals and procedures. Most members may be anxious about what the team and they, as individual members, are supposed to do. Task relationships are often guarded, cautious, and noncommittal. Understanding leadership roles and getting acquainted with other team members facilitates development. The second stage, <u>storming</u>, begins when competitive or strained behaviors emerge. Initially, the storming process may involve resistance and impatience with the lack of progress. Team members may challenge the leader, or they may isolate themselves from group discussion. If conflict spreads, frustration, anger, and defensive behavior may appear. The next stage is <u>norming</u>. At the beginning of this stage the dominant view might be: "We are in this together, like it or not. Let's make the most of it." If the group gets to the end of this stage, most members may like their involvement. The members begin to develop a sense of belonging and commitment. Although some groups never reach their performance potential, regardless of how long they exist, by the <u>performing stage</u>, members usually have come to trust and accept each other. To accomplish tasks, diversity of viewpoints is supported and encouraged. Leadership within the team is flexible and may shift among members in terms of who is most capable of solving a particular problem. In terms of relationship behaviors, the group accepts the reality of differences and disagreements and works on them cooperatively and enthusiastically. The <u>adjourning stage</u> involves terminating task behaviors and disengaging from relationships. This stage is not always planned and may be rather abrupt. Adjournment of a work team charged with a particular task should be set for a specific time and have a recognizable ending point.

[Page 496]

5. Falling between the extremes of all-out warfare and groupthink are teams with norms that support productive controversy. <u>Productive controversy</u> occurs when team members value different points of view and seek to draw them out to facilitate creative problem solving. To ensure constructive controversy, work team members must establish ground rules to keep them focused on issues rather than people and defer decisions until various issues and ideas are explored.

[Pages 498–500]

6. A <u>virtual work team</u> meets and does its tasks without everyone being physically present in the same place or even at the same time. Virtual work teams can be functional, problem solving, multidisciplinary, or self-managing. The following are some of the current best practices for managing virtual work teams: use a variety of communication technologies; pay attention to the quality of the communication transmissions; encourage the team members to discuss cultural differences; be sure that someone is responsible for facilitation the communication process; encourage team members to interact one on one, without feeling obligated to copy every email message to the entire team; and train team members to match their choice of technology to the task.

CHAPTER 18
ORGANIZATIONAL CULTURE
AND CULTURAL DIVERSITY

LEARNING OBJECTIVES

After studying this chapter, you should be able to:

❖**1**❖   Describe the core elements of a culture.

❖**2**❖   Compare and contrast four types of organizational culture.

❖**3**❖   Discuss several types of subcultures that may exist in organizations.

❖**4**❖   Describe several activities for successfully managing diversity.

OUTLINE

❖**1**❖   Describe the core elements of a culture.

    I.   The Elements of Culture

        1. **Culture**—is the unique pattern of shared assumptions, values, and norms that shape the socialization, symbols, language, narratives and practices of a group of people.

            a. As illustrated in Figure 18.1, these elements form the base of a culture but they can't be observed directly.

            b. They can only be inferred from a cultures more visible elements—its socialization activities, symbols, language, narratives, and practices.

        2. **Shared Assumptions**—are the underlying thoughts and feelings that members of a culture take for granted and believe to be true.

        3. **Values**—basic beliefs about a condition that has considerable importance and meaning to individuals and is stable over time.

            a. <u>Norms</u>—are rules for the behaviors of group members.

        4. **Socialization**—is a systematic process by which new members are brought into a culture.

            a. The most powerful way to socialize people into a culture is through consistent role modeling, teaching, coaching, and enforcement by others in the culture.

1. At the societal level, socialization takes place within the family, in schools and religious organizations, and through the media.

2. At the industry level, socialization often occurs through organized activities conducted by industry associations.

5. **Symbols**—are anything visible that can be used to represent an abstract shared value or something having special meaning.

   a. Symbols are the simplest and most basic form of cultural expression.

   b. Symbols may be expressed through logos, architecture, uniforms, awards, and many other tangible expressions.

6. **Language**—is a shared system of vocal sounds, written signs, and/or gestures used to convey special meanings among members of a culture.

7. **Narratives**—are the unique stories, sagas, legends, and myths in a culture.

   a. Narratives often describe the unique accomplishments and beliefs of leaders over time, usually in heroic and romantic terms.

   b. The basic story may be based on historical fact, but as the story gets told and retold, the facts may be embellished with fictional details.

8. **Practices**—are the most complex but observable cultural form.

   a. Taboos—are behaviors that are forbidden in the culture.

   b. Ceremonies—are elaborate and formal activities designed to generate strong feelings. Usually they are carried out as special events.

      1. In most societies, important ceremonies celebrate the birth, marriage, and death of the society's members.

❖2❖   Compare and contrast four types of organizational culture.

II.   **Basic Types of Organizational Culture**—the four pure types of organizational culture are bureaucratic, clan, entrepreneurial, and market.

1. **Bureaucratic Culture**—is where the behavior of employees is governed by formal rules and standard operating procedures, and coordination is achieved through hierarchical reporting relationships.

   a. The long-term concerns of a bureaucracy are predictability, efficiency, and stability.

   b. The focus of attention is on the internal operations of the organization.

   c. To ensure stability, the tasks, responsibilities, authority for all employees is clearly spelled out.

   d. These cultures are often found in organizations that produce standardized goods and/or services.

2. **Clan Culture**—refers to the attributes of tradition, loyalty, personal commitment, extensive socialization, teamwork, self-management, and social influence.

   a. Its members recognize an obligation beyond the simple exchange of labor for a salary.

      1. They understand that contributions to the organization (e.g., hours worked per week) may exceed any contractual agreements.

   b. The clan culture achieves unity with a long and thorough socialization process.

      1. Long-time clan members serve as mentors and role models for newer members.

      2. These relationships perpetuate the organization's values and norms over successive generations of employees.

      3. Members of a clan culture are aware of their unique history and they have a shared image of the organization's style and manner of conduct.

      4. They have a strong sense of identification and recognize their need to work together.

      5. Shared goals, perceptions, and behavioral tendencies foster communication, coordination, and integration.

      6. Peer pressure to adhere to important norms is also strong.

3. **Entrepreneurial Culture**—is characterized by high levels of risk taking, dynamism, and creativity.

   a. There is a commitment to experimentation, innovation, and being on the leading edge.

      1. This culture does not just quickly react to changes in the environment; it creates change.

      2. Effectiveness means providing new and unique products and rapid growth.

   b. Individual initiative, flexibility, and freedom foster growth and are encouraged and well rewarded.

4. **Market Culture**—values achievement of measurable and demanding goals, especially those that are financial and market based (e.g., sales growth, profitability, and market share).

   a. Hard-driving competitiveness and a profits orientation prevail throughout the organization.

   b. A market culture does not exert much informal social pressure on an organization's members.

c. Superiors' interactions with subordinates largely consist of negotiating performance-reward agreements and/or evaluating requests for resource allocations.

d. <u>Strong Culture</u> – an organization is said to have a strong culture when the more observable cultural elements project a single, consistent message.

1. In such organizations, managers and employees share a common behavioral style.

2. They share common norms that guide how they relate to one another.

3. A strong organizational culture doesn't just happen—it's cultivated by management, learned and reinforced by employees, and passed on to new employees.

5. **Changing an Organizational Culture**—one reason for change is to create a stronger, more consistent organizational culture.

a. Before an organization can improve its overall culture, it must first understand the culture that is present now in the organization.

b. When an organization focuses on understanding its culture, it is likely to discover that it doesn't have one organizational culture—it probably has several subcultures.

❖**3**❖   Discuss several types of subcultures that may exist in organizations.

III. **Organizational Subcultures**

1. **Organizational Subcultures**—exist when assumptions values and norms are shared by some—but not all—organizational members.   Organizational subcultures occur for a variety of reasons:

a. <u>Mergers and Acquisitions</u>—when one firm acquires another firm, or when two firms merge, it is likely they will discover that the two firms had different cultures.

b. <u>Departmental and Divisional Subcultures</u>—these subcultures may reflect departmental specialties, regional locations, or they may be created by the managers in charge of the departments.

c. <u>Occupational Subcultures</u>—organizational designs that group members of a profession together reinforce and sustain occupation-based subcultures.

1. Subcultures within organizations often reflect business or functional specialties (e.g. manufacturing, R&D, accounting, engineering, marketing, and human resources).

2. Occupational socialization practices can be strong sources of cultural indoctrination, especially for professionals.

d. <u>Geographically Based Subcultures</u>—different subcultures are found in each country where the company has operations.

e. Created by Managers—differences in the personalities and leadership styles of managers are another reason units in an organization have different subcultures.

2. Subcultures Due to Workforce Demographics

   a. Workforce Demographics—describe employee characteristics such as ethnicity, age, and gender.

   b. The fact that people with different demographic backgrounds live side by side doesn't mean that they share the same culture.

   c. The presence of subcultures sometimes creates problems for employees and employers (e.g., firm acquisitions).

   d. Multicultural Organization—has a workforce representing the full mix of cultures found in the population at large, along with a commitment to utilize fully these human resources.

❖**4**❖ Describe several activities for successfully managing diversity.

IV. **Managing Cultural Diversity**

1. **Cultural Diversity**—encompasses the full mix of the cultures and subcultures to which members of the workforce belong.

   a. Today, efforts to manage diversity effectively usually involve finding ways to manage people representing the wide variety of subcultures found in an organization, regardless of the basis for those subcultures.

2. **Organizational Goals for Managing Cultural Diversity**—the specific approach that an organization uses to transform its culture depends on the organization's goals. The three main goals that most organizations strive to achieve are:

   a. Legal Compliance—complying with laws and regulations that prohibit discrimination, such as Title VII of the Civil Rights Act, is a necessary first step for any organization.

      1. The basic premise of such laws and regulations is that employment decisions should be based on job-related qualifications, not membership in a demographic group.

      2. The basic premise of affirmative action regulations is that organizations should actively recruit job applicants to build a workforce that reflects the demographics of the qualified labor force locally.

   b. Creating a Positive Culture—a positive organizational culture is one in which everyone feels equally integrated into the larger organization.

      1. Members of majority and minority subcultures feel respected; everyone has an equal chance to express views and influence decisions; and everyone has similar access to both formal and informal networks within the organization.

2. The most common methods used to assess organizational culture are employee surveys and focus groups.

3. In addition to asking employees directly about the organizational culture, some organizations conduct cultural audits to evaluate the language used in organizational documents and advertising, the visible symbols that decorate public spaces, the types of awards given to employees, the types and quality of food available in the company cafeteria, policies regarding holidays and absences, and the types of social activities sponsored by the organization, among other items.

c. Creating Economic Value—a third reason that organizations are striving to manage diversity effectively is because they believe that they can use diversity to create greater economic value.

1. With a diverse workforce and positive organizational culture in place, many managers believe their companies will be able to: develop products and services for new markets, attract a broader range of customers, improve customer satisfaction and increase business from repeat customers, and reduce costs, including those associated with litigation.

2. To date, little research is available publicly to document the economic benefits of a diverse workforce and positive organizational culture.

3. **The Process of Change**

a. Diagnosis—before managers begin designing new approaches to managing diversity, they first need to be sure that they understand how current practices affect the amount and nature of diversity—both in the organization as a whole and within its smaller units.

b. Vision—until leaders formulate a clear vision and persuade others to join them in being dedicated to that vision, they will not be able to generate the enthusiasm and resources needed for large scale cultural change.

c. Involvement—for a plan to be effective, those who are affected must buy into it. The best way to ensure that is through early involvement.

d. Timing—planned change usually follows an evolutionary—not revolutionary—path. Realistic expectations about how quickly change will occur are important to the long-term success of change efforts.

4. **Diversity Training**—most types attempt to provide basic information about cultural differences and similarities and sensitive participants to the powerful role that culture plays in determining their work behavior.

a. Awareness Training—is designed to provide accurate information about the many subcultures present in the organization.

b. Harassment Training—is aimed at ensuring that employees understand the meaning of harassment and the actions the company will take when someone complains of being harassed.

5. **Creating Family-Friendly Workplaces**—organizations need to survey their employees to find out their preferences and should then consider offering a variety of options to meet employees' needs.

6. **Holding Managers Accountable**—research shows the success of diversity training inititatives is greater in organizations that evaluate the effectiveness of the training and in those that offer rewards to managers who make diversity-related improvements in their business units.

7. **Challenges**—cultural awareness training programs may backfire if they seem to reinforce stereotypes or highlight cultural differences that employees have tried to erase in order to fit the company's culture.

MATCHING

<u>Directions</u>: Select the term that best identifies the statement listed below. Place the letter of the correct term in the space provided.

A. Ceremonies	K. Multicultural Organization
B. Strong Culture	L. Narratives
C. Socialization	M. Bureaucratic Culture
D. Clan Culture	N. Organizational Subculture
E. Cultural Diversity	O. Awareness Training
F. Shared Assumptions	P. Market Culture
G. Value	Q. Taboos
H. Symbol	R. Entrepreneurial Culture
I. Ceremonies	S. Culture
J. Harassment Training	T. Language

_____ 1. Dominated by a single majority culture or subculture, and members of other cultures or subcultures are expected to adopt the norms and values of the majority.

_____ 2. The unique stories, sagas, legends, and myths in a culture.

_____ 3. The attributes of tradition, loyalty, personal commitment, extensive socialization, teamwork, self-management, and social influence.

_____ 4. Behaviors that are forbidden in a culture.

_____ 5. Is anything visible that can be used to represent an abstract shared value or something having special meaning.

_____ 6. A shared system of vocal sounds, written signs, and/or gestures used to convey special meanings among members.

_____ 7. Underlying thoughts and feelings that members of a culture take for granted and believe to be true.

_____ 8. A unique pattern of shared assumptions, values, and norms that shape the socialization activities, language, symbols, and ceremonies of a group of people.

_____ 9. Involves the more observable cultural elements that project a single, consistent message.

_____ 10. An organization in which employees value formalization, rules, standard operating procedures, and hierarchical coordination.

_____ 11. The systematic process by which new members are brought into a culture.

_____ 12. Elaborate and formal activities designed to generate strong feelings and usually carried out as special events.

_____ 13. The achievement of measurable and demanding goals, especially those that are financial and market-based.

_____ 14. A basic belief about a condition that has considerable importance and meaning to individuals and is stable over time.

_____ 15. Has a workforce that represents the full mix of cultures found in the population at large, along with a commitment to fully utilize these human resources.

_____ 16. This exists when assumptions, values, and norms are shared by some, but not all, organizational members.

_____ 17. The full mix of the cultures and subcultures to which members belong.

_____ 18. Exhibits high levels of risk taking, dynamism, and creativity.

_____ 19. Are elaborate and formal activities designed to generate strong feelings.

_____ 20. This is designed to provide accurate information about the many subcultures present in an organization.

TRUE OR FALSE

Directions: Write True or False in the space provided.

❖1❖

_____ 1. Organizational cultures are influenced by larger societal and industry cultures and smaller employee group subcultures.

_____ 2. Values are the underlying thoughts and feelings that members of a culture take for granted and believe to be true.

_____ 3. Symbols are the simplest and most basic observable form of cultural expression.

_____ 4. Ceremonies include the unique stories, sagas, legends, and myths in a culture.

_____ 5. Taboos are elaborate and formal activities designed to generate strong feelings.

❖2❖

_____ 6. Different organizational cultures may be appropriate under different conditions, with no one type of culture ideal for every situation.

_____ 7. A bureaucratic culture is characterized by experimentation, risk taking, and being on the leading edge.

_____ 8. In a market culture, social relations among coworkers are emphasized, with many economic incentives tied directly to cooperating with peers.

_____ 9. In a clan culture, there is a commitment to experimentation, innovation, and being on the cutting edge.

_____ 10. The need to determine which attributes of an organization's culture should be preserved and which should be modified is constant.

❖3❖

_____ 11. When organizational cultures of the merged firms are similar, the chances of success decrease.

_____ 12. Organizational designs that group members of a profession together reinforce and sustain occupation-based subcultures.

_____ 13. Although most countries have several subcultures, only one culture exists in most organizations.

_____ 14. Gender roles may seem to be more powerful in some ethnic communities than others, and they may be more powerful in some generations than others.

_____ 15. A multicultural organization has a workforce representing the full mix of cultures found in the population at large, along with a commitment to utilize fully these human resources.

❖4❖

_____ 16. Cultural diversity encompasses the full mix of the cultures and subcultures to which members of the workforce belong.

_____ 17. A variety of laws make it illegal for employers to discriminate against employees on the basis of personal characteristics that are unrelated to the jobs.

_____ 18. Planned organizational change usually follows an evolutionary path.

_____ 19. Harassment training is designed to provide accurate information about the many subcultures present in the organization.

_____ 20. The success of diversity training initiatives is greater in organizations that evaluate the effectiveness of the training than in those that offer rewards to managers who make diversity-related improvements.

MULTIPLE CHOICE

Directions: Select the best answer in the space provided.

❖1❖

_____ 1. _____ is the unique pattern of shared assumptions, values, and norms that shape the socialization activities, language, symbols, and ceremonies of a group of people.
a. Multiculturalism
b. Culture
c. Pluralism
d. Religion

_____ 2. All of the following elements of culture are observable, except:
a. language
b. socialization
c. values
d. practices

_____ 3. _____ are the underlying thoughts and feelings that members of a culture take for granted and believe to be true.
a. Shared assumptions
b. Value systems
c. Shared practices
d. Narratives

_____ 4. Which of the following statements about socialization is true?
a. The most powerful way to socialize people into a culture is through consistent role modeling, teaching, coaching, and enforcement by others in the culture.
b. At the societal level, socialization takes place within the family, in schools and religious organizations, and through the media.
c. At the industry level, socialization often occurs through organized activities conducted by industry associations.
d. All of the above

_____ 5. Logos, parking priorities, office location, and furniture are examples of _____.
a. bonuses
b. status
c. symbols
d. image

_____ 6. One well-known saga, which appears on the company's web site, is about how Mary Kay Ash founded a successful company while struggling to support herself and her children as a single parent. This is an example of _____.
a. a folklore
b. an icon
c. a narrative
d. socialization

_____ 7. A _____ at Merck is to put profits ahead of ethical responsibilities to doctors, nurses, and patients.
   a. culture
   b. taboo
   c. value
   d. rule

❖2❖

_____ 8. In the _____ culture, the behavior of employees is governed by formal rules and standard operating procedures, and coordination is achieved through hierarchial reporting relationships.
   a. clan
   b. market
   c. bureaucratic
   d. entrepreneurial

_____ 9. The _____ culture achieves unity with a long and thorough socialization process.
   a. clan
   b. entrepreneurial
   c. market
   d. bureaucratic

_____ 10. A(n) _____ culture suits a company's start-up phase.
   a. technological
   b. market
   c. bureaucratic
   d. entrepreneurial

_____ 11. Which of the following statements about a market culture is <u>false</u>?
   a. The relationship between individual and organization is contractual.
   b. It promotes a feeling of membership in a social system.
   c. Managers are expected to cooperate with managers in other departments only to the extent necessary to achieve their performance goals.
   d. Hard-driving competitiveness and a profits orientation prevail throughout the organization.

_____ 12. Regarding organizational culture, which of the following is a true statement?
   a. A strong organizational culture doesn't just happen; it's cultivated by management.
   b. Organizational culture has the potential to enhance organizational performance, individual satisfaction, the sense of certainty about how problems are to be handled, and so on.
   c. More and more employees have begun to feel that organizational cultures established decades ago are out of step with contemporary values.
   d. All of the above

❖3❖

____ 13. A(n) _____ exists when assumptions, values, and norms are shared by some—but not all—organizational members.
a. organizational subculture
b. multicultural organization
c. cultural diverse organization
d. all of the above

____ 14. Today, _____ percent of workers in the United States are foreign born—the highest rate in 70 years.
a. 10
b. 15
c. 5
d. 20

____ 15. A _____ organization has a workforce representing the full mix of cultures found in the population at large, along with the a commitment to utilize fully these human resources.
a. monolithic
b. multicultural
c. pluralistic
d. market

❖4❖

____ 16. An organization's _____ diversity refers to the full mix of the cultures and subcultures to which members of the workforce belong.
a. cultural
b. affirmative
c. demographic
d. industrial

____ 17. The most common methods used to assess organizational culture are _____ and

_____.
a. cultural audits; sensitivity training
b. oral interviews; sagas
c. employee surveys; focus groups
d. customer feedback; narratives

____ 18. With a diverse workforce and positive organizational culture in place, managers will be able to _____.
a. attract a broader range of customers
b. reduce costs, including those associated with litigation
c. develop products and services for new markets
d. all of the above

_____ 19. Organizations that succeed in managing diversity do so because top management is committed to _____.
   a. achieving legal compliance
   b. instituting a positive organizational culture
   c. using diversity to create economic value
   d. all of the above

_____ 20. _____ is designed to provide accurate information about the many subcultures present in the organization.
   a. Harassment training
   b. Awareness training
   c. Multicultural training
   d. Ethnicity training

ESSAY QUESTIONS

❖1❖

1. Define *culture* and explain the core elements of culture.

❖2❖

2. Identify and discuss the three types of organizational cultures.

❖3❖

3. Define *workforce demographics* and *multicultural organizations* and their relationships to subcultures.

❖4❖

4.   Compare and contrast awareness and harassment training.

CHAPTER 18
ORGANIZATIONAL CULTURE
AND CULTURAL DIVERSITY

MATCHING SOLUTIONS

1. J - Harassment Training
2. L - Narratives
3. D - Clan Culture
4. Q - Taboos
5. H - Symbol
6. T - Language
7. F - Shared Assumptions
8. S - Culture
9. B - Strong Culture
10. M - Bureaucratic Culture
11. C - Socialization
12. I - Ceremonies
13. P - Market Culture
14. G - Value
15. K - Multicultural Organization
16. N - Organizational Subculture
17. E - Cultural Diversity
18. R - Entrepreneurial Culture
19. A - Ceremonies
20. O - Awareness Training

TRUE/FALSE SOLUTIONS

Question	Answer	Page	Explanation
1.	True		
2.	False	512	<u>Shared assumptions</u> are the underlying thoughts and feelings that members of a culture take for granted and believe to be true. <u>Values</u> are basic beliefs about something that has considerable importance and meaning to individuals and are stable over time.
3.	True		
4.	False	516	<u>Narratives</u> are the unique stories, sagas, legends, and myths in a culture. Narratives often describe the unique accomplishments and beliefs of leaders over time, usually in heroic and romantic terms. <u>Ceremonies</u> are elaborate and formal activities designed to generate strong feelings.
5.	False	517	<u>Ceremonies</u> are elaborate and formal activities designed to generate strong feelings. Usually they are carried out as special events. <u>Taboos</u> are culturally forbidden behaviors.
6.	True		
7.	False	518	An organization that values formalization, rules, standard operating procedures, and hierarchical coordination has a <u>bureaucratic culture</u>. The long-term concerns of a bureaucracy are predictability, efficiency, and stability. Managers view their roles as being good coordinators, organizers, and enforcers of written rules and standards. Tasks, responsibilities, and authority for all employees are clearly defined. High levels of risk taking, dynamism, and creativity characterize an <u>entrepreneurial culture</u>. There is a commitment to experimentation, innovation, and being on the leading edge.
8.	False	518–519	In a <u>market culture</u>, social relations among coworkers aren't emphasized, and few economic incentives are tied directly to cooperating with peers.

9.	False	518	In an <u>entrepreneurial culture</u>, there is a commitment to experimentation, innovation, and being on the cutting edge. In a <u>clan culture</u>, the behaviors of employees are shaped by tradition, loyalty, personal commitment, extensive socialization, and self-management.
10.	True		
11.	False	521	When organizational cultures of the merged firms are similar, the chances of success increase.
12.	True		
13.	False	523	The fact that people with different demographic backgrounds live side by side doesn't mean that they share the same culture.
14.	True		
15.	True		
16.	True		
17.	True		
18.	True	531	
19.	False	534	<u>Awareness training</u> is designed to provide accurate information about the many subcultures present in the organization. <u>Harassment training</u> is aimed at ensuring that employees understand the meaning of harassment and the actions the company will take when someone complains of being harassed.
20.	True		

MULTIPLE CHOICE SOLUTIONS

Question	Answer	Page	Explanation
1.	b	512	A <u>culture</u> is the unique pattern of shared assumptions, values, and norms that shape the socialization activities, language, symbols, and ceremonies of a group of people. Cultures develop in both large and small groups of people.
2.	c	512–513	Assumptions, values, and norms form the base of a culture but they can't be observed directly. They can only be inferred from a culture's more visible elements—its socialization activities, symbols, language, narratives, and practices.

3.   a   512–516   <u>Shared assumptions</u> are the underlying thoughts and feelings that members of a culture take for granted and believe to be true. A <u>value system</u> comprises multiple beliefs that are compatible and support one another. <u>Shared practices</u> include taboos or ceremonies. <u>Narratives</u> are the unique stories, sagas, legends, and myths in a culture.

4.   d   514   <u>Socialization</u> is a systematic process by which new members are brought into a culture. The most powerful way to do so is through consistent role modeling, teaching, coaching, and enforcement by others in the culture. At the societal level, socialization takes place within the family, in schools, and religious organizations, and through the media. At the industry level, socialization occurs through organized activities conducted by industry associations.

5.   c   514   A <u>symbol</u> is anything visible that can be used to represent an abstract shared value or something having special meaning. Symbols are the simplest and most basic observable form of cultural expression. Symbols may be expressed through logos, architecture, parting priorities, uniforms, office location, furniture, and so on.

6.   c   516   <u>Narratives</u> are the unique stories, sagas, legends, and myths in a culture. They often describe the unique accomplishments and beliefs of leaders over time, usually in heroic and romantic terms.

7.   b   517   The most complex but observable cultural form is shared practices. These practices include taboos or ceremonies. <u>Taboos</u> are behaviors that are forbidden in the culture. A taboo at Merck is to put profit ahead of ethical responsibilities to doctors, nurses, and patients.

8.   c   518   In a <u>clan culture</u>, the behaviors of employees are shaped by tradition, loyalty, personal commitment, extensive socialization, and self-management. In a <u>market culture</u>, the values and norms reflect the importance of achieving measurable and demanding goals, especially those that are financial and market based. In a <u>bureaucratic culture</u>, the behavior of employees is governed by formal rules and standard operating procedures, and coordination is achieved through hierarchial reporting relationships. In a <u>entrpreneurial culture</u>, flexibility creates an

environment that encourages risk taking, dynamism, and creativity.

9.	a	518	Tradition, loyalty, personal commitment, extensive socialization, teamwork, self-management, and social influence are attributes of a <u>clan culture</u>. It achieves unity with a long and thorough socialization process. Long-time clan members serve as mentors and role models for newer members. These relationships perpetuate the organization's values and norms over successive generations of employees.
10.	d	518–519	High levels of risk taking, dynamism, and creativity characterize an <u>entrepreneurial culture</u>. There is a commitment to experimentation, innovation, and being on the leading edge. An entrepreneurial culture suits a new company start-up phase.
11.	b	519	The achievement of measurable and demanding goals, especially those that are financial and market-based (e.g., sales growth, profitability, and market share) characterize a <u>market culture</u>. Hard-driving competitiveness and a profit orientation prevail throughout the organization. A market culture doesn't exert much informal social pressure on an organization" members. Supervisor" interactions with subordinates largely consist of negotiating performance-reward agreements and/or evaluating requests for resource allocations. Social relations among coworkers aren't emphasized. Managers in one department are expected to operate with managers in other departments only to the extent necessary to achieve their goals.
12.	d	519–520	The need to determine which attributes of an organization's culture should be preserved and which should be modified is constant. All of the statements listed are true.
13.	a	521	An <u>organizational subculture</u> exists when assumptions, values, and norms are shared by some—but not all—organizational members.
14.	a	523–524	Today, 1 in 10 workers in the United States is foreign born—the highest rate in 70 years.
15.	b	527	A <u>multicultural organization</u> has a workforce representing the full mix of cultures found in the population at large, along with the a commitment to utilize fully these human resources.

16.	a	527	An organization's <u>cultural diversity</u> refers to the full mix of the cultures and subcultures to which members of the workforce belong. <u>Demographic diversity</u> reflects the degree of mix of characteristics of the people who make up an organization's workforce.
17.	c	529	The most common methods used to assess organizational culture are employee surveys and focus groups.
18.	d	529	Organizations are striving to manage diversity effectively because they believe that they can use diversity to create greater economic value. With a diverse workforce and positive organizational culture in place, many managers believe their companies will be able to develop products and services for new markets; attract a broader range of customers; improve customer satisfaction and increase business from repeat customers; and reduce costs, including those associated with litigation.
19.	d	530	As is true for many other managerial responsibilities, effectively managing cultural diversity is a continuing process, not a one-time program or short-term fad. Organizations that succeed in managing diversity do so because top management is committed to achieving legal compliance, instituting a positive organizational culture, and using diversity to create economic value. Such managers recognize that significant organizational changes may be needed to achieve these goals, and they are willing to commit resources to making such changes.
20.	b	534	<u>Awareness training</u> is designed to provide accurate information about the many subcultures present in the organization.

ESSAY SOLUTIONS

[Pages 512–517]

1. A <u>culture</u> is the unique pattern of shared assumptions, values, and norms that shape the socialization activities, language, symbols, and ceremonies of a group of people. <u>Shared assumptions</u> are the underlying thoughts and feelings that members of a culture take for granted and believe to be true. A <u>value</u> is the basic belief about a condition that has considerable importance and meaning to individuals and is stable over time. A value system comprises multiple beliefs that are compatible and support one another. <u>Socialization</u> is a systematic process by which new members are brought into a culture. Individuals learn the ropes and are introduced to the culture's behavioral norms. A

symbol is anything visible that can be used to represent an abstract shared value or something having special meaning. They are the simplest and most basic observable form of cultural expression. From a cultural perspective, language is a shared system of vocal sounds, written signs, and/or gestures used to convey special meanings among members. The elements of this system include shared jargon, slang, gestures, signals, signs, songs, humor, jokes, gossip, rumors, proverbs, metaphors, and slogans. Narratives are the unique stories, sagas, legends, and myths in a culture. They often describe the unique accomplishments and beliefs of leaders over time, usually in heroic and romantic terms. The most complex but observable culture form is shared practices. These practices include taboos or ceremonies. Taboos are behaviors that are forbidden in the culture. Ceremonies are elaborate and formal activities designed to generate strong feelings.

[Pages 518–519]

2. The four basic types of organizational cultures are:

    a. *Bureaucratic culture* is an organization governed by formal rules and standard operating procedures, and coordination is achieved through supporting relationships. Long-term concerns of a bureaucracy are predictability, efficiency, and stability. The focus of attention is on the operations of the organization. Tasks, responsibilities, and authority for all employees are clearly defined.

    b. *Clan culture* includes the attributes of tradition, loyalty, personal commitment, extensive socialization, teamwork, self-management, and social influence. Its members recognize an obligation beyond the simple exchange of labor for a salary. They understand that contributions to the organization may exceed any contractual agreements. The clan culture achieves unity with a long and thorough socialization process. Members share feelings of pride in membership. They have a strong sense of identification and recognize their independence.

    c. *Entrepreneurial culture* exhibits high levels of risk taking, dynamism, and creativity. There is a commitment to experimentation, innovation, and being on the leading edge. This culture does not just quickly react to changes in the environment, it creates change. Effectiveness means providing new and unique products in order to grow rapidly. Individual initiative, flexibility, and freedom foster growth and are encouraged and well rewarded.

    d. *Market culture* values achievement of measurable and demanding goals, especially those that are financial and market-based. Hard-driving competitiveness and a profits orientation prevail throughout the organization. Market culture doesn't exert much informal social pressure on an organization's members. Superior's interactions with subordinates largely consist of negotiating, performance-reward agreements and/or evaluating requests for resource allocations. Social relations among coworkers aren't emphasized, and few economic incentives are tied directly to operating with peers. Managers in one department are expected to cooperate with managers in other departments only to the extent necessary to achieve their goals.

[Pages 523–527]

3. <u>Workforce demographics</u> describe employee characteristics such as ethnicity, age, and gender. However, the fact that people with different demographic backgrounds live side by side doesn't mean that they share the same culture. A <u>multicultural organization</u> has a workforce representing the full mix of cultures found in the population at large, along with a commitment to utilize fully these human resources. Multicultural organizations strive to permit many subcultures to coexist while ensuring that no one subculture dominates the others.

[Page 534]

4. <u>Awareness training</u> is designed to provide accurate information about the many subcultures present in the organization. Conducted over the course of one or two days, activities may include information sharing intended to educate employees about differences between subcultures, educating employees about the negative consequences of stereotypes, and helping employees understand their own subculture's unique perspective. <u>Harassment training</u> is aimed at ensuring that employees understand the meaning of harassment and the actions the company will take when someone complains of being harassed.